THE SCANDAL
OF GEORGE III'S
COURT

For Adrian Lukis and Caroline Langrishe, with much love and many thanks for cocktails, friendship and memories to treasure!

THE SCANDAL OF GEORGE III'S COURT

Catherine Curzon

PEN & SWORD
HISTORY

AN IMPRINT OF PEN & SWORD BOOKS LTD.
YORKSHIRE · PHILADELPHIA

First published in Great Britain in 2018 by
PEN AND SWORD HISTORY
an imprint of
Pen & Sword Books Ltd
Yorkshire – Philadelphia

Copyright © Catherine Curzon, 2018

HB ISBN 978 1 47387 251 6
PB ISBN 978 1 52675 163 8

The right of Catherine Curzon to be identified
as the author of this work has been asserted by them in accordance
with the Copyright, Designs and Patents Act 1988.

Printed and bound in the United Kingdom
by TJ International, Padstow, Cornwall

Typeset in Times New Roman 11/13.5 by
Aura Technology and Software Services, India

Pen & Sword Books Ltd incorporates the imprints of Pen & Sword
Archaeology, Atlas, Aviation, Battleground, Discovery,
Family History, History, Maritime, Military, Naval, Politics, Railways,
Select, Social History, Transport, True Crime, Claymore Press,
Frontline Books, Leo Cooper, Praetorian Press, Remember When,
Seaforth Publishing and Wharncliffe.

For a complete list of Pen and Sword titles please contact
PEN & SWORD BOOKS LIMITED
47 Church Street, Barnsley, South Yorkshire, S70 2AS, England
E-mail: enquiries@pen-and-sword.co.uk
Website: www.pen-and-sword.co.uk

Or

PEN AND SWORD BOOKS
1950 Lawrence Rd, Havertown, PA 19083, USA
E-mail: Uspen-and-sword@casematepublishers.com
Website: www.penandswordbooks.com

Contents

Acknowledgements

A big and not at all scandalous thank you to the team at Pen and Sword, particularly Jon, because what's better than cake and good company? Huge thanks as ever to Lucy, my fierce and fabulous editor, for raising the difficult questions!

To all at The Foxglove and The Peppercorn, for tea, gin and a comfy corner, thank you, thank you, thank you and a big (but not too big) woof from Pippa.

To all the readers who have ever stopped by the virtual salon or opened one of my books, I am in your debt. Let me repay you with tea, but please don't all come knocking at once.

As ever, big hugs and a scandalous 'merci' are due to friends all over the world for their encouragement, friendship and fabulousness. And what would I do without the mighty Terriers, who drag me out of the eighteenth century now and then? Kathryn, this is all your fault for buying *that* ticket. You're to blame.

To Pippa, Nelly and the Rakish Colonial - you keep the home fires burning.

And that makes you the most awesome of all.

List of Illustrations

23. The humbug or an attempt at tragedy, with the Jordan [struck through and replaced by] Joram Upsett, showing Mrs Jordan and the Duke of Clarence. 1791.
24. Ernest Augustus, King of Hanover. H R Cook, after G Saunders.
25. Fashionable Contrasts - or The Duchess's little shoe yielding to the magnitude of the Duke's foot. James Gillray.1792.
26. His Royal Highness the Duke of Kent. Thomas Cheesman, after Muller.
27. His Royal Highness Frederick, Duke of York. John Jackson. 1822.
28. The Modern Circe or a Sequel to the Petticoat, showing Mary Anne Clarke and Wardle. Isaac Cruikshank. 1809.
29. Fanny Burney. Charles Turner. 1840.
30. A man disappearing into a cracked chamber pot which has the legs of woman; implying the illicit relationship between the Duke of Clarence and Mrs. Jordan. James Gillray. 1791.
31. Horatio Walpole, Earl of Orford. W Evans. 1811.
32. George III as he was in his final illness. Charles Turner. 1820.

Cast of Characters

The House of Hanover
In a world of dukes and duchesses, princes and princesses, it's easy to confuse your Cumberlands. Here's a quick guide to the siblings and children of George III. Their significant others are in italics - official spouses only, or we could be here a long, long time!

The King and Queen
George III
Charlotte of Mecklenburg-Strelitz

The King's Siblings… and Their Spouses
Princess Augusta, Duchess of Brunswick
 Charles William Ferdinand, Duke of Brunswick-Wolfenbüttel
Prince Edward, Duke of York and Albany
Princess Elizabeth
Prince William Henry, Duke of Gloucester and Edinburgh
 Maria, Duchess of Gloucester and Edinburgh
Prince Henry, Duke of Cumberland and Strathearn
 Anne, Duchess of Cumberland and Strathearn
Princess Louisa
Prince Frederick
Caroline Matilda, Queen of Denmark and Norway
 Christian VII of Denmark and Norway

The King's Children… and Their Spouses
George IV
 Caroline of Brunswick
Prince Frederick, Duke of York and Albany
 Princess Frederica Charlotte of Prussia

William IV
    Adelaide of Saxe-Meiningen
Charlotte, Princess Royal
    Frederick I of Württemberg
Prince Edward, Duke of Kent and Strathearn
    Princess Victoria of Saxe-Coburg-Saalfeld
Princess Augusta Sophia
Princess Elizabeth
    Frederick VI, Landgrave of Hesse-Homburg
Ernest Augustus, King of Hanover
    Frederica of Mecklenburg-Strelitz
Prince Augustus Frederick, Duke of Sussex
    Lady Augusta Murray (annulled)
    Lady Cecilia Buggin
Prince Adolphus, Duke of Cambridge
    Princess Augusta of Hesse-Cassel
Princess Mary, Duchess of Gloucester and Edinburgh
    Prince William Frederick, Duke of Gloucester and Edinburgh
Princess Sophia
Prince Octavius
Prince Alfred
Princess Amelia

Introduction

'Love, and Scandal, are the best Sweeteners of Tea […] but, in my Opinion, Scandal is the sweetest of the two, and least dangerous.'

Henry Fielding's words, first spoken at Drury Lane in 1728, are as true today as ever. As the twenty-first century unfolds, the public's thirst for scandal shows no sign of waning. Each generation may think that its scandals are the most shocking that have ever been revealed and that there can be nothing as sordid as that morning's tabloid revelations, but each generation is soon proved wrong.

In fact, gossip, scandal and all manner of dubious dealings have long since fuelled the engine of societies across the world and for the Georgians, there was nothing more delicious than a little salacious tidbit, all the more so if its tentacles reached as far as the throne room itself.

When it came to the Hanoverian kings of Great Britain, the gossip-hungry public was in for a real treat. One thing was certain, as long as the four King Georges sat on the throne, there was always *something* shocking in the headlines.

When my first book, *Life in the Georgian Court,* was published in 2016, it was a source of great delight for me to see how many people just couldn't get enough of Georgian scandal. The response to the brief collection of shockers contained in that book was so great that it gave me a wonderful insight into just how much we still love a bit of eighteenth century drama. I decided that the time had come for a second helping.

You will find some of the scandals from my first book retold here, for some are too juicy *not* to include. In those cases. each one is examined in far greater depth, offering an insight into some classic royal embarrassments from the supposedly dull court of George III. After all, one could hardly dip into the scandals of George III's reign without including both Mrs Jordan and Mrs Robinson, not to mention the tragedy of Caroline Matilda. Diving into newspapers, letters and memoirs of the era, one can almost hear the frustrated monarch stamping his feet on the throne room floor and asking why people couldn't just *behave*!

This jaunt through the scandals of the court of George III will take readers from the palaces of Britain all the way to Denmark. Far from being an exhaustive compilation of every scandal that gripped the Georgian public - for that you would need many volumes of encyclopedia - think of this as a cornucopia of some of the most eyebrow-raising episodes. The reign of George III was an eventful time in the history of the family that came from Hanover, bringing with it the most shocking and rip-roaring period in the history of the British Isles. You will not find in-depth political analysis here, though there are, of course, many excellent volumes that provide this, but instead a rogue's gallery full of lovers, lords and layabouts. Some of them were irresistible, some of them were reprehensible and one or two managed to be both!

Think of this book as your window into the coffeehouses of eighteenth century Britain, complete with a fire blazing in the grate and a gossipmonger sitting happily beside the hearth sharing larger than life tales with those who stumble into her purview! Where better to spend a few hours than deep in the scandalous Georgian court?

Long before the days of spin doctors, press relations and a well-massaged media, in the eighteenth century, it was a case of *anything goes*. From shady business deals gone sour, mistresses bent on revenge and shadowy rumours of men who wielded the power to get away with murder, not to mention clandestine weddings, illegitimate children and the shadow of the executioner's blade, the Georgians had it all. Welcome to a world where even the most well-bred and illustrious wearer of the most magnificent crown in the land could be caught with their breeches down, in more ways than one!

Chapter 1

The Fair Quaker

'This week has seen the exposure of a stupid and mischievous fable respecting the family of George III which has been floating about for half a century, which is in some quarters, we believe, an article in the popular historic creed.'[1]

Unlike George III, I have never been one for rules. Yet when one is writing a book, one must by necessity have *some* rules, or where would we all be? So we find ourselves at the opening of this book, at the pinnacle of the mountain, if you will, looking down on illegitimate spouses and children, murderous valets and scheming sorts, and in these very first pages, the rules will be broken.

Call it authorial privilege.

The scandalous stories within these pages are all events that occurred during the reign of George III and involved one or more of his family members. So you shall not find the imprisoned Sophia Dorothea of Celle examined here nor the case of the outrageous Bartolomeo Pergami and his magnificent whiskers, but there are plenty of other memorable sorts to take their not-so-illustrious places.

But here at the start, before we have even met the cast who make up our stories, the one rule that has been established is to be broken, for the tale of Hannah Lightfoot might have occurred during the time of George III, but it didn't become a true scandal until many, many years later. Yet it strikes me as the perfect story to open our journey with, for it paints a picture of a George III that we won't come across again. Instead that unfortunate king is forever caught in the public consciousness as one of two things - either the monarch who lost America, or the man who lost his mind. Yet in these pages we will meet a man of piety and duty, married to a wife of similar standards and opinions and heading a court full of brothers, sons and even the occasional daughter who seemed determined to create havoc, moral standards be damned.

George was the second child born to Frederick, Prince of Wales, and his wife, Augusta of Saxe-Gotha. At his birth he was so weak that few expected him to live. Yet he defied the odds and didn't only survive, but flourished. Frederick, George's father, was the favourite grandson of George I but was rather less popular with his own father, George II, and the pair was bitterly estranged.

Frederick died when George was just 12-years-old and suddenly, quite out of nowhere, the sheltered young man found himself next in line to the British throne. The prolonged estrangement of the Wales household from that of the sovereign's thawed as Frederick's widow Augusta sought out what help she could to raise her bereaved brood and where would be a better place to start than with the old king himself? The estrangement was swiftly healed as the fatherless family was reunited with the monarch and George II, once again, clasped his grandchildren and daughter-in-law to the royal bosom.

Time was short, for the old king wasn't getting any younger and no one knew how many years remained before George, now Prince of Wales, would take his place. In the event, he was just 22-years-old when he assumed the throne in 1760 and unlike the other Georges with their love of the ladies, this George was single but definitely *not* in the mood to mingle. But what of the years between Fred's death and that of George II? Were there adventures in the youth of George III? Some say yes.

So it was that the young man was drawn back into the heart of the royal family and as he was trained in the ways of kingship, his devotion and piety only increased. The history of the House of Hanover was littered with scandal that arose, the young man couldn't help but think, from too much indulging of base desires. It was those desires that had landed his great grandmother, Sophia Dorothea, in prison for thirty years[2], and had seen his predecessors bring a legion of mistresses into the royal palaces. This had caused a rift between George I and his son, George II, that was later echoed in the estrangement of George II and Frederick, Prince of Wales. Frederick died before George III was an adult, but familial rot was a fact of life for the esteemed House of Hanover.

In his youth, George witnessed firsthand the power of scandal when his bereaved mother, Augusta, sought out a new male role model for her fatherless son. She didn't choose a member of the royal family but a Scottish politician, John Stuart, 3rd Earl of Bute. Bute was a long-time friend of the Prince and Princess of Wales, whom he had met during a card game at Egham Races when rain forced the horses back into their stables and the spectators undercover. Intelligent, respectful, a little bit stern and very respectable indeed, Augusta thought Bute was the perfect choice to guide her son into manhood.

Yet the public didn't share Augusta's adoration of Bute, whom they suspected of winning the role not due to his brain, but another part of his anatomy entirely. Bute was tall, handsome and famed for his fabulous legs. In short, he was just the sort of man to comfort a grieving widow.

If you get my drift.

Horace Walpole[3] - who else? - had much to say on the matter of Augusta's attachment to Bute. He prudently refrained from making any conclusions of his own, but he was happy to record the rumours in his wonderfully gossipy journals. It is a quintessentially Walpoleish tale, scandalous, saucy and just the sort of story that kept the court wheels turning.

> 'It had already been whispered that the assiduity of Lord Bute at Leicester House, and his still more frequent attendance in the gardens at Kew and Carlton House, were less addressed to the Prince of Wales (the future George III) than to his mother [Augusta]. The eagerness of the Pages of the Back-Stairs to let her know whenever Lord Bute arrived [and some other symptoms] contributed to dispel the ideas that had been conceived of the rigour of her widowhood.'[4]

And Bute, as Walpole noted, was doing little to dispel such rumours. In fact, if one was being particularly critical, one might almost accuse him of encouraging them. After all, he made no effort to blend in, and seemed to delight in being the centre not only of royal attention, but of the public's chatter too.

> 'On the other hand, the favoured personage [Bute], naturally ostentatious of his person and of haughty carriage, seemed by no means desirous of concealing his conquest. His bows grew more theatric, his graces contracted some meaning, and the beauty of his leg was constantly displayed in the eyes of the poor captivated Princess.'[5]

In the press, Bute and Augusta became the targets of merciless swipes and she was caricatured as *The Wanton Widow*. Though these swipes began before George came to the throne, they went on for years. When Bute became Prime Minister, they got louder still, eventually forcing his resignation. Bute was a talented and experienced statesman but he found himself helpless against accusations of rising to the top on the strength of his prowess in Augusta's bedroom. The allegations led John Wilkes[6] to pen a far from respectful bit of poetry.

> 'Where all must rise, or not coherent be,
> And all that rise must rise in due degree,
> Then in the scale of various Pricks, 'tis plain
> Godlike erect, BUTE stands the foremost man.'

Rest assured that the rather obvious double entendre is exactly what Wilkes was aiming for. By his usual standards, this was positively affectionate!

I never said he was subtle.

It's important to note that there is absolutely no evidence whatsoever that Bute and Augusta were lovers, but that didn't matter to the Georgian scandal mongers. It was a lesson well-learned for George who, though protected to some extent from what was being written about his mother, was hardly completely ignorant of it. Bute had been appointed to guide the fatherless Prince of Wales safely through adolescence and there was nothing more to it than that, but gossip rarely listens to the facts. Instead George saw first-hand how a decision taken with the very best of motives could easily become something else, something sordid and forbidden. It was not a lesson he would quickly forget.

And he didn't come to the throne without knowledge of those aforementioned dalliances of his predecessors either. George I openly lived with his long-term mistress, Melusine von der Schulenberg, and she was mother to three illegitimate children by him. His son, George II, was bitterly estranged from George I[7] and kept plenty of mistresses of his own, chief among them the famed Henrietta Howard, Countess of Suffolk. He in turn was estranged from *his* son, Frederick, Prince of Wales, father of George III[8]. Though Frederick and George III were close as father and son, the young king would have been all too aware of the not always happy romantic history of the House of Hanover. It was because of this chequered family past that George was determined to be the man who broke the mould. He would take no mistresses nor father any illegitimate children, making him unique among the King Georges.

Yet the weight that George bore on his slender shoulders was heavy, for the fate and moral fibre of a nation was now depending on him. Much was made of the fact that he was the first of the Georgian kings to be born and raised in Britain, and when Frederick died he left a letter for his son that clearly mapped out his expectations for the young man's eventual reign. The letter was catchily titled, *Instructions for my son George; drawn by my-self, for his good, that of my family, and for that of this people, according to the ideas of my grandfather, and best friend, George I.*

Frederick's words were written out of 'the tenderest paternal affections' and he entrusted the letter to the Princess of Wales, who was in turn entrusted with reading it to the young man and passing it into his custody when he became king. As well as wise words on balancing the books, keeping the politicians and courtiers sweet and the importance of stressing his Englishness, Frederick reminded George that above all things, his life must be one of faith.

> 'I conclude, with recommending you, the Princess, the rest of my children, and all your subjects, to the protection of God Almighty; which, depend upon it my son, you will have, if you fear and obey Him.'[9]

George III feared and obeyed the word of God to his dying day. Even in the throes of madness, when he could not recognise his own family and was strapped down to a restraining chair, his doctors praised him when he stopped jabbering and chattering long enough to pray for his own recovery. He followed the highest moral standards and expected his family to do likewise. This is the king, let us not forget, who would one day issue a *Royal Proclamation For the Encouragement of Piety and Virtue, and for the Preventing and Punishing of Vice, Profaneness and Immorality*, aimed at improving the moral health of the nation.

So much for our leading man; what about his leading lady for this particular chapter?

Hannah Lightfoot was born, according to the scant details that remain of her life, in 1730 in St John[10], Middlesex. She was the daughter of a shoemaker,

Matthew, and Mary, his wife, and was raised a Quaker. Hannah's father died when his little girl was just three-years-old and she went to live in London with her uncle, who was a linen draper. When she was in her early twenties, Hannah married a grocer named Isaac Axford, but the marriage was not a happy one. Before two years had passed, Hannah was estranged from Axford and by 1756, the Fair Quaker had disappeared forever. Years later she was still being sought as the newspaper advertisement below shows, but Hannah would never emerge from whatever seclusion she had found. It looked, to all intents and purposes, as though she was dead and buried.

> 'HANNAH LIGHTFOOT, Spinster, or HANNAH AXFORD, the wife of ISAAC AXFORD, alias the Pretty Quaker.
>
> If any person can, and will give information and proof, whether Hannah Axford, the wife of Isaac Axford, late of Ludgate-hill, in the City of London, Grocer, and whose maiden name was Hannah Lightfoot, and who formerly lived in St. James's Market, and was generally known by the appellation of "the pretty Quaker," was living on the 4th of December, 1759, and if since dead, when and where she died, shall be handsomely rewarded by Mess. Hill and Meredith, Attornies, Gray's Inn, London, to whom the Information is required to be given.'[11]

So what became of Hannah Lightfoot, and how did the name of an unassuming Quaker girl come to be linked with the most morally upright king of the Georgian era?

Hannah's husband did not share her faith and it was decided that a *Testimony of Denial* would be issued against her in January 1756. As John Gough writes in his 1799 history of the Quakers, this testimony would result in Hannah being forever banished from Quaker society. How she responded to her banishment we cannot know, for Hannah was never reliably referred to in the historical record again. Though she cropped up in the occasional will, it appeared that even her mother didn't know whether her daughter was alive for she noted in her own will that she hadn't seen Hannah for years. The abandoned Isaac Axford, meanwhile, described himself as a widower when asked and even remarried in 1759. Of course, it's perfectly believable that, after Hannah's disappearance, he *didn't* know if she was still living, so let us not look on him too darkly or accuse him too harshly.

Besides which, if Hannah *was* still alive and Isaac Axford was indeed a bigamist, then there was a rather more illustrious bigamist at large than that in 1761.

The king himself.

The seeds of this scandalous story appear to have first been sown in a newspaper entitled *The Citizen*. The inaugural edition of that far from august journal was published on 24 February 1776 and, in the time-honoured tradition of the press, the first issue promised to contain quite a scoop.

> 'The History and Adventures of Miss L..htf..t, the Fair Quaker; wherein will be faithfully portrayed some striking pictures of female constancy and princely gratitude, which terminated in the untimely death of that young lady, and the sudden death of a disconsolate mother.'[12]

This mention of the mysterious Miss Lightfoot appears to be the first, but it would not be the last. Intriguingly, the story makes no claims that it refers to George III and could just as easily be applied to any prince from anywhere in the world yet seeing as it was on the front page of a British newspaper, the connection would be an easy one to make.

The story, such as there is one, is simple enough. Supposedly when George was still Prince of Wales and in his teens, he caught a glimpse of the as yet unmarried Hannah, by then in her early twenties, through the window of the drapery shop. As soon as their eyes met, the pair fell in love and George, still young, and not yet the serious gentleman he would become, was determined to court her.

Supposedly.

Of course it *could* be true, for young George did have a weakness for a pretty face, and there would be no wrong in a young man setting his cap at an eligible girl, but the romance, so the gossips claimed, didn't stop there. As the story gained traction, the more romanticised versions of the tale claimed that George could not forget Hannah, and it's here that things start to get confusing.

Three versions of the story began to circulate. Firstly it was claimed that the royal family engaged the Duchess of Kingston[13] to convince Isaac Axford to marry Hannah. They hoped that this would be enough to keep the Prince of Wales from proposing to her, alongside the promise of a large financial consideration. The second claimed that George couldn't forget Hannah even after her marriage, so conspired to spirit her away from Isaac Axford after her marriage. She went willingly and despite now being Mrs Axford, bigamously married the adoring prince *anyway*. Third was the most scandalous of all. This last theory posited that George married Hannah just before she was wed to Isaac. The wedding to Axford went ahead as planned and as soon as the ceremony was concluded, Hannah left her grocer behind and ran into the arms of her prince. Kept in luxurious seclusion by the Prince of Wales, later George III, she lived as his wife and was even mother to his firstborn. Both this theory and the second cast either the prince or the Fair Quaker as a bigamist.

If the third theory was true, then some commentators began to argue that the constitutional repercussions would potentially be massive. Had George married Hannah before his official wedding to Charlotte of Mecklenburg-Strelitz took place and before she said *I do* to Isaac Axford, then he was a bigamist and Hannah 'had as fair a claim to the queenly crown as Elizabeth Woodville'[14]. Any children born of that marriage would be the rightful heirs to the throne, the marriage to Charlotte would be null and void, the Prince Regent would not have succeeded and- and—

Are you breathless yet?

In fact, all of this is rather romantic supposition, supported by not even a whisker of evidence. The most popular version of the gossip was careful to go for the *slightly* less scandalous route. This posited that George was already married by the time he supposedly hitched himself to the beautiful young Quaker. Therefore it was his second, morganatic[15] marriage that would be illegal, and *those* children would be illegitimate, having no constitutional impact whatsoever. Whatever the truth of the Lightfoot mystery, the marriage of George and Charlotte was binding.

With constitutional crises off the table, let us pause and wonder at the likelihood of any of the most drastic outcomes. This was George III, let us not forget, the king who was responsible for the Royal Marriages Act, the man who would one day have his own son's marriage annulled because he had not obtained permission to contract it. Now there have always been hypocritical monarchs, just as hypocrites can be found in any walk of life, but this seems a step too far even for fiction, let alone for King George III.

Yet the rumour stuck, though few took it very seriously, and over the years, the scandalous revelations became rather less so. The supposed marriage became nothing more than a bachelor romance, the whispers of children ever more quiet. Indeed, by the time Nathaniel Wraxall, that esteemed historian of the age, came to consider the question of Miss Hannah Lightfoot, it was hardly enough to raise even a single eyebrow.

> 'Stories were indeed generally circulated, of his Attachment to a young Woman, a Quaker about this Time of his Life; just as Scandal, many Years afterwards, whispered that he distinguished Lady Bridget Tollemache by his particular Attentions. The former Report was probably well founded; and the latter Assertion was unquestionably true; but, those Persons who have enjoyed most Opportunities of studying the King's Character, will most incline to believe that in neither Instance did he pass the Limits of innocent, Gallantry or occasional Familiarity.'[16]

King George III, it seemed, was just not that kind of guy and for every scandalous book that breathlessly repeated the legend, it gained little traction or credence. Instead it just became one of *those* stories; a bit of drama, a bit of scandal and a lot of fiction. The story became more muddied, the supposed timeline more jumbled and nobody could produce a shred of evidence. In fact, it looked set to die a death and would likely have done so were it not for a resurgence of interest in the 1820s, when it was claimed that the marriage took place *before* that of Hannah and Axford. If this was the case, there might well be a little bit of a constitutional issue.

You know, just a tiny one.

It wasn't helped by the likes of the estimable Hester Thrale[17] who, in her position as editor of Wraxall's memoirs, added a footnote that said '[Hannah's] son by him (King George) is still alive.' Hester was not the sort of woman you would want to pick a fight with but her footnote contained no qualifying information or evidence whatsoever. It reads merely as though she was repeating the gossip that had been chattered about for decades. Yet Hester's note reignited interest in the case and suddenly, quite out of nowhere in the year after King George III's death, Hannah Lightfoot's name was in the press once more. The pages of the *Monthly Magazine* came alive with new versions of the legend, with the recollections of various Axfords and Wheelers and Lightfoots who all had a slightly different memory. Hannah, it was claimed, had variously died soon after the marriage or decades later, had met the prince at the opera or the drapery shop, and might even be called Whitefoot.

With precious few facts known about her, Hannah soon became all things to all people. To the newspaper editors and owners she was cold, hard cash. As one correspondent balefully reported, 'the history is very poor stuff, but the publication of it is significant, as showing to what tricks these newspapers, whose trade is to set class against class, are now obliged to resort.'[18]

The story that wouldn't die resurfaced in 1848 with the curious case of Princess Lavinia, daughter of Olivia Serres and, if she was to be believed, the illegitimate granddaughter of a very illustrious chap. Olivia had long since declared that her true father was the king's brother, Prince Henry, Duke of Cumberland and Strathearn, something she insisted George III had not only known about, but had promised financial support for. Olivia and her daughter were determined to pursue the family claim. Whether Olivia was a swindler or just delusional is a matter for debate but she dressed her servants in royal livery and referred to herself as *Princess Olive of Cumberland*, whilst claiming that George III had acknowledged her parenthood and promised her a very fat payment, which she never received. At her death in 1834 her daughter, Lavinia, took up the baton and carried it all the way to the Court of Probate.

Here Lavinia claimed that she was the rightful heiress to a £15,000 bequest promised to her mother by George III. Of course it had never been paid, and now she was ready to fight the case to the end. Central to her argument was the claim that George had married Hannah when both were single and that he had fathered children by the Quaker. If this was true it would mean that George IV and the reigning Queen Victoria had no legitimate claim to the throne - something Lavinia herself would have.

To support these outrageous claims Lavinia produced a marriage certificate confirming that the wedding had taken place. Taken at face value, the papers in her possession appeared to verify that the ceremony just happened to have been carried out by a Dr Wilmot, a member of Lavinia's own family. She even had the will of Hannah Lightfoot, made before her supposed death in 1768 in which the Fair Quaker referred to herself as *Hannah Regina*. Lavinia claimed that Hannah had been stolen away from George's arms and forced to marry Axford. She spun a wonderfully gothic, utterly improbable yarn in which none other than William Pitt himself donned a disguise that would make Sherlock Holmes proud and took to the dark alleyways of London, searching in vain for the missing Quaker.

'Provided I depart this life I recommend my two sons and my daughter to the kind protection of their royal father my husband, His Majesty George the Third, bequeathing whatever property I may die possessed of to such dear offspring of our ill-fated marriage.'[19]

The extract above is from what Lavinia had intended to be her smoking gun. It was a letter dated 1762, supposedly written and signed by Hannah Lightfoot, or *Hannah Regina*, as she signed, and witnessed by the Lords Dunning and Pitt[20]. Unfortunately, Pitt had signed as the Earl of Chatham, several years before he *was* the Earl of Chatham, and the letters supposedly from George III himself bore no resemblance whatsoever to his handwriting.

It went just as well as you might expect.

It should be noted that the only volumes written in support of these claims or, indeed, the only voices that were raised to shore up the veracity of the Lightfoot story, were those belonging to the more spurious sort of gossips. Lavinia's claims found their supporters amongst those who loathed the House of Hanover or simply fancied a little mischief, and were determined to shift a few books on the back of a scandalous scoop. After all, when faced with passages such as the following, one can hardly imagine that the author might be considered an impartial historian. Particularly distasteful is the suggestion that George's much-publicised battle with mental illness might be a direct result of a guilty conscience thanks to his treatment of Hannah!

'With the characteristic obstinacy which afterwards led [George III] to persist in the unconstitutional taxation and coercion of America, till he lost it to this country, he married Hannah Lightfoot, and when he had children by her, coolly abandoned her at the age of twenty-three, and married Charlotte of Meclenburg [sic] Strelitz.

[…]

The domestic history of George III is one of the most awful that ever befell a monarch. The consequences of his concealment of his first marriage, were terrible to his peace of mind, and to that of more than one of his children, and in this fact are we to seek for the true causes of the overthrow of his intellect.'[21]

Ouch.

The court, under the auspices of the Lord Chief Justice Cockburn[22], rejected the claims of Lavinia Serres. It declared her documents 'were rank and foolish forgeries'[23], probably created by her mother, whose entire life had been dedicated to securing her imagined rights to be royal. The court declared that regardless of what Lavinia had been raised to believe, she had no royal blood running in her veins. Let this be an end to the whole sorry affair, the establishment hoped. Just like her mother before her, Lavinia would not let the matter rest and continued to campaign for recognition until her death in 1871.

More recently those eighteenth century documents presented by the so-called *Princess Lavinia* have been declared to be nineteenth century forgeries. DNA testing on those who claim to be descended from the children of Hannah Lightfoot and George III has likewise found no case to answer at the time of writing.

What became of Hannah Lightfoot we cannot know yet there remains one last delicious footnote. A painting by Sir Joshua Reynolds can be found at Knole House in Kent (the ancestral home of the Earls and Dukes of Dorset and the Barons Sackville) which some believe shows the face of Hannah Lightfoot, captured for posterity. It was recorded in 1817 as showing, 'Miss Axford, the Fair Quakeress', though we cannot know for sure that this is Hannah who would, of course, have been *Mrs* Axford. Or Mrs King, if we're feeling naughty.

The fate of Hannah Axford remains unknown and it seems most likely that she was indeed dead by 1759. Her final resting place and the life she lived before she passed away remains one of the era's most tantalising mysteries to this day.

Chapter 2

The Sins of the Sisters

'Last Night, on receiving the agreeable News of her Royal Highness the Princess Dowager of Wales being safely delivered of a Princess, the Flag was displayed from the Castle, the Great Guns were fires, and the Night concluded with ringing of Bells, and other Demonstrations of Joy.'[1]

Princess Caroline Matilda of Great Britain was born on 22 July 1751 to Augusta of Saxe-Gotha, Dowager Princess of Wales, and the late Frederick, Prince of Wales. She never met her father, who died at the age of 44 just a few months before her birth, and she was one of nine children born to the couple. Among her siblings was, of course, the adolescent George, Prince of Wales, later fated to rule as George III. That boy, who was barely 13-years-old when his sister was born, served as godfather at her christening. Throughout Caroline Matilda's life, he would be the one who often steered the path of her fate, in concert with their formidable and ambitious mother.

The young princess spent her early years rambling in the gardens at Kew, far away from the gossip-driven, power-hungry court. In fact, her youth was relatively simple and she was never happier than when cantering on her mount through the bucolic landscape or tending her gardens and the small patch of land given over to her care. Yet Caroline Matilda was a royal princess, the granddaughter of the king and sister of the heir to the throne and in Georgian Britain, that made her a very valuable commodity indeed.

From her childhood, Caroline Matilda was trained in the necessities of being a good wife. She learned languages, became an accomplished musician and singer and was drilled in manners, deportment and etiquette. Even as a child, she was being trained for the job to come and when she was nine-years-old, that training became more important than ever.

'This morning at about seven o'clock, departed this life, at his palace at Kensington, his Sacred Majesty our most gracious

Sovereign; a Prince endowed with all royal virtues.— The grief
and consternation which this unexpected event has occasioned,
is legible in every countenance, and will be deeply felt by all
his subjects, who regarded him as their common father.'[2]

With the death of George II and the accession of George III, Caroline
Matilda's value as a wife rocketed up and all over Europe, eligible bachelors
squared their shoulders. A canny arrangement might secure a dynasty or
cement an alliance, shore up shaky lands or even stave off a war.

Across the sea in Denmark, King Frederick V watched events in England
with interest. As Caroline Matilda's uncle by marriage[3], Frederick had been
at the front of the queue to win the hand of the young princess for his
son, Crown Prince Christian. In fact, so keen was Frederick that he initially
approached George II when the boy, who was two years Caroline Matilda's
senior, was still a toddler. Frederick wasn't particularly bothered *which*
British princess he snagged so long as he managed to get *one*.

Those early negotiations bore little fruit and no doubt Frederick thought
he had missed the boat when the newspapers reported on gossip from the
continent that 'A marriage is very much talked of in Germany, between
Frederick William, Prince Royal, and Hereditary Prince of Prussia […] and
the Princess Caroline Matilda of England, youngest sister to his Majesty'[4].
However, not for the first and certainly not for the last time, the press was
wide of the mark. In fact, Frederick William actually went on to marry
Elisabeth Christine of Brunswick-Wolfenbüttel. Given that Frederick
William was later to prove himself to be a serial philanderer and bigamist
you might think that Caroline Matilda had had a very lucky escape. In fact,
her fate proved to be far unhappier than Elisabeth Christine's would ever be.[5]

The Danish king approached Walter Titley, a diplomat who had been
the British envoy to Denmark for over thirty years[6], and asked once again if
there might be any British princesses in need of a prince. George III initially
considered his sister, Princess Louisa as an ideal candidate. It soon became
clear to everyone that Louisa's health was too frail to risk the journey to the
Oldenburg court, let alone the duties expected of the wife to the heir to the
throne, and negotiations for her hand stalled[7].

The next obvious candidate was the young and sheltered Caroline
Matilda. At not yet even 14-years-old, she was given no say in her fate but
her brother, George III, was very well aware of how valuable a marriage
to Denmark would be. George might be young but he was not without
feeling and he sought assurances about the character of the youthful

Christian, concerned that his sister not be subject to any unpleasant surprises on her arrival in Denmark. He received promising word from Titley, who assured him beyond a doubt that the inexperienced young princess need not fear.

> 'The amiable character of the Prince of Denmark is universally acknowledged here, so that the union appearing perfectly suitable, and equally desirable on both sides, I hope soon to have an opportunity of congratulating you, my Lord, upon its being unalterably fixed and settled.'[8]

The marriage was announced at the State Opening of Parliament on 10 January 1765 when the king told members of the House that, 'I have now the Satisfaction to inform you, that I have agreed with My good Brother the King of Denmark, to cement the Union which has long subsisted between the Two Crowns, by the Marriage of the Prince Royal of Denmark with my Sister the Princess Caroline Matilda, which is to be solemnized as soon as their respective Ages will permit.'[9]

The decision was made and if George's own doubts had been set at ease by Titley, young Caroline Matilda had no such confidence. As she sat for a miniature that was to be sent over to her new fiancé, the teenage girl must have wondered what her life was about to become. She had been raised in such a sheltered environment that the thought of leaving her family behind for a strange new world was not one that she particularly relished.

And little did she know what she was headed for. Christian was far from the perfect specimen he was being portrayed as yet nobody had any idea what drama lay in store. And from Denmark, the good reviews just kept on coming.

> '[Christian] is regular and sober, [he] eats heartily but drinks little or no wine. His temper is compassionate and good, but equitable and firm. He has a quick apprehension, with a sound and not uncultivated understanding, and his mind is well seasoned with the principles of virtue and religion. He is now impatient for the accomplishment of his marriage, and as he is hitherto under no prepossession, there is the greatest reason to believe that he will find his happiness in that union.'[10]

Contrary to Titley's claims, the teenage Crown Prince Christian was already something of a handful and had been for quite a while. His mother, Louise of Great Britain, died before Christian turned three and her husband was plunged into mourning. He took little interest in his four children and passed them over to the care of the household, where Christian was allowed to run riot during his very early youth. All of that changed when he hit the grand old age of six. It was then that he began his training for the throne under the eye of his chamberlain, Christian Ditlev Reventlow, and tutor, Elie Salomon François Reverdil. The two men could not have been more different.

Reventlow was brutal and determined to beat the little boy until he was a hardened man, ready to face all that the world could throw at him. He had almost half a decade of unchecked, barbaric rule over the young prince before the gentle, academic Reverdil was given his position. However by that time, the heir to the throne was already exhibiting behaviour that might suggest he was prone to seizures. The more Christian foamed at the mouth, the harder he was beaten. And worse still, his father continued not to take any interest in him and instead devoted himself to the boy's new stepmother, Juliana Maria of Brunswick-Wolfenbüttel. Christian must have wondered if anyone cared for him at all and once he had a taste of power, it's little wonder that he became a troubled and self-centred young man.

Christian began to believe that he was imbued with extraordinary physical and mental abilities, seeing himself as a mighty figure who was destined to become a legendary warrior-king. Neglected by his surviving, drink-loving parent, he was resented by his stepmother She had a son of her own, Christian's half-brother Frederick, who she would have liked to install as heir to the throne. Regularly beaten by his chamberlain and allowed to mix with some very questionable friends, it's hardly surprising that Christian's behaviour grew more outrageous with every passing year.

Just a fortnight before Christian turned 17, his father died. That troubled little boy was now a king and his bad teenage behaviour was given full and free reign. He delighted in tormenting the ladies of his court and terrorised them with jokes and spiteful pranks. His courtiers and cabinet prayed that marriage might calm his spirits and appealed to George III to send Caroline Matilda without delay. When George tarried, concerned about his sister's youth, Denmark hit the king in his weak spot: international relations.

Britain couldn't risk Denmark forming a new alliance with France and Robert Gunning, Minister Resident at the Danish court[11], was swift to capitalise on this. He wrote to the British king: 'If the marriage takes place before a renewal of the French treaty, the influence of so amiable a Princess, as her Royal Highness is, on so young a Prince [...] will operate powerfully in favour of the mutual interests of the two kingdoms.'[12]

And with that, the king capitulated.

> 'Last night, between seven and eight o'clock, her Royal Highness the Princess Caroline Matilda, youngest sister to our most gracious Sovereign, was married by proxy to the King of Denmark, his Royal Highness the Duke of Gloucester standing proxy for his Danish Majesty. [...]'[13]

Just a day after the rushed nuptials took place and a whole twelve months earlier than she had expected, 15-year-old Caroline Matilda was bound for Denmark. Her dowry of £100,000 left just ahead of her. She wept bitterly at the news, especially when she heard that none of her familiar attendants would be allowed to join her in her new home. Far from offering comfort, her mother had no sympathy. After all, Augusta was a woman of immense ambition who had herself arrived in England as a bride when she was just 17.

It was time, she told her daughter, for duty to come first and with duty, came ceremony.

> 'The Princess Caroline-Matilda of England will go to Copenhagen, by the way of Holland, the Circle of Westphalia, this Electorate [Hanover], and Lower Saxony. Two of the Court Coaches, with several footmen and other domesticks, will set out Tomorrow for Holland, to wait for her Royal Highness, and in a few days a Chamberlain and a Gentleman of the Bed-chamber will go to Wildehausen, in the Circle of Westphalia, to accompany her Royal Highness from thence to Harbourg. At Harbourg her Royal Highness will be received and complimented by a company of young Ladies, elegantly dressed, who will threw flowers before her all the way from the place of her landing.'[14]

The Bluestocking, Elizabeth Carter[15], wrote of Caroline Matilda's fate as 'worse than dying; for die she must to all she has ever seen or known,' and indeed, wrenched from the world in which she had grown, she might as well have been journeying to the moon. The crossing was stormy and dangerous and all Caroline Matilda had to comfort her was a letter from her brother, George III. In it he stressed the importance of three things: not to get involved in politics, not to upset the in-laws and, most importantly, not to expect too much. Indeed, the king warned his sister, that to seek happiness was to virtually guarantee you would never have it. Better instead to have plenty of children and find happiness in them, for that was the greatest blessing any wife could wish for.

The young queen suffered from seasickness during the crossing and by the time her party reached Rotterdam, she was eager to set foot on solid ground again. She did so to great fanfare.

> 'Hamburgh, Oct 21. On Saturday the 18th instant the Queen of Denmark landed at Altona, and it is impossible to describe the crowds of people, as well upon the Elbe as on the shore, and in every street through which her Majesty was to pass, waiting to see their Queen. The river was covered with boats ornamented with Danish and British colours, as were all the ships with their respective ones, both at Altona and Hamburgh.'[16]

It must have been utterly bewildering for the young woman who had been so sheltered to suddenly be thrust into a starring role that she didn't even want. She missed her sisters desperately and now also had to bid farewell to Lady Mary Bowlby, the friend and attendant who had been allowed to accompany her on the crossing. Caroline Matilda's care was entrusted to Louise von Plessen, who was to help the new queen find her feet. Caroline Matilda took one look at her new companion and developed an instant dislike to her, wrongly but understandably convinced that Louise had mischievous intentions.

Over time that suspicion would transform into love and Caroline Matilda grew deeply attached to Louise, whom she viewed as a replacement for the mother she had lost. It was a role that Louise was eminently better suited to than the ambitious and scheming queen dowager, Juliana Maria.

Upon her arrival in Denmark, Caroline Matilda was taken straight to the city of Roeskilde and into the presence of her new husband, the mercurial Christian. As the king, tiny and frail, took his healthy, solidly built bride in his arms, he was as taken with her as he was with any novel distraction before the excitement inevitably wore off. The couple were married in the chapel of Christiansborg Palace on 8 November 1766 and for the week of festivities that followed, all appeared to be well.

The honeymoon period would not last.

Juliana Maria had ambitions of her own and chief among them, the rumour-mongers claimed, had long been the removal of Christian. She was very much the storybook *wicked stepmother*, devoted to ridding herself of her troublesome stepson so that her own child, Frederick, could assume the throne. Frederick was hardly the most mentally robust candidate and this would mean that Juliana Maria could neatly sideline him too, thus snatching the role of regent for herself.

Even after the queen dowager's death, rumours persisted that she had attempted to poison Christian in the nursery, that she had encouraged or paid his carers to drown him or had somehow been responsible for him manifesting the symptoms of what were most likely schizophrenia. If even only the slightest element of this is true, and it's likely that Juliana Maria *did* harbour ambitions to become regent, then the arrival of Caroline Matilda would surely spell disaster for her plans. Now an heir was just a matter of time and when that heir was born, Frederick would be pushed further and further back along the line of succession. Each time he was, Juliana Maria's influence would diminish.

Yet Juliana Maria knew that Christian believed it was hardly the done thing for a young, rich, wild chap about town to settle down to a game of happy families. He wanted to play the field and as early as December (just two months after her arrival in Denmark) Caroline Matilda was writing home to tell her brother, George III, of trouble in the House of Oldenburg.

> 'I have been more than once mortified with the superior knowledge and experience for which the queen takes care to praise herself, and offended at the want of respect and attention in the prince [Frederick, her new half-brother-in-law]. As such unmerited slights cannot be resented without an open rupture, I rather bear with them than disunite the royal family, and appear the cause of court cabals, by showing my displeasure. It seems the king teaches his subject, by example, the doctrine of possessive disobedience.'[17]

Not only were there problems with the brother-in-law, but Caroline Matilda was also beginning to taste the bitter pill of her husband's disinterest. He might have a wife, but that didn't make him any less likely to visit the brothels and bawdy houses of Copenhagen whilst Caroline Matilda waited at home, isolated in her new world. The French envoy rejoiced at the news, for hadn't the entire purpose of the marriage been to bring Great Britain into the bosom of the Danish court, thus forever pushing France out into the cold? In fact, it did no such thing.

Louise von Plessen thought she knew just what was required to bring the king back to the marital bed. She encouraged Caroline Matilda to *treat him mean, keep him keen*, and play hard to get. So, when Christian *did* visit her chambers, he was told that the queen was too busy to see him and was sent away again. If Louise hoped that this would drive the king wild with desire, she was sadly mistaken[18]. Christian had never taken rejection well and he simply stopped visiting altogether, believing that his wife was indifferent towards him. Christian's anxious ministers knew that this state of affairs simply couldn't be allowed to continue and they hit the king in his weakest spot: his manhood.

So long as the king failed to produce an heir, the ministers chorused, the people of Denmark would begin to wonder if it was a question of *wouldn't* or *couldn't*. Did he *want* his subjects to question his ability to perform? Christian initially brushed off the warning and declared that it was unfashionable to love one's wife, so he was merely keeping up with the vogue. The more he brooded on it though, the more it niggled at him: might he *really* be thought impotent?

Finally, Christian and Caroline Matilda consummated their marriage and the 16-year-old queen fell pregnant. In the months that followed Christian's, behaviour grew increasingly more manic until Reverdil, by now Cabinet Secretary, decided that his former charge might benefit from a change of air[19]. As Christian fretted and ranted and considered giving up his throne altogether, the promise of a trip away seemed like the perfect balm. Caroline Matilda was desperate to accompany her husband but he wouldn't hear of it. As a result, the two exchanged bitter words before his parting.

Christian set off on his trip around Denmark, sending back regular romantic missives to Caroline Matilda that had actually been written by Reverdil, and dutifully copied out by the king. When he returned home and she realised that her husband was as cold and indifferent to her as ever, Caroline Matilda was heartbroken. Yet still she tried to win back his affections, indulging his every whim and attempting to mould herself into the ideal wife. Instead his behaviour grew worse than ever. Christian mocked her in public and flaunted his relationship with his mistress, Anna Catherine Benthagen, aka *Støvlet-Cathrine*[20], a prostitute, actress and career courtesan. Ironically given Caroline Matilda's later love of donning male attire, Catherine often dressed in the uniform of a male officer to indulge her husband's love of attractive ladies in men's clothes.

Although Støvlet-Cathrine's immense influence over the king was soon nipped in the bud by his ministers, who convinced her to quit the city and the king in return for a generous annuity, this didn't mark a change in his behaviour towards Caroline Matilda. Once again she was abandoned in favour of the brothels of Copenhagen and even Christian's outlandish attempts at an acting career.

This time the neglected queen didn't sit at home and brood. Instead the pregnant Caroline Matilda donned her cloak and, accompanied by Louise and a footman, took walks through the city streets. This was unheard of but Caroline Matilda soon set something of a trend. Before long, *all* the noblest ladies wanted to be seen mixing with the public.

Caroline Matilda gave birth to a son, Crown Prince Frederick, on 28 January 1768. Shortly afterwards, Louise von Plessen received her marching orders and was replaced by the watchful sister of Christian's close friend, Count Holck. She felt more isolated than ever and that sense of isolation grew in May 1768 when Caroline Matilda learned that her 19-year-old sister, Princess Louisa, had died. Louisa and Caroline Matilda had been very close in England and Louisa was actually considered as a possible bride for Christian, but had been saved from that fate by her frail health. Stuck hundreds of miles from her grieving family, Caroline Matilda took comfort in her newborn son even as she mourned her late sister.

Despite the birth of his son and heir or perhaps even *because* of it, the king soon had itchy feet again. Before long, plans were underway for yet another royal tour. Though this one would even include Great Britain, he had already decided that his wife would not accompany him. He wanted to escape her, and where better to do so than on the other side of the North Sea?

Christian travelled across the continent towards Calais, where he planned to board the British royal yacht, *Mary*, prior to travelling to Britain. It was during this journey that he made a fateful and for some, fatal decision.

In Ahrensburg, just outside Hamburg, Christian was introduced to a Prussian doctor named Johann Friedrich Struensee. Educated at the University of Halle, Struensee's charm and intellect endeared him to Enlightenment thinkers and he became a member of the circle of Schack Carl Rantzau, an influential Danish nobleman. It was Rantzau who introduced him to Christian and recommended him as a useful chap to know. The doctor and the monarch got along famously and Struensee seemed to be a sensible sort; in fact, he was just the type of company that a schizophrenic young sovereign might benefit from spending time with. Christian appointed

Struensee as his physician and he joined the royal party, travelling with his new employer into the heart of the British court.

When the group reached Britain, Struensee had just celebrated his thirty-first birthday. They arrived to find a king who, quite unlike the flighty, fun-loving Dane, preferred a peaceful, uneventful life. The official reception that he encountered was rather cooler than had been anticipated. The court was still in mourning for Princess Louisa and George III wasn't even in London to greet the new arrival. He had travelled to Windsor to indulge in a little contemplation, and had to be swiftly recalled. Though Christian had hoped to escape his wife, instead he found himself assailed by her mother, who questioned him ceaselessly about her daughter's wellbeing.

The British people loved Christian, but his erratic behaviour raised eyebrows at court. Horace Walpole was shocked at how little care he showed for the wife and child he had left behind. The king who had once claimed that it was 'unfashionable to love one's wife'[21] now scandalised Walpole when, during a performance of *The Provoked Wife*, '[Christian] clapped whenever there was a sentence against matrimony; a very civil proceeding, when his wife is an English princess!'[22].

Christian returned home to Copenhagen in January 1769, eight months after he had departed and after a detour to France, where he enjoyed some riotous celebrations. It seemed that absence had made the heart grow fonder and for a short time he was rather taken with his British bride all over again. This period ended as quickly as it had begun and as the year wore on, both husband and wife were plunged into ill health.

For Christian, the complaint was both mental and physical. His whirlwind trip across the continent had exhausted him and his delusions were growing ever more extreme. He took to being tied down and thrashed with newspapers, acting out a bizarre scenario in which he fancied himself to be being broken on the wheel. Far from bringing him satisfaction, at the end of these interludes he was more distressed than ever. Caroline Matilda, meanwhile, was simply and utterly at the end of her tether. She gave up any pretence of self-care and in November 1769, Gunning became so concerned for her long-term prognosis that he sent an urgent dispatch to the Secretary of State, Lord Rochford, warning him that tragedy might not be far away.

> 'I am extremely sorry to acquaint your Lordship that the state of the Queen of Denmark's health has lately presented some very unfavourable symptoms; which have given such

apprehensions to her physicians, as to make them think that a perfect reestablishment may be attended with some difficulty, unless her Majesty can be persuaded to pay unusual attention to herself. I am so thoroughly sensible how deeply it would affect the King [George III] to receive information of a still more alarming nature, and so anxious to prevent it, that I cannot help desiring your Lordship to represent to his Majesty that, though there appears no immediate danger, yet the situation the Queen of Denmark is at present in is too critical not to make it highly necessary to obviate worse symptoms, and as this happy effect depends very much upon her Majesty's own care, I believe she would be wrought upon by nothing more successfully than by some affectionate expostulations from the King, upon the very great importance of her life.'[23]

So the queen was wasting away… but what of Struensee?

The physician had made a quiet but strong impact on his employer and crucially was able to undermine the position of the seemingly unshakeable Holck. Holck was removed from his position in 1770 and his role as king's companion was filled by Enevold Brandt, a close confidante of Struensee. The doctor and the king's new friend encouraged Christian to take more exercise and to drink less alcohol. Struensee's reward was a promotion to Councillor of State. He had bigger ambitions that that though, intending to make it to the very highest echelons of the court. For this, he had to win the backing of the courtiers. Central to achieving that was the popular queen, the woman who would rule as regent *when*, not *if*, her husband's mental state rendered him unable to do so.

Caroline Matilda had no time for Struensee though. To her, he was another Holck, just one more power hungry man at court. You can imagine how delighted she must have been when concerns for her health meant that she was obliged to become a patient of Struensee herself, regardless of her own wishes on the matter. How relieved Caroline Matilda must have been when she learned that Struensee was actually far from being another dissolute glory seeker in the mould of Holck. Instead he was a thoughtful and intelligent man who advised her that she should spend more time outdoors, as well as less time alone. Just as her husband had, the queen soon took the dashing doctor into her confidence, and Struensee mediated between the unhappy couple, winning the trust of both.

It was smallpox that provided the catalyst to transform that friendship into romance. An epidemic of the often fatal disease seized Denmark and among the very small number of people who championed inoculation was Struensee. Despite the intense disapproval of the court, Struensee inoculated the little crown prince and cared for him as his body adapted to the treatment. At Struensee's side throughout her son's short illness was Caroline Matilda and as they wiled away the long hours of night, the couple's friendship blossomed into romance.

Christian's mental health had by now deteriorated drastically and when Struensee was promoted again, this time to Councillor of Conference and the queen's *very* Private Secretary, there could be no doubt how the wind was blowing. Struensee warned Caroline Matilda that her husband would soon be incapable of ruling and someone else would need to steer the ship of state. If Caroline Matilda didn't seize the day, then Juliana Maria *certainly* would. That was all it took, and soon Denmark's newest power couple began positioning themselves to take the reins of the kingdom.

Oddly, almost as soon as the affair began, Christian warmed to his wife, and began to hold her in a higher regard. Together, the trio of king, queen and doctor seemed to get along in a way that Caroline Matilda and Christian never had before. Though this was no ménage both husband and wife seemed far more at ease, and at 18, Caroline Matilda was finally flourishing, no longer the unhappy young woman she had once been.

She donned male attire to ride astride through the towns and countryside of Denmark and even took part in archery contests, scandalising the public and court alike. Her inseparable shadow, Struensee, was in the ascendant. He and Caroline Matilda's passion blazed and with it, his influence only increased. By now virtually insane, Christian looked to his wife and doctor for guidance in all things yet Struensee knew that if he wanted *real* power, he needed *real* office.

He wanted to be Prime Minister.

Securing the position was to prove virtually no challenge for Struensee, especially given the precarious state of the current incumbent, Count Johann Hartwig Ernst von Bernstorff. Bernstorff had been in government for over two decades but he and Christian had never really got along. With Struensee and his friend, Rantzau, now powerful figures at court, the seasoned Bernstorff knew just what was on the horizon and he surely wasn't surprised when Christian dismissed him in 1770, citing a wish to restructure the government. Struensee studded the new administration with his own favourites and that all-encompassing *restructuring* ensured one thing: no man held more power than the doctor. Now all decisions must be officially signed off not by the ministers, but by the king or his representative, Struensee. He was the regent in all but name to a king who ruled absolutely, thanks to the *Lex Regia*, a document that set out the Danish constitution.

> 'The hereditary kings of Denmark and Norway shall and must be regarded by their subjects as the only supreme chiefs on earth. They shall be above all human laws, and whether in matters spiritual or matters temporal, shall recognise no other superior than God; […] The whole realm of Denmark and Norway, its provinces, dependencies, islands, fortresses, rights, jewels, money of every kind, its army, navy, everything now enjoyed, everything that may be acquired hereafter, are the inalienable property of the sovereign alone; and can never be divided or separated from the crown.'[24]

It really *is* good to be the king, or at least the man who tells him what to do. Now whenever anyone appealed directly to Christian, they were met with the same, stock reply.

Apply to Struensee.

What George III must have made of all this, we can only guess. He wrote to his sister and urged her not to support the dismissal of Bernstorff but she rebuffed him in no uncertain terms, informing him that she would manage her own affairs, thank you very much. Gunning warned George III that Caroline Matilda was a woman, 'whose power is affirmed to be unlimited, and on whose will all depends.'[25]

The genie was out of the bottle.

Across the court gossip about the queen and the doctor raged, but with the couple commanding such power, there was little anybody could do to fight back. They might intrigue, of course, but one wrong step against Struensee was akin to making a wrong step against the king. The consequences could be dire. Caroline Matilda's contemporary biographers cast her as a wide-eyed innocent abroad, who was exploited by the shrewd and cunning Struensee, but is that really fair?

Certainly she was young and very isolated, but was she really as easily manipulated as all that? Of course, Caroline Matilda was still a teenager but she had been forced to grow up fast, from a child to a bride to a queen to as near as dammit to a regent. There can be little doubt that her swift climb from depressed child-bride and mother, staring at the wall and dreaming of home, to the woman at the centre of the court was rapid. That it came about as a consequence of her relationship with the physician is clear, but one might question whether Caroline Matilda was as exploited as she might have at first appeared...

Struensee was worldly, his royal lover was far from it, and perhaps she really was romanced into giving her lover what he desired. Perhaps though, faced with her ambitious mother-in-law and troubled husband, Caroline Matilda had really discovered herself and had realised exactly what she was capable of. The powerful, influential queen who now strutted through Copenhagen in male dress was the woman Caroline Matilda had always wanted to be.

It was not the woman that Juliana Maria wanted as a daughter-in-law.

How things might have been different if the meddling Struensee hadn't appeared on the scene. With Christian teetering on the verge of complete madness, had Caroline Matilda remained a shy, unhappy young lady, then the Queen Dowager could have claimed what she saw as her rightful place as regent. Here she might have remained unchallenged, ruling until her infant step-grandson took his seat on the throne. Instead the power that she craved had been snatched away by the shameless queen and her passionate lover.

Now the *Time of Struensee* could begin.

The couple enacted a vast number of sweeping reforms, many of them striking at the heart of the nobility. The Council of State was abolished and with that decisive move, the poor of Denmark celebrated. They regarded this all-powerful council of nobles as a body that had controlled and kept them down for too long. Struensee then passed a law declaring that any debtor who owed money could be arrested by their creditors. Since most of those nobles owed money to *someone*, they fled the capital. They were bound for their country seats where they hoped to buy some time. With the nobles flocking to leave Copenhagen for the countryside, they were hardly anticipating another unwelcome surprise. Yet one was to come, and Struensee told the nobles who wished to hold office that things had changed. They must forfeit their impressive formal roles in favour of lowly new positions. From there they would start from the bottom rung, receiving promotion only when and if they had earned it.

Struensee strove for a classless society in which being a member of the noble classes or the clergy afforded no special privileges that had not been earned. Roles in government were made available to all, regardless of their birth and that wasn't the only change. Over a thousand reforms were introduced in a matter of months and there were few in Denmark who didn't feel the impact of the new regime, whether for better or worse. Torture was abolished and serfs were no longer subjected to the enslavement they had toiled under for generations. Taxes on the wealthy were hiked up and the revenue from these was used to fund vaccination and health treatments for the poor, whilst virtually every area of Danish life experienced one upheaval or another. In the short-lived *Time of Struensee*, the world changed for the people of Denmark.

And the people were not happy.

The rich, the clergy and the nobles all had good reason to dislike the new world that was emerging from the rule of Caroline Matilda and Struensee, but the poor seemed to have less cause for dissent. Still, they had a dislike of the physician who had come from nowhere to wield immense power, seeing his zeal for reform as a worrying sign of power running rampant. Not only that, but he wasn't even Danish. Nor were those German friends of his who were now installed in the most powerful positions in the land. Royal decrees were no longer written in Danish, as they had been when issued by Christian, but in Struensee's mother tongue of German. Copenhagen, it seemed, was fast becoming an annex of Germany. All of these worries wouldn't be unfamiliar to anyone who had witnessed the much-anticipated arrival of George I, the German king, to Great Britain in 1714.

The *Time of Struensee* was rapidly hurtling towards disaster. Little did the doctor know that he had provided the very fuel that would feed the flames.

One of the most drastic reforms Struensee made was the total abolition of censorship. In fact, this had been one of the few things that kept the rumours about the queen and the doctor from reaching the widest possible audience. Now those rumours could be circulated far and wide without fear of recrimination. Tales and caricatures depicting Bacchanalian scenes and orgies worthy of Caligula became widespread. They were printed in pamphlets that were distributed throughout the country and even pinned up on the walls of the palaces by disgruntled, anonymous courtiers. In Britain, where George III learned of events with increasing dismay, the gossip mill was beginning to churn.

> 'All the Noblemen who were in favour with the King of Denmark when he was at this Court, are dismissed from their employments; and his Physician, who was also with him here, is now actually at the head of affairs; some say these changes have been brought about by Ladies.'[26]

For Juliana Maria of course, all of this was a dream come true. She quickly embraced her role as the figurehead of the old regime, serving as a potent symbol of the incapacitated King Christian VII and a time when Germans didn't appear to reign supreme in the House of Oldenburg. Her supporters spread rumours alleging that the little crown prince was neglected by his mother, who was too busy intriguing with Struensee to care for her son. Her enemies claimed he was treated worse than a dog, caged and fed from the floor if he was fed at all. The truth, of course, was somewhat less dramatic than that.

The young prince had been spoiled by his adoring and attention-starved mother but now, under the stewardship of Struensee, he was no longer indulged. Instead his diet was kept plain for the sake of his weak constitution and it's true that the doctor encouraged a stricter regime than the young prince was used to, but the accusations of violent cruelty were unfounded.

Yet as the saying almost goes, something was rotten in the state of Denmark.

Struensee had risen too quickly and too dramatically. There was no way that his ambition would remain forever unchecked and though his affair with the queen was central to that rise, it was also the thing that undid him. Christian might have been happy to be spared the burden of ruling but those who saw their king as easily exploitable were determined to bring him back to the centre of power.

Everyone in the Copenhagen court knew of the attachment of the doctor to the queen. Under the new regime, wrote the courtiers, Christian 'was considered of little more importance than his dog Gourmand'[27].

'Nothing could be more licentious than the Court of Matilda,' writes one of those present. 'Her palace was a temple of pleasure, of which she was the high-priestess; everything was found there calculated to excite and gratify sensual desires.'[28]

Things were running out of control.

The queen had always been a stocky girl and during her tenure in Denmark she had grown rather plump. Yet during 1771 that plumpness seemed to take on another significance. No announcement was made of a royal pregnancy but Gunning suspected that Caroline Matilda was with child. It was his duty to inform George III but the job was fraught with danger. If Caroline Matilda was not pregnant, Gunning risked incurring the wrath of the already nervy British king. Of course, if she *was* pregnant and Gunning did nothing, he would face that wrath anyway. After waiting in vain for somebody to say *something* about Caroline Matilda's condition, Gunning finally seized the bull by the horns and put pen to paper.

> 'As no declaration has yet been made of Her Danish Majesty's pregnancy, I have long entertained scruples with regard to the propriety of mentioning it, but as nobody now seems to make the least doubt of its truth, I am at length convinced I ought no longer to suppress so important a piece of intelligence.'[29]

His suspicions were proved correct in July 1771 when the 19-year-old queen gave birth to a daughter. Soon, all of the court was buzzing with talk of just who the little girl's father might be. The people of Denmark had not been expecting a birth because, tellingly, no official announcement of the pregnancy had been made. This breach of protocol did nothing to silence the rumours of questionable paternity. All it did was make them even louder.

> 'A letter from Copenhagen of the 23rd mentions that the Queen of Denmark was then in a perfect state of health and suckles herself the Princess she was lately delivered; which is considered as an extraordinary instance of maternal affection in a personage of her exalted rank in these days.'[30]

Officially, Princess Louise Auguste of Denmark's[31] father was the king, Christian VII. Unofficially of course, he was Johann Friedrich Struensee. Though the court celebrated as though this was a royal birth, the press, unfettered by censorship, went to town. Struensee, they wrote 'had shamelessly dishonoured the King's bed, and introduced his vile posterity in the place of the pure blood of Oldenburg'[32]. Strong words indeed, made all the stronger by the fact that it was Struensee who was present at the birth, *not* Christian.

Gunning wrote to George III that Caroline Matilda was 'now in full possession of the most absolute power, and free from all imaginable control', and one can only imagine what must have gone through the king's mind. Yet Gunning couldn't be totally honest with his employer about Christian's perilous state of mind, for fear of offending the British king whose own battles with mental illness were well known. With this in mind, he took a different approach and aimed instead for diplomacy. Perhaps, Gunning ventured, George might attempt to negotiate with Struensee to ensure that Danish aims matched those of Great Britain. They could even bring the two nations together with Russia in an all-powerful alliance that would shut down any threat from France once and for all.

George III would do no such thing. Gunning's suggestion that he should enter into negotiations with the doctor put the final nail in his career coffin and when Caroline Matilda asked her brother to remove the envoy from his post, George obliged. Gunning was transferred to a new role in Prussia, away from the intrigue of British queens.

All entreaties from Caroline Matilda's family in Great Britain to draw back from the brink were met with furiously imperious replies from the queen, who was a nervous and lonely girl no longer. She was the Queen of Denmark and Norway, she told them, and she would rule precisely as she saw fit. Little Louise Auguste was christened on her mother's birthday and on that same day, Struensee saw to it that the king had the title of *Count* conferred on both himself and Brandt. The once lowly doctor had secured the final piece of the power jigsaw and when the king issued a decree stating that his former physician was officially empowered to issue decrees that carried the same weight as those given by the king personally. Struensee was now Regent in all but name.

Apply to Struensee, indeed.

Those who had ridden to power on the back of their friend, Struensee, saw all too well that his new regime couldn't last. Rantzau, the man who had introduced the doctor to the king so very recently, was the first to seek a new berth. Anticipating the imminent collapse of Struensee and Caroline

Matilda's court, he quietly allied himself to the Queen Dowager, Juliana Maria. Even Struensee seemed to suspect that his days were numbered and his nerves became raw, his mental and physical wellbeing suffering as a result. He became convinced that there were plots against his life and as the people grew restless, Struensee even considered leaving Denmark altogether. Perhaps because of his power, perhaps because of his daughter, he remained. Struensee confided in Reverdil that it was his love for the queen that kept him at court. Romantic words indeed, but one suspects that his love of power might have played its part too.

Robert Murray Keith, Gunning's successor at the Danish court, continued to update George III with the situation in Scandinavia. He could not gain access to the queen, he wrote, for all her audiences were approved by her lover. If only he might secure a private meeting he was sure that he could impress upon her the sense of at least *considering* the reinstatement of Bernstorff, which was her brother's wish, but the chance of winning even a moment alone with the queen seemed virtually impossible. George III swallowed his pride and wrote a letter to Caroline Matilda in which he urged her to reconsider the course on which she had set her nation, begging her to send away the divisive doctor and recall the respected statesman.

She did not reply.

On 16 January 1772 the queen and her lover hosted a glittering masked ball at Christiansborg Palace, to which the cream of Copenhagen society was invited. Christian, jabbering, insensible and occasionally suicidal, was to join the festivities as a co-host. The young man who had once loved theatre and show now kept to the shadows as best he could, spending the party in the company of friends while his wife paraded her finery on the dance floor. Little did she realise that, among the assembled guests, were those who had joined a conspiracy against Struensee and Caroline Matilda. This was to be the party to end all parties.

The party to end a marriage.

The glittering bash appeared to pass without any drama and as the guests melted away, the conspirators[33] gathered in the queen dowager's apartments. Their mission was simple: subdue Struensee and Caroline Matilda and secure the king's signature on a document that placed Juliana Maria in full control of the kingdom.

Christian woke from a deep sleep to find the conspirators in his bedroom. He was petrified, believing they had come to assassinate him, but when the queen dowager explained their mission, he quickly regained his composure. Juliana Maria told her regal stepson that the queen and her lover were at the head of a plot to dethrone him and that he must act quickly to save his crown and possibly his life.

Christian signed the orders that were presented to him without hesitation. The reins of power passed smoothly from Struensee to Juliana Maria. The brief *Time of Struensee* came shuddering to a halt.

Struensee and Brandt were arrested, bound and taken to Kastellet, a fearsome fortress that was a far cry from the sumptuous palaces that they had so recently called home. Here they were shackled to the wall and left to languish as though they were the lowest criminals. Caroline Matilda spent a restless evening in her own rooms, unaware of the coup that had occurred in the darkest hours of the night.

The queen was roused in the early hours and told that Rantzau had requested an immediate audience. It was here, in her antechambers before dawn, that Caroline Matilda heard of Struensee's arrest. She reacted with violent distress, raging and panicking to the extent that the guards thought she might do herself harm or even pitch herself from the window to her death. Believing that Christian would set things right she begged to see him, but instead Rantzau gave her a note that her husband had written.

> 'Madam, I have found it necessary to send you to Kronborg, your conduct obliges me to it. I am very sorry, I am not the cause, and I hope you will sincerely repent.'[34]

In his confusion, the troubled king had dated the order 1771.

Caroline Matilda and her daughter were taken to the glowering edifice of Kronborg and shown to their quarters. Their new home was an octagonal tower room with barred windows. The young queen, now mired in disgrace, would never see Copenhagen again.

Christian VII was paraded through the streets of the capital, where a festive atmosphere had dawned. Behind the scenes, Struensee's favourites and appointees were swept away. Some were arrested, some exiled, but all were replaced by Juliana Maria's adherents. The days sped by and Caroline Matilda forgot her sadness and grief at losing Struensee and was instead overwhelmed by anger. The British envoy, Robert Murray Keith, found his efforts to visit the queen constantly frustrated and though the doctor might have been clapped in irons and thrown into a bare, damp cell without causing a diplomatic storm, the same could not be said for Caroline Matilda.

The British crown commanded an immense military force and the last thing that the new Danish regime wanted was to inflame the ire of George III. In London the streets buzzed with gossip despite all efforts by the crown and government to keep the embarrassing scandal secret. The king's political opponents, however, saw the conduct of the Danish queen as an excellent opportunity to create mischief. Soon there was hardly a soul at the British court who hadn't heard whispers of Caroline Matilda's disgrace. Despite the efforts of the royal family to keep Caroline Matilda's seriously ill mother, Augusta, from learning of her daughter's troubles, George III took it upon himself to break the unhappy news. Augusta was devastated when she heard of her daughter's fate.

It was one more scandal in a court that was overwhelmed by them, and George was mortified by his sister's unhappy fate. Though officially nothing had been said, gossip was seeping out. The public and court waited for the next twist in the story, wondering if this unhappy affair might conceivably drag the two countries into war. In fact, George III took the events in Denmark with a pinch of salt. He thought that his sister had become willful and difficult during her marriage and when he received a letter from Christian, it gave him pause for thought. Its contents also seriously weakened any resolve George might have had to appeal for mercy on behalf of his sister and her lover. No doubt composed by Juliana Maria, the letter catalogued the shocking conduct of Caroline Matilda and Struensee in lurid detail. George's intervention via Murray Keith somewhat lessened the harsh conditions of his sister's imprisonment, but Caroline Matilda remained a captive in her adopted land. She refused to see the clergymen who came to save her immortal soul and found comfort only in the little girl who remained at her side.

For Struensee, meanwhile, things were considerably more unpleasant. Charged with usurping the royal authority, he was subjected to torture intended to drag from him a confession that he had plotted to depose the king. He refused to admit to any such thing and continued to protest that his relationship with the queen was purely platonic. He still believed that she reigned in Copenhagen and this alone gave him hope. When he learned that she too was imprisoned and would be spared punishment if he confessed, Struensee's resolve deserted him. To save Caroline Matilda, he would say anything his interrogators demanded.

Distraught and broken, Struensee admitted that he and Caroline Matilda had been lovers. Over the course of days he recounted each intrigue, every liaison, and through it all, he wept bitter tears. He was rewarded with material comforts including better food, wine and toiletries, but his words had doomed both him and the woman he loved. When Caroline Matilda's own cross examination began she stuck to her guns, refuting allegations of wrongdoing until Struensee's confession was shown to her. Still she responded with distressed denials, but her interrogator, Joachim Otto Schack-Rathlou, had an ace up his sleeve.

If Struensee had lied about their affair, he told the queen that the physician should face execution for such a slander against her good name. Though she knew the confession must have been extracted under torture, Caroline Matilda was forced into a corner. Should she save her honour, her lover would die; should she save her lover, her crown and reputation would be lost to her forever, yet Struensee would live. It was an easy choice.

Rathlou showed Caroline Matilda a document he had prepared in which she appeared to confirm Struensee's story in her own words. If she signed, he promised her that the disgraced doctor would not be put to death. With little choice, Caroline Matilda took up the pen and signed her name to the confession. It was enough to secure a royal divorce, meaning disgrace for the unhappy queen. On the matter of the little princess's paternity, rather tactfully, the court had nothing to say. After all, to question the legitimacy of one child would call into question that of the other. He was heir to the throne, and that would be a bridge too far.

In response to the brutal prosecution case against her, Caroline Matilda prepared a statement to be read to the court.

> 'I should utterly despair had not my intentions been always for the welfare of the King and the country. If I have possibly acted incautiously, my youth, my sex and my rank must plead in my favour. I never believed myself exposed to suspicion, and, even though my confession appears to confirm my guilt, I know myself to be perfectly innocent. I understand that the law requires me to be tried: my consort has granted me this much; I hope he will also, through the mouth of his judges, acknowledge that I have not made myself unworthy of him.'[35]

With Caroline Matilda's marriage at an end, all that remained was to decide her punishment.

Murray Keith had ideas of his own on that score. Disgraced she might be, he argued, but Caroline Matilda was still the sister of the king of Great Britain. This meant she was a princess, a woman of royal blood and privileges. Therefore she should be given into the care of her brother and allowed to return to her homeland.

With the court musing on the appropriate punishment for the now former queen, things were rather more cut and dried for Struensee and Brandt. Both were found guilty and sentenced to a brutal punishment. They were each to have one hand severed prior to be being broken on the wheel and beheaded.

Just three days after sentencing, the prisoners were conveyed to the eastern gate of Copenhagen, where an enormous crowd had gathered before a purpose built scaffold. Many of those present had camped out to ensure a good seat and they weren't to be disappointed. Dressed once more in the fine garments he had worn for the masque on the night of his arrest and unchained for the first time in months, Struensee was surprisingly composed. Brandt, his co-condemned, was positively cheerful.

Brandt was the first to die. Trembling, Struensee followed his friend and colleague to the scaffold and prepared for the axe. Horrifyingly, Struensee suffered a severe convulsion when his hand was severed and leapt to his feet, causing the executioner to give him a glancing blow, rather than behead him. He was seized by his hair and forced down onto the block so that the headsman might swing one more. This time, the blow was fatal.

As Struensee's reign reached its bloody end, Juliana Maria savoured her triumph. At the same time Caroline Matilda nursed her broken, betrayed heart. Now George III, under Murray Keith's direction, finally began to fight for her. He requested that his sister be given into his care, yet the Danish government demurred. *Hand her over*, the king demanded firmly, *or our nations go to war*.

This time, the Danes capitulated. Although the fate of Caroline Matilda's marriage was fuelling gossip in the chattering classes, the government agreed to entrust her to the care of George III whilst prohibiting any publication of the divorce ruling. She would retain her title and receive an annual stipend but she would not be allowed to see her son again. In addition, she must hand her daughter over to Christian.

A tearful Caroline Matilda agreed unhappily to these stipulations, comforted only by the knowledge that she would soon be on route for sanctuary in Britain. Here she could return to the countryside where she had been so happy and to the company of the family who had been her greatest comfort. Yet fate had one final twist.

Queen Charlotte, the wife of George III and a woman to whom virtue and piety was everything, put the brakes on her husband's plans. She would not allow a woman of such loose morals to come into contact with her children, Charlotte declared, nor should Caroline Matilda get any ideas about seeking refuge in Hanover, where the atmosphere was so light and cheery that she was bound to get into more mischief. Instead, Charlotte and George decided, Caroline Matilda should be sent to Celle, from whence the equally ill-fated Sophia Dorothea had hailed all those years earlier.

With her unhappy goodbyes to the daughter she would never see again still ringing in her ears, Caroline Matilda set off for Celle. She left behind the jewels her husband had given her, wishing to take nothing that might remind her of Christian. George handled this situation with the guidance of his ministers and, keen to avoid further offence, assured the Danish king that he might think of it as retaining the jewels for safekeeping, as opposed to feeling that they had been flung back in his face. Caroline Matilda was to be treated as befit a queen, regardless of what had gone before.

> 'By order of the King of Great Britain, our most Excellent Sovereign, the Royal etiquette will be observed in all points towards the Queen his sister. Her Majesty will be served in gold; and all the Royal household are already arrived from Hanover.'[36]

As Caroline Matilda settled into her new home at Celle she was once more accompanied by Louise von Plessen. Murray Keith, the consummate diplomat who had fought her corner, was richly rewarded for his robust care of the young lady. He was promoted to the position of ambassador at the Viennese court whilst George, as was befitting of a king known for his rigid moral code, did all he could to keep the sorry affair out of the public eye. When Caroline Matilda wrote to him three years later and asked for his assistance in a coup that would return her to the throne as regent, her brother wanted no part of it.

She was running out of time.

> 'On Thursday Evening last one of His Majesty's Electoral messengers arrived from Hanover with the melancholy Account, that Her Majesty Caroline Matilda, Queen of Denmark and Norway, died at Zell on the 10th Instant, about

Midnight, of a Malignant Fever, after an Illness of Five Days, to the great Grief of Their Majesties and all the Royal Family.'[37]

Queen Caroline Matilda died in Celle on 10 May 1775, aged just 23, a victim of scarlet fever. Despite rumours that her wicked stepmother-in-law had poisoned her, the disgraced queen's death was entirely natural.

For all his wishes to keep the scandal secret, George did not succeed. The newspapers reported on the gossip and across Europe, everyone knew what had really transpired in Denmark. Or at least, they *thought* they did.

> 'It is well known, that the intrigues of the QUEEN MOTHER and her party occasioned the execution of STRUENSEE, the most enlightening Minister that ever presided in the Danish Cabinet; and drove into exile CAROLINE MATILDA, the most accomplished princess in Europe.'[38]

In the centuries that followed, the tragic tale of the British princess and her star-crossed lover inspired writers, filmmakers and artists - from those early coffeehouse gossips to the silver screen of the twenty-first century. The scandalous love story of Caroline Matilda and Struensee, the queen and the doctor, continues to be told.

Chapter 3

Carry On Cumberland

In 1769 a shockwave of sexual scandal surged through London's high society. It rattled the windows of the royal palaces, filled the courtroom with saucy drama and left the public and press hungry for the next twist in an eyebrow-raising scandal. To a modern audience, the very idea that the king's brother might find his sex life held up for detailed public scrutiny is barely believable. For the Georgians, it was just the way of the world.

Prince Henry, Duke of Cumberland and Strathearn, had never really stood out amongst his brothers. In fact, Cumberland and his brother, George III, really couldn't have been more different in terms of intellect and, more importantly for the pious king, the direction in which their respective moral compass was pointing. George was a man who believed in keeping one's house in order and he was unique amongst the Georgian kings for the fact that no sexual scandal attached itself to his name. He hoped that his brothers might follow his example and lead lives that were beyond reproach but as his part in the creation of the Royal Marriages Act 1772 shows, he was wrong.

Whilst the king was occupied with the business of ruling, Cumberland seemed set for an uneventful and relatively comfortable life in the navy. He would, his brother hoped, be utterly without controversy, excitement or scandal.

His brother would prove to be sadly mistaken.

Someone who was *never* without excitement was Henrietta Vernon. This society beauty was the daughter of Henry Vernon, a Member of Parliament, and she was determined to achieve big things. Her sister had already made some serious inroads for the influential family and was maid of honour to Queen Charlotte, so winning Henrietta's hand in marriage would be a tempting prospect for any eligible bachelor of note.

That eligible bachelor turned out to be none other than Richard, Baron Grosvenor, future Earl of Grosvenor, and quite a catch in himself.

Lord Grosvenor was worth an absolute fortune and what he lacked in good looks and moral fibre, he more than made up for with his bank balance. Grosvenor's favourite hobby was womanising. He was known for his love of the company of prostitutes and ladies from the seamier side of town. Eventually his despairing doctors could no longer keep up with his frequent and ever more damaging battles with venereal disease and they declared that only one treatment would do: Lord Grosvenor must find a Lady.

In a twist worthy of a romantic novel, Grosvenor met that lady during a rainstorm in 1764. Whilst visiting Kensington Gardens, the heavens opened above the pox-ravaged noble, and he was forced to take shelter from the rainstorm in a lodge. There he found Henrietta and Caroline Vernon, who were also waiting out the deluge.

Happy news indeed.

Being a consummate gentleman, as well as a chap who liked the company of the ladies, Grosvenor gallantly asked whether the young ladies might accept a lift home from him in his luxurious carriage. Both accepted of course, for Grosvenor was no stranger to them. As a hugely wealthy and influential courtier, he often accompanied the royal dukes on their social engagements or out riding, so a lift in his carriage put them at no risk either in terms of their personal safety or their all-important reputations.

The Grosvenor family was famed for its wealth, typified by the grand London home, Grosvenor House, which caused wags to remark on its eye-watering proportions.

> 'When Grosvenor House, Millbank, was the extreme house on one of the ways leading out of London, somebody asked another, in passing, "Who lived in it?" "Lord Grosvenor," was the reply. I do not know what estate his lordship has," said the querist, "but he ought to have a good one; for nobody lives beyond him in the whole town.'[1]

Grosvenor accompanied the ladies to the carriage and settled into its opulent confines alongside them. Henrietta was not yet 20 but was already well-versed in the importance of employing her womanly wiles when faced with one of the richest men in the country. Of course she knew all about Lord Grosvenor and that this wasn't just *any* old carriage: this was the carriage that might carry her into a life of luxury.

Henrietta, wide-eyed and beautiful, commented innocently on the splendid quality of the vehicle's upholstery. How could one possibly infer any ulterior motive from a compliment when given by a young lady of such fine breeding and so little ambition? Grosvenor, of course, was entirely smitten by this beautiful young woman who was fourteen years his junior and commented that not only was she welcome to ride in the carriage, but to also become mistress of it if she would just say the word.

The young lady did indeed say the word and less than a month after they sheltered from the storms together, the couple was married. This may seem mind-bogglingly speedy to our modern eyes but in eighteenth century noble circles, there was nothing untoward about it whatsoever. In fact, one might imagine that readers who were acquainted with Grosvenor's wild ways might have even breathed a sigh of relief to learn that he was finally settling down. After all, this was the person described by diarist Joseph Farington as one of the 'most profligate men, of his age, in what relates to women'. Perhaps *relief* is a step too far then, as those in the know were instead whispering a quiet prayer for the young lady unfortunate enough to be the hellraiser's bride!

> 'This morning was married at St. George's Church, Hanover Square, by the Rev. Mr. Taylor, one of his Lordship's Chaplains, the Right Hon. Lord Grosvenor, to Miss Vernon, daughter of Henry Vernon, Esq; and niece to the Earl of Strafford. They went immediately from church to his Lordship's at Coombe in Surry [sic].'[2]

Talk about a whirlwind courtship! Be warned though, for this is no historical romance. There are no choirs of cherubs, no cupid's arrow and *definitely* no happy ending. As *The Gentleman's Magazine* ruefully commented once the sorry scandal of the lady and the duke began to unravel, such a speedy courtship and trip to the altar 'may serve as a caution to youth against entering for life into hasty connections.'[3]

The couple settled into married life together and for some time, all seemed well. Yet in truth, things were far from peachy. Henrietta swiftly realised that her husband was no bargain after all. She might have the run of the monumentally grand Grosvenor House, but she also had a spouse who wasn't about to toe the line. Saturnine, riddled with disease, pockmarked and blessed with a reputation for being anything *but* a gentleman, Lord Grosvenor wasn't ready to settle down.

Marriage didn't calm Grosvenor's baser instincts and he continued to visit brothels and gamble away enormous amounts from his fortune, losing as much as quarter of a million pounds in one night - and that figure *hasn't* been adjusted for inflation!

Lord Grosvenor had a thing for blondes and was a regular client of the notorious procuress, Ann Sheldon. In fact, the rakish nobleman made regular appearances throughout her memoirs. She claimed that they met when she had approached Grosvenor on a mission of charity regarding a member of her household who had fallen pregnant, but talk eventually turned to the matter of her business and, of course, a professional agreement was soon reached. Ms Sheldon might try to have us believe that she was innocence personified when it came to her own behaviour, but she was more than happy to arrange liaisons for others!

> 'Lord Grosvenor had a very great partiality for *lasses* with *golden locks*, I offered to recommend him one of that description, whom I had every reason to believe would meet with his approbation. He readily accepted of my proposal, and appointed to meet her at Mrs. *Townshend's*, a very miserable place indeed near *Argyle-buildings*. His Lordship was very well satisfied with my recommendation, and behaved very generously to me on the occasion. Thus did I become acquainted with a nobleman so well known in the annals of the gallant world, and have ever since that time, lived upon terms of good humour with him.—
>
> His Lordship, indeed, expressed a wish at this period to know my address, and accompanied the request, with offers of service to me; but as I was then connected with a gentleman who deserved every mark of regard and attention from me, I begged his Lordship to excuse my receiving him; and he was pleased to approve of the reasons I gave for such a conduct.'[4]

What a catch.

Grosvenor had a particular penchant for prostitutes from the poorest areas of London and Ann Sheldon put out something resembling a casting call on behalf of her illustrious client. The baron would choose his favourites from Mrs Sheldon's hand-picked line-up and soon, of course, those venereal diseases were raising their ugly heads again.

Henrietta despaired of her husband, yet she found an unlikely hero in Cumberland, in whose company she often found herself at royal engagements, either by accident or by design. With the heir[5] and spare born, Henrietta had no further obligation to the husband who had made her so miserable and she emerged as a glittering star of the social world once more. For a woman whose beauty was so remarked upon, to imagine that she might enjoy liaisons with a duke without anyone noticing was laughable, yet that is exactly what Cumberland and Henrietta attempted to do.

To drive the final nail into the coffin, Grosvenor discovered his wife reading a letter from her lover as she recuperated in bed from the birth of her second child. Thinking quickly, Henrietta told him that the letter was intended for a maid rather than herself and handed Grosvenor the note. He took it in good humour and showed its contents to Henrietta's mother, but no further action was taken. When nothing further was said, Henrietta allowed herself to believe that her husband hadn't fully understood the content of the note, and had failed to grasp that the couple was having an affair. Little known to Henrietta however, Grosvenor had asked the household staff to observe her coming and going and report back to him. With the promise of a generous payment for intelligence received, soon the network of spies extended throughout the city and beyond, with seemingly everyone keeping an eye out for the lady and the duke. Cumberland actually wore a variety of comical disguises for their trysts but it wasn't enough, he was instantly recognisable to anyone who had seen the prints that showed his typically Hanoverian features, not to mention the distinctive white eyelashes that some of his family displayed.

> 'I shall be at *St. Albans* on Saturday Evening, attended only by — and —. I suppose I need say no more to a cavalier of your spirit and resolution. I propose to put up at the sign of the —: but if you do not find me there, you know the other house. If no misfortunate be the consequence of this meeting, I shall flatter myself that all danger is at an end, and that I may meet the man I love with less fearful apprehension than I have lately fallen to the share of,
>
> Your most truly enamoured,
> G—. [Henrietta]'

'I Congratulate you, my charming girl, and I most sincerely congratulate myself, on the prospect before us. I will set sail to be at *St Alban's* at the moment of assignation; and be assured that I will elude the search of every other eye. Permit me to anticipate my happiness.

Yours, wholly yours,
C— —. [Cumberland]'

These letters, not at all unique between the lovers, marked the beginning of the end, thanks to an assignation at the White Hart in St Albans. Between any other couple, it's likely that nobody would have noticed but between a man already well known for his gallivanting and a woman whose husband was infamous for doing some gallivanting of his own, it's no surprise to discover that the press was all over the scandal.

The couple's clandestine meeting was observed. Thanks to an anonymous well-wisher, as Britain prepared to celebrate Christmas, the atmosphere in the royal palaces and at Grosvenor House was doubtless very frosty indeed. The names might have been judiciously expunged from the newspaper report, but there wasn't a soul alive in London society who didn't know exactly who the story referred to.

The tale that caused the trouble was a curiously uneventful one in which Cumberland and Henrietta were discovered by Lord Grosvenor together at the White Hart. Though they were indeed alone in a bedchamber, when Grosvenor burst in on them the couple was dressed and enjoying a game of cards together. The rumpled bed, he claimed, certainly appeared to have been put to good use no matter how innocent the scene appeared. It was the start of one of the most celebrated scandals of the era, and one that left the ultra-pious George III reeling.

Like all gentlemen, the king would certainly have partaken of *The Gentleman's Magazine* and when he read the following passage, his heart must have leapt into his chest. This was a sovereign who longed for a quiet life, yet he seemed destined to have anything but.

'An assignation at the White Hart at St. Albans between, Lady G—, and a certain great D—e was disconcerted by the forcible intrusion of my lord's gentleman, who about two o'clock in the morning burst the chamber door open, and found the lovers sitting together in close conversation. An affidavit has since been made in the Commons with a view to a divorce and a suit is likely to commence in which the ablest lawyers will be employed.'[6]

Across the city, gossip swirled about the identity of this mysterious, anonymous lady and her nameless duke. The Georgians revelled in scandal. It greased the wheels of society and kept the coffee houses and salons in business, and what was juicier than a *royal* scandal?

Nobody was more furious at the public embarrassment of such reports than Lord Grosvenor. It was one thing to be a man about town, known for gambling and flitting about the alleyways of Covent Garden and Ann Sheldon's 'dirty parts of Westminster', it was quite another to be cuckolded by your own wife. And with a royal duke! Especially a royal duke who was considered one of the more stupid inhabitants of the palace.

With his wife the talk of the town, Lord Grosvenor instructed his lawyers, Partington and Garth, to take action against her. That instruction became legal reality in March 1770, when a libel was entered in Doctors' Commons, the ecclesiastical court of the diocese of London that had the power to annul a marriage. Crucially though, the Commons wouldn't be able to grant the baron a divorce, but only a legal separation. Although he wouldn't be able to marry as a result of *this* suit, an annulment in Doctors' Commons would get Lord Grosvenor off the hook for alimony: he could walk away without having to give his wife so much as a penny.

Knowing what we do of the leading players in this particular scenario, with its injured party a shameless lord who liked nothing better than frequenting the lowest brothels, two passages in particular make for interesting reading in the suit. The first, describes Baron Grosvenor himself, suddenly transformed from a chap who cared for little beyond the pleasures of the flesh and the track into a gentleman who must surely be destined for sainthood. His lawyers clearly planned to make this the epitome of a bitter estrangement.

> 'That the said Richard lord Grosvenor, from the time of his aforesaid marriage with the said Henrietta now lady Grosvenor, always behaved towards her with true love and affection, and did all in his power to render her completely happy; and was and is a person of sober, chaste, and virtuous life and conversation, and one who would not be guilty of a breach of his marriage-vow; and for, and as such a person, he, the said Richard lord Grosvenor, was and is generally accounted,

respected, and esteemed to be, by and amongst his neighbours, friends, acquaintances, and others: and this was and is true, public, and notorious.'[7]

Can this really be the same man? The man who met Ann Sheldon to discuss the admission of her 'big-bellied chare-woman' to the lying-in hospital and managed to end the conversation in a discussion of the blondest prostitutes in town and their procurement? The man who offered Ann *services* and, later, more besides? Indeed, this supposedly pure, loving and faithful gentleman was so utterly blameless that he set up Ann as part of his *seraglio*, so that he might indulge his no doubt pious whims whenever the mood took him.

'I immediately entered into his Lordship's service; but as his frequent visits gave the people with whom I lived, occasion to suspect my calling, and his Lordship's practices, I returned again by his desire to *Lambeth*, and took a house in the *Marsh*, where a hundred thousand lords and commoners might have come daily and nightly, without notice or observation.'[8]

We digress.

So who had poor, blameless Lord Grosvenor yoked himself to upon marriage, we might wonder? Let us turn once more to the libel lawsuit and see how Messrs. Partington and Garth describe the lady in question, who appears to be some sort of Whore of Babylon, in league with Beelzebub himself.

'That the said Henrietta lady Grosvenor, being unmindful of her conjugal vow, and not having the fear of God before her eyes, but moved and instigated by the devil, did contract and carry on a lewd and adulterous conversation with his royal highness Henry-Frederick duke of Cumberland; and they, the said lady Grosvenor and his said royal highness the duke of Cumberland, frequently had the carnal use and knowledge of each other's body, and thereby committed the foul crime of adultery together, as is herein after more particularly unmentioned; and this was and is true.'[9]

Poor Lord Grosvenor. An innocent, loving, betrayed husband saddled with an immoral wife who— wait a minute, something seems wrong here, doesn't it? Of course, Lady Grosvenor *did* commit adultery, there's really little point in denying it, but the absolute hypocrisy of the philandering baron is mind-boggling. The press thought so too, and labelled Grosvenor *the Cheshire Cornuto*[10], in mocking recognition of his own unapologetically bad behaviour against his wife. Whilst the lawsuit alleged that the duke and the lady had been gadding about all over London, rumpling beds across the south and rarely if ever spotted apart from one another in public, the gentlemen of the press were well aware that Grosvenor was no shrinking violet.

For some reason, Grosvenor was willing to gamble on the fact that Henrietta wouldn't counter-sue for his own misdemeanours. If she did, the suits would effectively cancel each other out, with each party guilty of adultery to one degree or another. Before the trial began, Grosvenor requested an audience with the king at which he offered to make the matter *go away for a small consideration.* George, however, sent him on his way, declaring he knew nothing of the details of the case. So what was Grosvenor's motive in making this unusual offer? Was it simply an effort to avoid an embarrassing public scandal or might it be more sinister, positioning himself ready to blackmail the king into elevating him to a dukedom[11]? After all, George III loathed public embarrassment, and this stood to be one of the biggest. It threatened to be one of the most expensive too, with Grosvenor demanding damages of an eye-watering £100,000.

Whilst Grosvenor enjoyed his *seraglio*, the lovers were making use of a house in Pall Mall owned by a milliner named Mary Reda. Here the couple could spend uninterrupted and intimate hours together, away from the prying eye of the society gossips, or so they hoped. Their sex lives might be splashed all over the courts and the papers, but the press reserved its most withering criticisms for none other than Lord Grosvenor, their *Cheshire Cornuto*.

Still, this was and often still is a world in which husbands and wives are not afforded the same treatment and so it proved in the case of Lord and Lady Grosvenor. There was no question that the number of his transgressions had far outstripped hers, but there was equally no debate about which of the parties had sinned the most seriously. He was simply seeking a little sexual recreation, whereas she was imagined as being party to all manner of intrigues!

> 'At the time we highly condemn lady G— for her infidelity to Cornuto, we will not pretend to say his l—p had no connexions with the rest of the sex. But there is no parallel in

the transgression between a husband and a wife; for besides the risk on her side of a spurious issue to inherit his titles and estate, a woman's affections and esteem must be gained before she submits to a lover; whereas he, heated by liquor, corrupted by the example of his boon companions, or accidentally meeting with an agreeable object, may trespass upon conjugal fidelity without transferring any share of his affection from the proper object of his wishes. Accordingly we find upon the trial, that all the ladies who could be mustered to prove his unconstrained desires, except one, were the mere transient objects of his passion, on whom he made no other settlement than an idle hour.'[12]

With their secret out, Lady Grosvenor and Cumberland began to meet without the need for subterfuge and were even invited to social engagements together. After all, both of them probably knew that there was absolutely no point in refuting the allegations against them. Better instead to mount a counter-attack than fight a battle that they couldn't hope to win.

'A great concourse of people daily assemble before the house of Lady Grosvenor,' wrote *Bingley's Journal*, one of the papers that most concerned itself with the affair, 'and we are well informed, that while the Duke is paying his visits to her Ladyship, a person stands within that wall with a *drawn sword*, as a guard to keep off the populace.'[13] Such a throwaway comment can leave us in no doubt that the jig was very definitely up.

The prince, meanwhile, might have had his critics, but he had his champions too. He had unquestionably enjoyed countless liaisons with a married lady, but as a correspondent with the *London Evening Post* noted, 'a Prince of the Blood-Royal is entitled to some respect from his subjects.' He was young, his defender pointed out, and 'his passions are the same as other youths'[14]. Sometimes, it's good to be a prince.

The trial of Grosvenor v. Cumberland for *criminal conversation* began at King's Bench before Lord Mansfield[15] on 5 July 1770 and it soon became a cause célèbre. Better known as 'crim con', criminal conversation was a suit usually brought by a husband against his wife, in which he sued her for committing adultery. Abolished in the UK in 1857, it is still in use in some parts of the world but it really enjoyed its heyday in the eighteenth century.

The trial was the hottest ticket in London, but both the Grosvenors and Cumberland kept away. Instead the duke accompanied his sovereign sibling for a hack on the opening day of proceedings.

The baron's prosecution team assembled a rich procession of witnesses, each one more outrageous than the last but none was more so than Countess Camilla D'Onhoff[16]. She testified that the couple frequently visited her house in Cavendish Square, more often than not disappearing off together for some time during their liaisons. Countess D'Onhoff explained that she was as surprised as anyone to see the duke in her home but Henrietta explained his presence away, claiming that she wished to discuss the naval career of her brother with Cumberland, who was known for his involvement in maritime affairs. Alas, said Henrietta, she wasn't able to see Cumberland at her own home because he and her husband didn't get on, though she really had no idea why.

So far so good, if the countess is to be believed, but discovery lurked around every corner or behind every closed door. Amid tales of disordered bed linen and packages of letters sent back and forth between the duke and his lover, Countess D'Onhoff had a smoking gun.

Or a weapon of some description, at least. Unfortunately for Grosvenor, although she was happy to testify before the Doctors' Commons, when it came to the King's Bench, the countess blanched, leaving only her earlier testimony to consider.

Countess D'Onhoff testified that she left the duke and the lady alone in the dining room for half an hour and, upon her return, found Henrietta lying back on a couch. Her petticoats were gathered up around her waist and the Duke of Cumberland was lying on top of her, his breeches unfastened. The couple was having sex, the countess told the court, and Cumberland didn't so much as pause when he sent her away with a furious flea in her blushing ear. Two hours later the couple departed, leaving Countess D'Onhoff in a state of distressed distraction. She knew nothing of the romance, she claimed, and would never have agreed to them meeting in her home if she had done.

Of course, Countess D'Onhoff wasn't so distressed that she didn't allow more rendezvous, having sought and received Lady Grosvenor's assurances that the couple wouldn't misbehave again. Naturally they did just that, and the countess ambled into the room only to witness an almost exact replay of the same scene. It was all getting a bit *Carry On Cumberland*, and it was after this second discovery that the couple moved their liaisons to the rooms of the aforementioned milliner, Mary Reda, where they could presumably enjoy their sexual encounters without countesses wandering in and out of the room.

With the duke frequently away at sea, he and Henrietta communicated by letters which were often delivered via intermediaries. Those letters went on to form the backbone of the prosecution case; indeed the baron had already leaked them to the press in the hope of winning some support for his cause. Britain was heartily amused to see that the prince, who had been viewed as an unintelligent dullard, really *couldn't* spell, and the public was able to revel in his long-winded and confusing love letters thanks to their serialisation in the popular press.

Grosvenor's lawyers might have had the greater number of witnesses, but Cumberland's legal team had assembled some *very* interesting characters. One after the other Grosvenor's witnesses testified to cracking beds, loud groaning and bedsheets strewn here and there, not to mention the duke's enormous and eccentric black wigs and pseudonyms including *Squire Robinson* or *Farmer Jones*. They described his reliance on comedy accents and his pretence - *perhaps* - of stupidity, not to mention his chronic inability to spell. Little wonder that an atmosphere of saucy farce pervaded.

Into this scandalous hearing entered five young ladies who had met the baron in their capacity as prostitutes. Between them, Abigail Mary de Boisgermain, Mary Howe, Mary Smith, Ann Tremilly and Mary Watson painted a sorry picture of the supposedly wronged Grosvenor. Far from the devoted husband whose heart had been broken by his errant wife, her legal team contested, he was 'vicious, lewd and debauched'. On one occasion, the court heard, when he was riding in a carriage with Lady Grosvenor, the lord spotted one of his mistresses, sometimes known as Charlotte Gwynne among other names, travelling in the opposite direction. He abandoned Henrietta, commandeered a horse from his servants and took off after Charlotte, returning a short while later as though nothing untoward had happened. He even tried to install the 17-year-old Charlotte as maid to Lady Grosvenor to keep her close at hand, but the young lady refused to take the role.

While Lady Grosvenor and the Duke of Cumberland enjoyed their trysts in the Pall Mall house of Mary Reda, Lord Grosvenor had not been sobbing at home alone. Instead he passed indulgent nights of decadence with his favourite prostitutes. Indeed, in 1769, Abigail Mary de Boisgermain even gave birth to a son by the baron, though the baby died soon after birth.

Henrietta was determined to go down fighting. The defence concluded that it was the right of the wronged Lady Grosvenor to 'be divorced from bed, board and mutual cohabitation with the said Richard lord Grosvenor her husband, by reason of his adultery, committed by him as aforesaid.'[17]

It seemed that Grosvenor was a man of base instincts, whereas the duke was a bit of a fool. Indeed, the court heard that 'they could not charge his

R.H. with intriguing merely for the sake of intrigue, as the *incoherency* of his letters, plainly proved him to be a real lover.'[18]

Those letters veer from discussions of meetings and appointments missed to shady asides from Lady Grosvenor when she hasn't heard from her lover for a few days, distracted as he was by the *many charms* of Portsmouth and its environs. This accusation was batted away by Cumberland, who blamed not the ladies of the port town, but the duties of his commission. Often addressing his lover as his *sweet angel*, Lord Grosvenor is referred to by the couple as *the brute* and back and forth went the letters, getting ever more routine until their secret meetings are barely even discussed. Instead the livery of the coachman who will transport the lovers into one another's arms is described with the note ending simply, 'you know the rest'.

Indeed we do!

Damaging, perhaps, but not half as embarrassing as the Duke of Cumberland's now public recounting of an erotic dream featuring his paramour, which must have sent the king's eyebrows flying up to his hairline.

> 'I then prayed for you, my dearest love, kissed your dearest little hair, and lay down and dreamt of you, had you on the dear little couch, ten thousand times in my arms kissing you, and telling you how much I loved and adored you, and you seemed pleased: But alas! when I awoke, found it all delusion; nobody by me, but myself at sea.'[19]

Lord Mansfield, known for his royalist sympathies, took just thirty minutes to sum up the proceedings for the jury. He told them that they must try to set aside questions of rank and privilege and judge the couple as nothing more than a man and woman, free of worldly goods and titles. The damages decided upon, he warned, should not be greater because they were to be awarded to a nobleman from a prince. The searing social commentator, Junius[20], scathingly echoed public opinion that such advice was patently absurd. As a supporter of the crown, he argued, Mansfield had merely attempted to ensure that the damages awarded wouldn't be too ruinous for the royal purse.

> 'An action for criminal conversation being brought by a peer against a prince of the blood, you were daring enough to tell the jury, that in fixing the damages, they were to pay no regard

to the quality or fortune of the parties; — that it was a trial between A. and B. — that they were to consider the offence in a moral light only, and give no greater damages to a peer of the realm, than to the meanest mechanic. I shall not attempt to refute a doctrine, which if it was meant for law carries falsehood and absurdity upon the face of it: but if it was meant for a declaration of your political creed is clear and consistent. Under an arbitrary government, all ranks and distinctions are confounded. The honour of a nobleman is no more considered than the reputation of a peasant, for with different liveries they are equally slaves.'[21]

Taking the opposing corner when he analysed the case years later, Henry Brougham, 1st Baron Brougham and Vaux, suggested instead that the judge's wording might well stem from Mansfield's royalist sympathies but ultimately, it little mattered if that was the case. Rather than join Junius in his chorus of disapproval, Brougham suggested that the judge's words to the jury indicated 'a sufficient respect for the equal rights of all classes of plaintiffs, and might be as unpalatable to the Aristocracy as it was pleasing to the Crown.'[22]

He *was* a lawyer, remember.

Whatever really lay behind Mansfield's summing up. he didn't have long to wait to hear if it had the desired impact. Three hours after leaving the court, he received the verdict of the jury at his house in Bloomsbury Square.

Lady Grosvenor was found guilty of adultery and her husband was awarded damages of £10,000. It was a fraction of the sum he had hoped for, but still a fortune. With added costs, the total bill stood at £13,000[23]. As so many celebrities do nowadays, Grosvenor promised that he would donate any damages received to charity because, as *Bingley's Journal* sneered, 'the wages of *sin* cannot be more properly applied than to the protection of the innocent.'[24] Whether the donation was ever made is not recorded.

Whatever the destination of the cash, the Duke of Cumberland could not hope to pay such an amount. Instead he enlisted the help of his brother, Prince William Henry, Duke of Gloucester and Edinburgh, to approach the king for a hand out. They quickly discovered that their sovereign sibling couldn't afford to bail out Cumberland either. George had no choice but to write to the Prime Minister, Lord North, seeking assistance to clear up the sorry affair for his brother.

'A subject of a most private and delicate kind obliges me to lose no time in acquainting you that my two brothers have this day applied to me on the difficulty that the folly of the youngest has drawn him into; the affair is too publick for you to doubt but that it regards the lawsuit; the time will expire this day seven night, when he must pay the damages and the other expenses attending it. He has taken no one step to raise the money, and now has applied to me as the only means by which he can obtain it promising to repay it in a year and half; I therefore promised to write to you, though I saw great difficulty in your finding so large a sum as thirteen thousand pounds in so short a time; but their pointing out to me that the prosecutor would certainly force the House, which would at this licentious time occasion disagreeable reflections on the rest of his family as well as on him. I shall speak more fully to you on this subject on Wednesday but the time is so short that I did [not] choose to delay opening this affair till then; besides, I am not fond of taking persons on delicate affairs unprepared, whatever can be done ought to be done; and I ought as little as possible to appear in so very improper a business.'[25]

In other words, 'keep me out of it, mate.'

Lord North assured the king that the costs would be paid from the public purse, meaning that the people of Great Britain would be left to foot the bill for the Duke of Cumberland's sex life. Though we might expect the duke to be ashamed, he appeared anything but. Likewise, the king might have told him a few home truths but it seems that the God-fearing George III felt more embarrassment at being even vaguely involved in the affair than his erring brother *ever* did.

'I cannot enough express how much I feel at being in the least concerned in an affair that my way of thinking has ever taught me to behold as highly improper; but I flatter myself the truths I have thought it incumbent to utter may be of some use in his future conduct.'[26]

Fat chance.

The affair didn't end there though, because the prosecution and defence were already busily gathering material in preparation for the forthcoming divorce trial in the Consistory Court. It was here that the legal case stalled as both sides presented ample evidence to support the wrongdoing of the other. There was to be no divorce, only a legal separation and an annual allowance for £1,200 for Lady Henrietta Grosvenor. Though the Lord Chamberlain forbade any reference to be made to the affair and subsequent legal proceedings on the stage, the free press had a field day for months, riding high on the saucy tale of the Grosvenors and the duke.

The couple was bound to one another until 1802, when Lord Grosvenor's dissolute life finally caught up with him. Just a month after her husband's death, Henrietta finally married her long-time lover, Lieutenant-General George Porter[27]. Porter was a member of Parliament and fifteen years Henrietta's junior. He and his new bride enjoyed a long and happy marriage, eventually dying within two months of each other in 1828.

For the Duke of Cumberland, however, there was plenty more scandal to come.

Chapter 4

Scandalous Siblings

'Says Dick to Tom, this act appears
Absurd, as I'm alive;
To take the crown at eighteen years,
The wife at twenty-five.
Quoth Tom to Dick, thou art a fool,
And little knowest life;
Alas! 'tis easier far to rule,
A Kingdom than a wife!'

Before we continue on our journey into the scandals of George III's court, there is one little bit of legislation that might prove relevant. It arguably changed the face of the British monarchy and the history of the country, and it was the response of a king in crisis, little knowing *how* to bring his troublesome siblings and their wild loving ways under control.

'But enough of that bill! Never was an act passed *against* which so much, and *for* which so little, was said.'[1]

It was, of course, the Royal Marriages Act 1772.

Sounds exciting, doesn't it?

In a world of mistresses and intrigue, it might seem odd that the catalyst for the change in the law came not from some hair-raising extramarital scandal, but from a marriage. And this wasn't a marriage sought for money or rank or diplomatic advantage, let alone one arranged when the bride and groom were too young to understand the meaning of the word. This was a marriage of love.

Prince Henry, that troublesome Duke of Cumberland and Strathearn, didn't spend *all* his waking hours scandalising the courts and romping with

Lady Grosvenor. In fact, just two years after that sorry affair had so captured the Georgian imagination, he was well and truly in love. The woman who had stolen his heart was Mrs Anne Horton, née Luttrell, the daughter of Simon Luttrell, 1st Earl of Carhampton. So far, so well-connected you might think, yet fate was to play a hand when the beautiful, accomplished and highly eligible Anne chose to marry Christopher Horton, a squire and commoner.

Anne was widowed within four years and, still a young woman, she was soon back on the market. Her *friendships* with illustrious, titled men memorably caused Horace Walpole to wryly note that she was 'the Duke of Grafton's Mrs Hoghton, the Duke of Dorset's Mrs Hoghton, everyone's Mrs Hoghton'[2], but she had her sights set far higher than mere dukes. After all, there were princes to charm.

When Cumberland first laid eyes on Mrs Horton, he was bowled over. The cynics among us might murmur that he was equally bowled over by Lady Grosvenor but whatever the truth of the matter, the more Mrs Horton declared herself a respectable lady, the more besotted he became. In fact, if the gentlemen of the press are to be believed, he declared his love for Anne on the very same evening that he first met her. She, of course, demurred, arguing that her valuable reputation was at stake, so what did the Duke of Cumberland do? Did he take some time to regroup, to be sure that his affections were true and sincere, or did he go all guns blazing into marriage?

If you plumped for the latter, you'd be right. He amended his declaration of love to a proposal of marriage and the lady readily accepted. Cumberland, it seemed, had learned nothing from his embarrassing clash with Lord Grosvenor, and was still dedicated *only* to pleasing himself. However, for a man with a reputation as a freewheeler, finally getting the ring onto a lady's finger was quite an achievement. His choice of bride met with the odd wry comment from a press who always found plenty of fodder in the Duke of Cumberland's escapades.

> 'The marriage of his Royal Highness the Duke of Cumberland to the Hon. Mrs. Horton, mentioned in the papers of yesterday, gains credit. […] This marriage may make sufficient atonement for the follies of youth: and in case of the Duke of Gloucester's and the Princess of Wales's deaths, he will stand first (by act of Parliament) in the Regency. Mrs Horton is a widow lady, daughter to Lord Irnham and sister to Col. Luttrell. The married pair are gone to Calais for a little while.'[3]

Cumberland did not seek the permission of his brother, the king. Nor did he even do George the honour of telling him about the marriage before it had taken place as the brothers had been estranged since the Grosvenor affair. Given the bad blood between them, when Cumberland sought an audience at Richmond Lodge with his sibling, George no doubt wondered what would be behind it. Doubtless he suspected that the news he was about to hear could not be good. When Cumberland arrived at the lodge, the two men took a stroll together. During a brief pause in their walk, Cumberland handed his brother a letter.

Or dropped the bombshell, so to speak.

> 'Sir,
> It is impossible for me to describe the emotions whilst I impart an event which I feel I never should have kept a moment secret from you if I had not found myself incapable of offering you the cruel alternative of it either being involved in any inconvenience by giving your consent to it; or of pronouncing my future misery for life by your refusal. Sir, I am married to Mrs. Horton Lord Ihrnam's daughter and nothing now remains to make me one of the happiest of men but your approbation which I trust the sensibility of your heart and the amiable qualifications of the object of my choice will strongly plead for and fully justify.
>
> Your most anxious and dutiful brother.'

Don't be fooled by the rather respectable sounding *Lord Irnham*, for Anne's father was a rogue to be reckoned with. He revelled in the nickname of *the King of Hell*, thanks to his regular visits to a place *called* Hell, one of Dublin's most notorious red light districts. The reputation of her brother, an unpopular politician, was not much better either.

Of course, Cumberland didn't *have* to ask George's permission to marry Anne, whom Walpole claimed was a 'coquette beyond measure' with 'the most amorous eyes in the world, and eyelashes a yard long,' but it would have been the polite thing to do. Furious, upset and worse still, grievously disappointed, the king ordered Cumberland from his presence. The affair of Lady Grosvenor had taught his brother nothing, it seemed, and George III was at his wits' end.

In fact, the marriage didn't scandalise Great Britain anything like as much as it scandalised and distracted the king himself. As a result of his brother's violently emotional response, the Duke and newly-minted Duchess of Cumberland left the country. The cat was out of the bag and as a final full stop, the press declared that Cumberland 'will not return to England till the K— will receive and acknowledge [Anne] as the D—s of C. We are also informed, that the R—l F—y is in great sorrow on this event.'[4]

Filled with righteous fury and indignation, the king had no intention whatsoever of recognising *any* Duchess of Cumberland. Instead he took up his pen, writing first to his mother, the Dowager Princess of Wales, to warn that the marriage could only bring about '[Cumberland's] inevitable ruin and [was] a disgrace to the whole family.' He then penned a second letter, this one to his favourite brother, Prince William Henry, Duke of Gloucester and Edinburgh, informing him of the misdeeds of this most troublesome of siblings.

Little did George know.

In fact, Cumberland wasn't alone in having arranged a clandestine marriage to a commoner. Even as Gloucester read the anguished revelations of what had happened in his absence, he had a secret of his own to keep.

Just the small matter of another secret marriage.

Of that, more anon.

In his fevered mind, George began to imagine any number of absurd scenarios that might arise from Cumberland's marriage. He pictured a world in which this union tore the country in two, of mass conflict and a return to the tumultuous days in which the arguments between 'the Yorks and the Lancasters were greatly owing to intermarriages with the nobility.'[5] In all honesty, it was ridiculous to imagine that Cumberland's new fancy could possibly end in a new civil war with the supporters of the crown on one side and those of his brother on the other. Cumberland had no interest in usurping the king. In fact, for a man who wanted to live life in line with his own wishes and not according to the rigid protocol and piety that bound his brother, the life of a monarch would have been suffocating to Cumberland.

Although Gloucester was concealing his own clandestine marriage, that didn't stop him from replying sympathetically to George. What must Gloucester have felt as his emotionally shattered brother poured out his heart? As he related his sadness and disappointment at the marriage of

Cumberland, one can only imagine the turmoil that must have seized the loyal Gloucester. For one day soon, he knew, he too would have to break his oldest brother's fragile heart.

The king became preoccupied with what he saw as Cumberland's betrayal and, with plenty of other unmarried siblings waiting in the wings, he was determined to put a stop to them thoughtlessly marrying the commoners who stole their hearts. He was encouraged along the path by his wife, Charlotte, who was even more extreme on matters of protocol and propriety than her husband, if that were possible. The only solution appeared to be to turn to the law and enshrine an act that expressly forbade any further such marriages from taking place. There was no attempt to pretend that this was driven by necessity for the wellbeing of the kingdom though, it was strictly a matter of personal family pride for the king. Ironic then that his first love had been Lady Sarah Lennox, a commoner who stole his heart. Duty kept George from marrying her, and it was a duty he would never allow his siblings and children to forget.

To this end, George and Lord North came up with the Royal Marriages Act. The king saw it as an immensely personal matter and warned the Prime Minister that nothing less than the total support of Parliament would do. 'I do expect every nerve to be strained to carry the Bill through both houses with a becoming firmness,' he wrote. 'For it is not a question that immediately relates to Administration, but personally to myself; therefore I have a right to expect a hearty support from everyone in my service, and shall remember defaulters.'[6]

The Royal Marriages Act was a blunt instrument aimed at enforcing George's will not only on his brothers, but on all members of the royal family. It specified that any descendent of George II who wished to marry could only do so with explicit consent from the monarch, given under the Great Seal and noted by the Privy Council. If the king refused to consent, as he alone could do, then the marriage could not go ahead. If it *did*, it would be considered illegitimate. The only exception to the rule was for those over the age of 25, who were offered a second option should the monarch refuse permission. In these cases, the disappointed parties could give notice of their wish to marry to the Privy Council. If Parliament did not refuse permission, twelve months after notice had been given, the couple could be married.

The full text of the bill, should you be champing at the bit to read it, follows. To get the full Georgian politician experience, be sure to be full of annoyance and righteous indignation by the time you reach the end!

'Whereas your Majesty, from your paternal affection to your own family, and from your royal concern for the future welfare of your people, and the honour and dignity of your crown, was graciously pleased to recommend to your parliament to take into serious consideration, whether it might not be wise and expedient to supply the defect of the laws now in being; and, by some new provision, more effectually to guard the descendants of His late majesty King George the Second, (other than the issue of princesses who have married, or may hereafter marry, into foreign families) from marrying without the approbation of your Majesty, your heirs, or successors, first had and obtained; we have taken this weighty matter into our serious consideration; and, being sensible that marriages in the royal family are of the highest importance to the state, and that therefore the Kings of this realm have ever been entrusted with the care and approbation thereof; and, being thoroughly convinced of the wisdom and expediency of what your Majesty has thought fit to recommend, upon this occasion, we, your Majesty's most dutiful and loyal subjects the lords spiritual and temporal, and commons, in this present parliament assembled, do humbly beseech your Majesty that it may be enacted: and be it enacted by the King's most excellent majesty, by and with the advice and consent of the lords spiritual and temporal, and commons, in this present parliament assembled, and by the authority of the same, that no descendant of the body of his late majesty King George the Second, male or female, (other than the issue of princesses who have married, or may hereafter marry, into foreign families) shall be capable of contracting matrimony without the previous consent of his Majesty, his heirs, or successors, signified under the great seal, and declared in council, (which consent, to preserve the memory thereof is hereby directed to be set out in the licence and register of marriage, and to be entered in the books of the privy council); and that every marriage, or matrimonial contract, of any such descendant, without such consent first had and obtained, shall be null and void, to all intents and purposes whatsoever.

Provided always, and be it enacted by the authority aforesaid, That in case any such descendant of the body of his late majesty King George the Second, being above the age of twenty-five years, shall persist in his or her resolution to contract a marriage disapproved of or dissented from, by the King, his heirs, or successors; that then such descendant, upon giving notice to the King's privy council, which notice is hereby directed to be entered in the books thereof, may, at any time from the expiration of twelve calendar months after such notice given to the privy council as aforesaid, contract such marriage; and his or her marriage with the person before proposed, and rejected, may be duly solemnized, without the previous consent of his Majesty, his heirs, or successors; and such marriage shall be good, as if this act had never been made, unless both houses of parliament shall, before the expiration of the said twelve months, expressly declare their disapprobation of such intended marriage.

And be it further enacted by the authority aforesaid, That every person who shall knowingly or wilfully presume to solemnize, or to assist, or to be present at the celebration of any marriage with any such descendant, or at his or her making any matrimonial contract, without such consent as aforesaid first had and obtained, except in the case above-mentioned, shall, being duly convicted thereof incur and suffer the pains and penalties ordained and provided by the statute of provision and praemunire made in the sixteenth year of the reign of Richard the Second.'

It wasn't George III's finest or most popular hour and William Pitt, 1st Earl of Chatham[7], advised that the sovereign should take care over this particular legal move. In his letters he laments the 'new-fangled and impudent' act, finding it 'wanton and tyrannical'. To George's political and public opponents, it seemed as though the king was indeed the tyrant that they had always suspected him to be. They wondered whether the princes and princesses, simply by being of royal blood, should really be deprived of a right all in Great Britain shared - to marry who they wanted.

However, when the bill went before the Lords on 26 February 1772, opponents in the House were less plentiful than they were on the streets. Although there were no great protests there were plenty of questions; ranging from whether George intended to attempt to control the marriages of *all* the descendants of George II, or only his own children, to the smallest minutiae imaginable regarding the specific wording chosen.

The Duke of Cumberland himself came to Westminster to argue that the bill was intended purely to spite *him*. He requested that a clause that allowed the Act to be applied retrospectively be erased, thus ensuring that his marriage to Anne could never be declared void.

> 'The bill now in agitation seems framed by the Minister with an intention of doing an injury to my family; I profess myself a married man, and I appeal to your Lordships humanity, whether any bill ought to pass this assembly, which contains a retrospective clause, evidently inserted to advert to an *ex post facto* matter? I trust your Lordships will not suffer so material an injury to be done me and my family.'[8]

Regardless of the doubts and criticisms from dukes and press and from some of the public, on 1 April 1772 the Act received royal assent[9]. Contrary to some misunderstandings of the Act, it didn't remove anyone who married *without* the monarch's approval from the line of succession, but any children of the marriage would be considered illegitimate and barred from sitting on the throne.

Given his own intervention in matters of marriage, George II might have found all of this wryly amusing or, more likely, responded to it by kicking his wig around his chambers and stamping his feet - he was that sort of chap. During the reign of the late king, *An Act for the Better Preventing of Clandestine Marriage* was put before Parliament by Philip Yorke, 1st Earl of Hardwicke. Better known by the far more succinct title of *The Marriage Act 1753*, this Act was the first legislation passed that required a formal ceremony of marriage to have taken place for a union to be considered legal. It laid down rigid stipulations regarding the reading of the banns and the need for licences, as well as acceptable venues for a legal wedding. Aimed at stopping clandestine marriages, the new legislation led directly to the popularity of trips to Gretna Green for the eloping Wickhams and Lydias of the world.

Perhaps ironically, the royal family was exempt from the law at the personal request of George II. He declared hotly, 'I will not have my family laid under these constraints!'. Considering that his successor was now pushing for a law to prevent the descendants of that very king from pursuing secret marriages, it was quite a turnaround.

George III might have hoped that would be an end to it and having lost his mother[10] during the process of getting the Act through Parliament, he was more than ready for a change in fortune. His letter to Lord North is that of a man in a celebratory mood, happy that a weight has been lifted from his mind.

'The account I have just received from you of the very handsome majority this day gives me infinite satisfaction,' wrote the king, and Lord North became a Knight of the Garter in recognition of his steering the Act through Parliament. 'I owns [sic], myself a sincere friend to our Constitution, both Ecclesiastical and Civil, and as such a great enemy to any inovations [sic], for, in this mixed Government, it is highly necessary to avoid novelties.'[11]

George III was delighted with the Act and optimistic that this would put an end to questionable marriages once and for all.

Not for the first time, he was wrong.

Remember that secret marriage I mentioned earlier? Like all secrets, it couldn't remain hidden forever and the Duke of Gloucester, the brother in whom George III had put so much of his trust and respect, was about to drop a cannonball right into the middle of the king's celebrations.

On 6 September 1766, five whole years before Cumberland and Anne tied the knot that led to the Royal Marriages Act, Prince William Henry, Duke of Gloucester and Edinburgh, had married someone who would be even less palatable to George III than the Duchess of Cumberland.

The lady was Maria Walpole, the illegitimate daughter of Edward Walpole and Dorothy Clement, a woman of decidedly humble origins. Lady Mary Wortley Montagu, that estimable chronicler of Georgian society, recalled hearing an early description that captures not only Dorothy's penury, but also her greatest asset, her eye-catching beauty.

> 'Lady Waldegrave's mother was the most remarkable beauty I have ever heard of. […] When she [the young Dorothy] was in the humble position of sitting on a dust-cart before the bishop's door, that lady [the bishop's wife] had the curiosity to call her in merely to see her nearer, and assured me that, in all her rags and dirt, she never saw a more lovely creature. Some time after she heard she was in the hands of a Covent-garden milliner, who transferred her to Neddy W. [Walpole], who doted on her to the day of her death.'[12]

Neddy was more formally known as Edward Walpole, son of Robert Walpole, the infamous politician and first Prime Minister of Great Britain. His family was influential, his name famed and Neddy and Dorothy adored one another, but for all his family connections, there was one thing that the happy couple lacked: a marriage licence. Although their relationship resulted in four children[13] who all went by the surname of *Walpole* and Edward and Dorothy lived as husband and wife, the couple had never actually married. In polite Georgian society, that was always going to be a big deal.

An ambitious woman like Maria was not about to let the circumstances of her birth hold her back. She inherited her mother's beauty and was a lively, witty conversationalist with excellent family connections, which saw her presented at court in 1758. When George III's childhood tutor, James, 2nd Earl Waldegrave, laid eyes on the 22-year-old Maria, he was smitten. Horace Walpole recalls that she was 'beauty itself! Her face, bloom, eyes, hair, teeth, and person are all perfect […] She has a great deal of wit and vivacity, with perfect modesty.'[14]

The couple was quickly wed and despite the large difference in age, the signs were good. Now the illegitimate girl had a title to match her intelligence, looks and charm, even if she didn't have the honourable birth to go with it. 'I am not surprised at Lady Waldegrave's good fortune' wrote Lady Mary Wortley Montagu archly. 'Beauty has a large prerogative.'[15]

Lord Waldegrave was more than twenty years his wife's senior and in 1763, just a month short of his fourth wedding anniversary, he fell victim to smallpox, leaving behind two children and his pregnant widow[16]. The redoubtable Maria wasn't the sort to let a small matter like losing her husband get her down and she was soon doing the social rounds once more, even though her reduced income could scarcely support her, and certainly wasn't enough to allow her to lead the life to which she had become accustomed. She was as stunning to behold as her mother before her and society was shocked when she rejected the suit of the wealthy and well-connected Duke of Portland, but they little knew her motive. For Maria had met a prince, and so a duke would never do.

Prince William Henry, Duke of Gloucester and Edinburgh, was seven years Maria's junior. Just as Earl Waldegrave had been, he was bewitched by the lady's beauty. Yet Gloucester, unlike Cumberland, shared the timid demeanour of their brother, the king, and he did not dare mention his infatuation to George. Maria wasn't so reticent and revealed the relationship to her uncle, Horace Walpole. Although it was 1766, and years before the Royal Marriages Act, Walpole counselled his niece to proceed with caution. The king was unlikely to give consent to a marriage between his brother and an illegitimate commoner, he told her, and even if he did, such would be the scandal that she and her husband would probably be shipped to Hanover out of harm's way, and Maria would likely be kept from her young daughters. With Walpole's gentle guidance, Maria asked if he might compose a letter to Gloucester to inform the duke that she was of too low a rank to be with him, whilst still being of too high a rank to be his mistress.

It all came too late to silence society gossip and the prince would not take Horace Walpole's politely phrased *no* for an answer. When he prevailed upon Maria not to end their affair she capitulated, and Horace Walpole thereafter refused to see or speak of the Duke of Gloucester and Edinburgh. Whilst society tittle-tattle cast the duke and the Dowager Countess of Waldegrave as lovers, the shrewd Walpole knew a thing or two about life and he suspected they must already be married, for both were highly religious and the king treated Maria respectfully at court. In fact, Walpole began to suspect that George knew of the marriage and had promised never to disclose it. In that supposition, of course, he was badly mistaken.

The couple married on 6 September 1766 in a secret ceremony in Maria's Pall Mall home. In all honesty, given the fact that Maria was welcomed at court and treated with the same dignity and respect shown to a visiting duchess, might we agree with Horace Walpole that George and Charlotte knew of the marriage and were simply choosing to keep the secret? On balance I think not, for George was not the sort of man who was willing to let a moral failing slip past unremarked. What is far more likely is that the monarch had his suspicions but didn't delve too deeply into the facts of the matter - a question of don't ask, don't tell. So long as he didn't know for sure, then he wasn't indulging in any deception, and he and Gloucester were so close that George wouldn't have risked losing his brother's valued friendship over a suspicion that he could happily choose not to pursue.

Maria took up residence at Hampton Court, deep within the innermost confines of the palace that were usually reserved for members of the royal family. She even had permission for her carriage to come and go from the inner courtyard, a distinctly royal privilege, and the press was quick to hint at more.

> 'We have it from the best authority, that when Lady Waldegrave pays her *private* visits to the Royal Family, she is always received by them in the title of Duchess of Gloucester.'[17]

Gossip was one thing but once the rumours began appearing in the newspapers, can we really believe that the king and queen didn't know what everyone else seemed so sure of? In May 1772, *The London Evening Post* took the bull by the horns and, at a time when the denials were coming from all corners, firmly laid the opinion of its editor out for all to see.

'There are many circumstances which make it believed, the King has not been ignorant of this marriage. Some time ago, when the Duke of Gloucester gave a grand entertainment to the Royal Family, Lady Waldegrave shewed [sic] her particular marks of attention. Either the Queen knew she was Duchess of Gloucester, or the Duke was unpardonably indiscreet to produce any other woman before her Majesty. The Duke is extremely acquiescing to the King, and takes particular care never to oppose his royal will. This clearly shews, [sic] that a clandestine marriage is not disagreeable at Buckingham-House. The contrast is striking. The brother, who has spirit to avow his marriage to the nation [Cumberland] is not to be forgiven. But the brother who keeps his marriage a secret [Gloucester], and may thereby occasion a contested succession to the crown, is caressed, promoted, has a grand Levee.'[18]

This odd state of affairs prevailed for some years but it couldn't go on forever. When Maria fell pregnant in 1772, the duke's moral compass could not allow him to keep the secret any longer. What must he have thought as he spilled out his heart to his brother, that same brother who had always seen Gloucester as a beacon of good sense and support? The same Gloucester, let's not forget, who had listened patiently to George's wailings about the moral collapse of the Duke of Cumberland, and the secret marriage that forced the passing of the Royal Marriages Act? Now not one but two princes were married to women who had troublesome politicians in the family and worst of all, they had contracted the marriages secretly.

'His R—l H—ss the Duke of Gl—r, on Wednesday declared his Marriage with Lady Waldegrave in Form to the K—, and acted a Part becoming a Man, while he acquitted himself of his Affection to his Brother and his Duty to his Sovereign.'[19]

It was all too much and George offered his brother an ultimatum. He could stay true to Maria and lose his brother, or remain loyal to the crown and forsake Maria. Gloucester chose love and just like Cumberland, he and his bride were banished. Both men bitterly regretted what had happened and as autumn drew on the estranged brothers vainly sought a reconciliation that would be years in the making. Yet the scandal here wasn't in the marriage itself, but in the reaction of George III, already suspected of black-hearted tyranny for his passionate pursuit of the Royal Marriages Act. Now he compounded his wrong, condemning his close friend and brother to an unhappy exile from court.

> '[…] the Duke of Gloucester is dying, not of a consumption, as hath been artfully and resignedly propagated, but of a broken heart, because his marriage with lady Waldegrave is not to be acknowledged.'[20]

For ten years the brothers were estranged and for ten years, George denied himself the company of his most precious brother. Gloucester's health and finances suffered and he and his little family eventually left England to escape their creditors. Yet George, in his self-appointed capacity as father-figure to his brothers, could not allow himself to show mercy. To do so, he reasoned, was to show tolerance of immorality, and that would never do. When Gloucester requested financial help, the king wrote to Lord North on the matter of his lost sibling, betraying a hint of remorse but still remaining clear about where the blame lay.

> 'My dear Lord, I cannot deny that on the subject of the Duke of Gloucester my heart is wounded. I have ever loved him more with the fondness one bears to a child than a brother: his whole conduct, from the time of his publishing what I must ever think a highly disgraceful step, has tended to make the breach wider; I cannot therefore bring myself, on a repetition of his application, to give him hopes of a future establishment for his children, which would only bring a fresh altercation about his wife, whom I can never think of placing in a situation to answer her extreme pride and vanity.'[21]

Perhaps, as the years passed, George began to believe that his family had given up on illicit marriages. If so, he was due to be dealt a devastating blow by his son, Augustus, not to mention the infamous George, better known as the Prince Regent. The Royal Marriages Act might have led to accusations of tyranny but it was to prove to be a rather blunt instrument, as we shall soon see!

Chapter 5

Perdita and Pickle

'In the theatre nothing is necessary to the amusement of two hours, but to sit down and be willing to be pleased.'

The words of Dr Samuel Johnson, gentleman of letters and master of pithiness, might have been written for the royal sons of George III. Whilst his sister was busy raising hell in Denmark and his brothers marrying ladies without a moment's thought for legality, he couldn't be blamed for hoping that his sons might have learned from the mistakes of their uncles. Augustus Frederick, the king's sixth son, had certainly learned nothing, and chose instead to uphold what appeared to be a burgeoning family tradition for clandestine marriages that George, Prince of Wales, would later continue when he wed the Roman Catholic widow, Mrs Maria Fitzherbert. Before they went anywhere *near* the altar, the sons of George III had some seriously wild oats to sow.

Though born four years apart, Mary Darby Robinson and Dorothea Jordan had more in common than their status of royal mistresses. Both knew what it was to be abandoned, first by their fathers, then by their princes, and both enjoyed success against some enormous odds, including smallpox, illegitimate pregnancy and careers that weren't always plain sailing. Whilst one of them fell into scandal *because* of her relationship, the other managed to stay perfectly respectable until her love affair ended.

This is a story of two actresses, two princes and two broken hearts. Although Mary and Dora didn't live their lives along parallel lines, I present them here as if they did. How better to compare and perhaps contrast (to borrow that favourite school essay technique) their experiences as women clasped, though briefly in one case, to the royal bosom?

Men were not kind to Mary Darby Robinson. From her father to her husband to her lovers, they all proved to be an unreliable bunch. Yet they flocked to her like moths to a flame and all too often, she was the one who ended up feeling the burn.

Mary was born in Bristol[1] as the fifth child[2] of Nicholas Darby, a member of the Society of Merchant Venturers, and his wife, Hester Vanacott. The couple had married in 1749 and they enjoyed a prosperous life, making their home in a house that had once been part of St Augustine's monastery. The building nestled in the shadow of the cathedral and Mary was born in a gothic chamber that overlooked the cloisters. Here, at the top of a winding staircase, beneath a door studded with fearsome iron spikes, the girl who would grow into a beloved actress, a scandalous mistress and a celebrated author, made her first entry onto the universal stage.

Mary's early life seemed idyllic to the little girl. Her father was prosperous and her mother devoted to her family, yet there were storm clouds on the horizon. Captain Darby was an ambitious man, not the sort who was content to rest on his laurels. Instead he sought adventure and even more wealth, and he decided that everything he wanted could be found in North America. His wife, fond of her comfy home and settled life, couldn't bring herself to encourage his plans to depart their homeland.

Whilst her parents battled over their opposing desires for the future of their family, Mary embarked on her education. She attended a Bristol school on Park Street that had been established by the celebrated bluestocking, Hannah More[3], and it was she who gave Mary her first taste of the stage. In 1764, Bristol was overcome with theatrical mania when the celebrated actor, William Powell, came to the city and gave a benefit performance of *King Lear*. The production was considered by some to be even better than David Garrick's interpretation and Powell and More became great friends behind the scenes.

When Powell visited the newly-built Theatre Royal in Bristol to revive his Lear, the Park Street students undertook an enthusiastic field trip to watch him perform. Mary was enraptured by what she saw, transported by Powell into another realm[4]. Her response to his co-star and wife, Elizabeth, was a little more muted and it appears that the rest of the audience agreed, for Mrs Powell did not trouble the stage with her presence again.

Mary became a voracious reader and it's tempting to speculate that this might have provided a way to escape the troubles at home, where her parents were still engaged in a battle of wills. Captain Darby was set on his scheme of going to America and if his wife wanted to continue to live in the splendour to which she had become accustomed, then he needed to find *some* way to keep the coffers full. He became convinced that there was a fortune to be made in whaling and began to develop a scheme to establish a whale fishery on the coast of Labrador in Newfoundland, a plan that sounded wild even to the most adventurous souls.

The voyage out to Labrador would be perilous and the territory that awaited offered little in the way of comfort. It would be a challenge but, armed with permission from the British government, it was a challenge that Darby was ready to accept. Hester was having none of it, especially when her husband revealed that he would be gone for at least two years. After some soul-searching she elected to remain in Britain with her children rather than be separated from them. She had no intention of facing the perilous sea journey whilst they remained at home to complete their education with neither mother nor father there.

Separated by thousands of miles, Captain and Mrs Darby initially exchanged loving letters but as the months sped past, those notes from the other side of the world became less frequent and less adoring. When the truth behind this change in her husband's manner became known, Hester was inconsolable.

'The cause of my father's silence was discovered to be a new attachment,'[5] Mary recalled in her memoirs, the years having lent her memories the wry edge that was so characteristic to her. 'A mistress whose resisting nerves could brave the stormy ocean, and who had consented to remain two years with him in the frozen wilds of America.'[6]

Reeling from this revelation, more misery was to follow in short order when Darby's scheme failed. The indigenous Inuit people he found in Labrador were hostile to his ambitious plans. They burned his settlement and scuppered his ships, whilst the crews fell victim to violent infighting. The ambitious Darby lost everything on the venture and at home, the luxurious life of Hester Darby and her children was about to change forever.

Over in Ireland, meanwhile, another little girl was making her first steps in a very different world. She was Dorothea Bland, who in 1761 was born to a Welsh mother and an Irish father in London. She was always thought of as an Irish girl though, for that's where she was brought up after her little family returned to their home in Dublin. Dora was not born in a cloister, nor did she enjoy the early privilege of the young Mary. Instead she was the daughter of a far less illustrious couple, but that would not hold back her meteoric rise into the beating centre of the royal heart.

Young Dora was not, on the face of it, an obvious match for the son of a king. She was illegitimate to start with, for Grace Phillips might have *called* herself *Mrs* Grace *Bland* but she wasn't actually married to her 'husband', Francis Bland. He was underage at the time of the ceremony and his own father had the match annulled and refused to offer the couple any financial assistance, but that didn't stop them trying to make a go of things. Grace was an actress, he was a stagehand and Dora was one of many siblings[7] who were brought up in Dublin. Yet Francis Bland couldn't rest with what he had and having lived a comfortable early life, the knowledge that his parents had disinherited him began to niggle as the years passed.

Bland took up a military position and eventually deserted Grace and his family when Dora was 13, abandoning his wife and children to an uncertain future. Just as Captain Darby deserted his family in the belief that there might be greener pastures elsewhere so too did Francis Bland. He went off to search for his own fortune. Just like Darby, he found another woman to soothe his fevered brow and left his (sort of) wife and children high and dry. Quite unlike the privileged Darbys, the struggling Blands had never known what it was to live in the lap of luxury. A hard life had just become considerably more difficult.

Mindful that she had to play her part in keeping the household from complete penury, Dora took a job as assistant to a milliner whilst Francis occasionally sent meagre purses of money back to his abandoned family. He enjoyed some success in the army and even more in romance, marrying Catherine Mahony, a rather well-to-do lady. Sadly for him his fortune was fleeting and in 1778 Francis Bland died, leaving Grace and his children without so much as a penny. Yet Dora's mother believed that her daughter, with her pretty face and flattering cascade of curls, could do better than millinery. Why, thought Grace, young Dora looked like an actress, and she reckoned that if she made the right connections, a career on the stage could be rather more lucrative than one in hats!

As with so many elements of Dora's early life, the details of her debut are questionable. Early biographers suggest she made her first appearance on stage as Phoebe in *As You Like It* at the tender age of 18. Later chroniclers of Dora's life suggest that her debut was actually a couple of weeks before *As You Like It* opened, as she took the role of Miss Lucy in Henry Fielding's *The Virgin Unmasked*. Jerrold states with authority that it was definitely the latter, as it pipped the bard to the post and appeared in the first week of November 1779. The curtain didn't go up on the Dublin production of *As You Like It* until a couple of weeks later.

Not long after that Dora hit on the formula that would prove the making of her. In true Georgian style, she decided that her unique selling point wasn't her beauty, her talent, her comic timing or even her sweet singing voice – it was instead her perfect legs!

Dora began to specialise in breeches roles in which she played young men, and when the audience saw her shapely calves, it went wild[8]. Dora, it seemed, had finally found her niche.

70

Lucky old Dora.

Meanwhile things were going from bad to worse for the Darby household. No sooner had Mary's younger brother fallen victim to smallpox (luckily, he survived) than the family learned that Darby was to return. Yet there was to be no reunion, for he was planning to establish a home in London with his mistress. Was there no shame to which he would not subject them, Hester must have wondered? Humiliation was something that Mary would one day become intimately acquainted with.

Though Darby would eventually go back to Labrador and enjoy great success there, he had no intention of returning to the bosom of his family. Instead he told them that they must all tighten their belts and lower their expectations. The family moved to London without Darby and it was here that Mary became a pupil of Meribah Lorrington. Lorrington was a remarkable woman; a true bohemian with a fierce intellect and a fatal weakness for booze, it was she who instilled in the young lady an undying love of literature. Though Mary had never boarded when she lived in Bristolian splendour, she moved into Lorrington's room at her new school and swiftly became a favourite student. Sadly the mercurial Lorrington's school was doomed to failure and she drank her way to ruin, leaving Mary and the rest of her pupils to seek new billets[9].

Mary continued with her education and eventually began giving classes of her own in the school that her go-getting mother had established with Lorrington's inspiration. Having recovered from her abandonment the redoubtable Hester had determined to make her own way in the world and was enjoying some small success. Cruelly, Darby demanded that the school be closed, wounded at his estranged wife's achievements. As her husband it was his right to express his will and Hester's establishment was forced to shut its doors whilst Mary went to finishing school at Oxford House.

By now just 15, Mary was already a beauty. Tall, graceful and seemingly imbued with endless talents, she had begun to make quite an impact on those who crossed her path. One man who saw the potential in the young lady was Oxford House's dance master, Mr Hussey. He also served as ballet master at Covent Garden theatre and mentioned her to Thomas Hull, the theatre manager, who was also a noted actor and dramatist himself.

Although once Hester's eyebrows might have shot up through her hairline at the prospect of her daughter pursuing a career on the stage, Mrs Darby had long since been forced to abandon her life of carefree gentility. Her husband had deserted her and forced the closure of the business she had put her heart and soul into, so the money had to come from somewhere. A daughter treading the boards might be just what was needed to keep the wolf from the door.

Under Hester's watchful eye, Mary was introduced to no less a man than David Garrick himself. Garrick was a titan of the Georgian stage and when he met Mary, he knew she was destined for great things. He offered her a one-night engagement as Cordelia opposite his Lear in the very play that had awakened Mary's interest in the theatre, and she was thrilled to accept.

Garrick encouraged Mary and Hester to visit Drury Lane as often as possible as she was preparing to make her debut. He wanted them both to become familiar with life in the theatre, so that Hester's mind might rest easy. Unfortunately, Mary caught the eye of a young captain and he began frequenting the box where she and her family sat. At first, Hester was dismayed at his attentions but when he made Mary a proposal of marriage, her attitude changed. This might be the break she had been looking for, after all, and a good marriage was infinitely more respectable than a theatrical life.

As Mary wrote, 'My mother, who but *half* approved a dramatic life, was more than *half* inclined to accept the addresses of [the] captain'[10], and decided that her daughter would accept the proposal. Imagine the horror of the women when it was discovered that the dashing young suitor was already married and wished only to seduce and use Mary. The engagement was off before it was on, and Hester was determined to watch her daughter's callers like the proverbial hawk from that moment forward.

If only someone had been watching out for Dora so keenly, but it seemed that Grace's eye for an honest man had failed her. When her daughter received a proposal from a gentleman named Lieutenant Charles Doyne, she persuaded Dora to reject him. After all, Doyne was a good man but not a rich one, and she was sure that Dora could do better. In Dora she saw a rising star who was destined for the very top and she wasn't about to have her snatched back down to earth by a mundane marriage to a 'nobody' of a soldier. With the unhappy lieutenant left to lick his wounds, Dora returned once more to her career.

Sadly Grace seemed rather less eagle-eyed when it came to the next man in her little starlet's life. Richard Daly, the very married, very lascivious manager of the Theatre Royal, Cork, had loaned Dora money to pay for treatment when her mother fell ill, and now he hoped to receive something in return for this supposed favour. Daly was the sort of chap who enjoyed a challenge and he had managed to survive no fewer than sixteen duels in the space of two years without having received so much as a scratch from his opponents.

As a man who was always 'embroidered, ruffled and curled'[11], Daly 'was remarkably handsome, and his features would have been agreeable but for an inveterate and most distressing squint'[12]. He wasn't about to let that hold him back though. Daly prided himself on seducing the ladies of his theatre company, and Dora was his next prey. After all, Dora, 'if not exactly beautiful, was irresistibly agreeable; her person and gait elegant and elastic; her voice, in singing, perfectly sweet and melodious, and, in speaking, clear and impressive; her enunciation, whether she spoke or sung, always gave full effect to words she had to deliver; her pronunciation was peculiarly elegant and correct.'[13]

Of course, all of that was probably of little import to Daly. He collected the ladies of his company like some men collected butterflies, and the next to be pinned to his metaphorical canvas was the impressionable young Dora. When she was just 20 she fell pregnant by her married lover. It was now that Grace swung into action and together, mother and daughter fled Ireland, her debts and Daly to begin a new life in England.

For Mary Darby, there was to be a new life of an entirely different sort. Her mother, Hester, hoped that she might marry her daughter off and found that one of the young lady's gentleman callers did indeed tick every box on her wish list for a son-in-law. As one of the many sensational reports regarding Mary's love life reveals, 'Satan appeared to her in the shape of an Attorney's clerk, all glittering with spangles, and bedaubed with lace'[14].

Satan was in fact a clerk named Thomas Robinson, who had been introduced to Mary's mother by a friend of the family. He claimed to be in receipt of a considerable inheritance and when Mary's brother fell ill with smallpox, Robinson nursed him as though he was already a member of the family. Perhaps inevitably Mary also came down with smallpox and she found her devoted suitor there at her side throughout, regardless of the danger to himself. Mary recovered and when she was barely 16-years-old, became Mrs Thomas Robinson.

Now that he had his wife, Robinson set about moulding her into the woman he decided she should be. He told her mother that Captain Darby would surely not approve of his daughter becoming an actress for in the theatre a young, beautiful woman would be prey to all manner of predators. Why, he said, Mary had only just recovered from a serious illness, she could hardly risk her health again by appearing in public night after night. If she did, she would soon be exhausted to the point of illness by such a fancy. Hester capitulated and wrote to Garrick, explaining that his would-be Cordelia had wed and was, alas, off the employment market.

At first all was rosy. Thomas introduced his new bride to his family and some noble acquaintances, though Mary noted that one or two of them, such as Lord Lyttleton, were better known as libertines rather than respectable gentlemen.

Little did she know!

Just as her mother had been before her, Mary was fated to be humiliated by her husband when he took a mistress. It was Lyttleton who informed her of his intrigues, surreptitiously handing her the address of a house on Princes Street in Soho. There she met a Miss Wilmot, the lady who had stolen her husband's flinty heart. Mary discovered that Thomas had even given his mistress a ring but when she challenged him to account for himself, he hardly seemed to care.

Worse was yet to come.

Not only did Mary have to contend with her husband's mistress, she also had her own pregnancy to deal with. Faced with a philandering husband and the overly-insistent attentions of his libertine friends, she must have mourned that career that had been lost to her before it began. Though Mary and her husband still lived a glittering social life, paid for by his increasing debts, she took little delight in it. After all, all the parties in the world couldn't make up for the betrayal of her husband. Every bit the happy couple in public, when they weren't dazzling at those society bashes, Thomas was generally nowhere to be seen.

There was still one thing in which Mary could find comfort despite her domestic discord, and this was her infant daughter, Maria. If she hoped that the new addition to the family might bring Thomas round, she was mistaken. Still he had no shame and no love for his wife: he even introduced her younger brother to his mistresses, as though this was quite the done thing.

All of those parties came at a price and, eventually, Mary came to realise that it wasn't only Thomas' sex life that was tangled. He was in debt up to his eyeballs and Maria was but a babe in arms when the family fled London for Wales, with Thomas fearing he might face a stint in prison when his creditors invariably caught up with him. His efforts to flee were in vain and in 1775, Thomas Robinson was finally hurled into the Fleet Prison. Here he remained for fifteen dreadful months, his loyal wife still at his side. During this period, Mary wrote her first book of poetry, a talent that would later earn her the soubriquet, *the English Sappho*. Thanks to the book she won the patronage of Georgiana Cavendish, Duchess of Devonshire, suggesting that Mary hadn't *quite* been forgotten by society!

For the girl from Ireland, however, things were going *much* better than they were for her English counterpart. Upon arriving in Leeds, Dora had been accepted into Tate Wilkinson's[15] theatre company and given the stage name of *Mrs Jordan*. Whilst her new prefix hinted at the respectability of an entirely non-existent marriage there was much more to it than that. The name Jordan was symbolic of her escape from Daly across the Irish Sea, a reference to the bible story of the Israelites crossing the River Jordan to reach safety. If this seems a little overcooked, let us not forget that Wilkinson was a man of the theatre and a noted impresario, he *really* knew how to sell an idea or, in this case, to sell a name.

So, whilst destiny had left Mrs Robinson miserable, it had handed a much needed bit of good fortune to Dora. She wasn't short on admirers either and when she fell in love with a lawyer named Richard Ford, it seemed as though she might at last have her happy ending. Famous, celebrated and secure with her loving Ford, Dora Jordan might finally be able to settle down.

And what of Mrs Robinson, whom we last saw languishing unhappily in the Fleet Prison beside her husband? Well, understandably, she had had quite enough of being in miserable thrall to her good for nothing spouse. Perhaps remembering those remarkable women who had formed the basis of her education, she didn't wilt under the pressure of this dreadful marriage, but instead flourished. Once more her dreams turned to the theatre and, having exhausted all charity from family and friends, Thomas encouraged his wife to finally make that much-delayed debut.

Finally Thomas' social network came in useful and Mary was introduced to Richard Brinsley Sheridan, that most quintessential Georgian theatrical gent. Sheridan owned the Theatre Royal in Drury Lane[16], and swiftly signed Mary up on a generous salary. He informed Garrick, who was now retired, that Mary was once again looking for a role. Without a moment's thought the acting great resumed his role as her mentor.

Years after it should have happened, Mary Robinson took to the stage of Drury Lane on 10 December 1776. She was Juliet to William Brereton's Romeo and though the notices weren't universally glowing, it seems that Mary's belief in her own talent was well-founded.

We shall draw a veil over the remainder of the company.

> 'She has elegance of person and beauty; the grace of her arms
> is singular, and what very few acquire, 'till after long practice.
> - Her walk is less pleasing; - but the art of filling the space is
> the most difficult part of an actor and can only be acquired by
> time. We may venture to pronounce her an acquisition and an
> ornament.'[17]

Mary's career was in the ascendant and Sheridan was quick to offer her the
lead in his new work, *The School for Scandal*. Pregnant with her second
child, Mary turned down the role. That child, Sophia, lived only six weeks.
Mary fell into a deep despair and took a leave of absence to mourn but
when she returned to the stage she found herself in high demand for roles
including Ophelia, Viola, Rosalind, and even Lady Macbeth.

Mr Robinson, meanwhile, was notable mainly by his absence. Having
a successful wife was proving rather useful and he enjoyed nothing more
than spending the hard-working Mary's money on his mistresses. He was so
profligate with *her* salary that Mary soon found her income insufficient to
support his freewheeling lifestyle.

The stage was set for drama and that stage, for now at least, belongs to Mary
Robinson.

When Mary was cast as Perdita in *A Winter's Tale* she could hardly have
guessed the impact it would have on her life for the decades to come. The
show was a hit and the royal family requested a command performance,
which was duly given on 3 December 1779. That night, resplendent in the
royal box beside his parents, King George III and Queen Charlotte, was
George, the then 17-year-old Prince of Wales. Wales loved beauty above
all things and when he laid eyes on Mary, he was smitten. This didn't go
unnoticed by the press either.

> 'There you shall see the famous Perdita of Drury-Lane, sitting
> at the play-house in the side box opposite the P— of W—.
> Look how wantonly she looks, thinking, Gracious Sir! Please to
> bestow one — upon a poor woman! Ho! Ho! Fine farce flow!'[18]

From his box, Wales sang Mary's praises just loudly enough for her to hear.
Of course she was flattered and declared herself to be artfully surprised and

just slightly alarmed at attracting such an illustrious admirer. Yet admire her he did and within days, Wales was sending Mary breathless love notes and expensive gifts, addressed to *Perdita*, signed by *Florizel*. They were hand-delivered by his friend, George Capel-Coningsby, Viscount Malden[19]. Eventually Mary replied and the couple began a correspondence that culminated when George sent Mary his miniature, along with a personalised, heart-shaped note. That note read, 'Je ne change qu'en mourant' on one side and on the other, 'Unalterable to my Perdita through life.'

Now, just like her prince, Mary was smitten too. Caring little for the husband who had so cruelly used her, she confessed in a letter to the prince that she shared his infatuation but begged him not to invite the anger of his family. Then, betraying the shrewd businesswoman beneath the blushing innocent, the consummate actress pointed out her own married state. Should she consent to become his mistress, her marriage would be forfeit. What was a girl to do?

> 'A certain young Prince, on the eve of being of age, has, we hear, been long enamoured of a lady called Perdita, and made her considerable presents, both in money and trinkets. The world does not scruple to say that they have met, and had a *tête-a-tète* together. It is further said, that before two months are at an end the fair one will, in dress and equipage, out-rival the first Duchess in the kingdom.'[20]

Mary declined the offer to disguise herself as a boy as she had done to such acclaim on stage, and to visit her would-be paramour in secret. With Malden still acting as their go-between, both knew that a meeting would be inevitable. Mary later recollected how that clandestine introduction, chaperoned by Malden and the Duke of York, eventually played out.

> 'Lord Malden and myself dined at the inn on the island between Kew and Brentford [as they awaited the meeting with the Prince of Wales]. Heaven can witness how many conflicts my agitated heart endured at this most important moment! I admired the prince; I felt grateful for his affection. He was the most engaging of created beings [ ] The interview was but of a moment. […] A few words, and those scarcely articulate, were uttered by the prince, when a noise of people approaching from the palace startled us. The moon was now rising; and the idea of being overheard, or of his royal highness

being seen out at so unusual an hour terrified the whole group. After a few more words of the most affectionate nature uttered by the prince, we parted. [...] Alas! My friend, if my mind was before influenced by esteem, it was now awakened to the most enthusiastic admiration. The rank of the prince no longer chilled into awe that being, who now considered him as the lover and the friend. The graces of his person, the irresistible sweetness of his smile, the tenderness of his melodious yet manly voice, will be remembered by me till every vision of this changing scene shall be forgotten.'[21]

Now Mary and Wales began to meet frequently, Perdita and Florizel enjoying their secret and scandalous liaisons. Mary swore afterwards that they were always chaperoned and perhaps they were, perhaps not, but one suspects that she was truthful. After all, this was a woman with no small amount of experience, not one to throw away her reputation and career for a few flattering words from a member of the royal family, no matter how prettily enchanting he might have seemed.

They spent long midnight walks in one another's company in those secluded avenues in the land surrounding the old Kew Palace. The prince sang to his charming companion and she found him utterly beguiling, as so many women would throughout his long and eventful life. Mary might have been the first woman to tumble into Wales' waiting arms, but she was far from being the last.

During their trysts Mary 'lamented the distance which destiny had placed between us', no doubt comparing the attentions of the prince to those of her disinterested, freeloading husband. In her memoirs, she remembered her feelings for the prince as those formed from the most noble, moral foundations. *Ah*, she cried, what a husband such a man would make[22].

> 'How would my soul have idolized such a *husband*! Alas! How often, in the ardent enthusiasm of my soul, have I formed the wish that that being were *mine alone*!'[23]

Mary might have assumed the role of the bowled-over innocent in her memoirs but the press rang with reports of her public flirtations with the prince who so desired her. On one occasion, she made such an impact that the sovereign himself requested her removal from the theatre.

No such thing as bad publicity, after all!

> 'A circumstance of rather an embarrassing nature happened at last night's Oratoria:— Mrs. R—, deck'd out in all her paraphernalia, took care to post herself in one of the upper boxes immediately opposite the Princes, and by those wanton airs, peculiar to herself, contrived as last to *basilisk* a certain heir apparent, that his fixed attention on the amorous object above, became generally noticed, and soon after astonished their M—s, who, not being able to discover the cause, seemed at a loss to account for the extraordinary effect. No sooner however were they properly informed, but a messenger was instantly sent aloft, desiring the *dart-dealing* actress to withdraw, which she complied with, tho not without expressing the utmost chagrin at her mortifying removal.
>
> Poor Perdita!
>
> — '*Queen* it not an inch further,
>
> 'But milk thy ewes and weep!'
>
> The *Maids of Honour* were thrown into the utmost consternation on the above *alarming* occasion!'[24]

Not half as much consternation as George III.

Yet Wales wasn't Mary's, nor could he be and the only role the prince could offer the actress was that of mistress. In many ways when one considers the actions of her father and her husband, who abandoned their wives for their own lovers, it's perhaps surprising that Mary accepted. In others, however, it really isn't that much of a shocker at all. There is no doubt some truth in her claims that she found the prince irresistible but she also knew a good arrangement when it was offered and the particular arrangement that was offered to Mary was impossible to turn down. If she gave up her husband and career, Wales swore, he would give her £20,000 and the position of mistress. He couldn't give her the cash right *now*, of course, it would have to wait until he turned twenty one. Perhaps an IOU would serve just as well though, he ventured.

Mary made a mistake.

Mary said yes.

She took her final bow at Drury Lane in 1780 and left the stage as a star, receiving rave reviews in a production of *The Miniature Picture*. That very night, she hastened from the company of her husband and soon bestowed all her womanly favours on the prince.

We cannot know exactly when the relationship was consummated. If anonymously published memoirs *purporting* to be written by Mary are to be believed (hint: they *aren't*), it was an unmitigated disaster. Mary awaited his princely arrival wearing a diaphanous negligé designed to make his royal heart beat faster. Their embraces grew hotter, their clothes fell away until… horror of horrors, Mary's 'hand which he [the Prince of Wales] thought could have created manhood under the ribs of death, was employed to no other purpose than to make him more humblingly sensible of his weakness'.[25]

At the moment of crisis, the future king's sceptre wilted.

There is far more at play in these anonymous memoirs than a simple scandalous story, of course. It is a political blunt instrument, walloping the prince again and again, painting him as an amorous youth with as little control over his body as he had over his gambling. In the hands of the author, Mary is the tempting *Perdita*, sexually irresistible, wanton, shameless. Together, once Wales had conquered his problem of prematurely peaking, the scandalous lovers painted London red.

Mary was soon a regular at all the best parties and she caused an uproar when she was invited to St James's Palace to join the birthday celebrations for George III. Here she sat proudly in the Lord Chamberlain's box, sending a very clear message about her new status to anyone who had recently come down from the moon, and had missed the speculation about her relationship with the Prince of Wales. Yet the prince wasn't satisfied with Mary merely being present. She had to be the star of the show and her celebrated bosom played its part in the scandalous proceedings that followed. When Lady Augusta Campbell gave the Prince of Wales a gift of two rosebuds from her posy, he took them graciously. Then, in full view of everyone, he had the flowers taken to Mary, where she displayed the blossom close to her bosom!

Mary felt 'proud of the power by which I thus publicly mortified an exalted rival' and from that day forward, she seemed invincible. She believed herself to be, at any rate.

We can't honestly know whether there was any truth in that earlier tale of the prince's inability to perform and as the years went by, he certainly gained enough practice and experience! Mary had stepped off a precipice into the unknown and had given up everything for a mercurial lover and the promise that, one day she would receive a payout to make up for the career she had abandoned. It was not one of her better decisions.

Soon Mary, well known by the nickname *Perdita*, was everywhere. The press couldn't get enough of the celebrated mistress and reported on her every move. When she wore a gown, *everyone* wanted it, when she visited a venue, it instantly became the place to be seen and just like today, she had her own entourage in tow to keep her looking perfect.

> 'The celebrated Perdita used to pay her Hair Dresser 50l. per Annum, but finding that she was often disappointed when she sent for him, she has taken a Hair-Dresser to reside in her House and whenever she goes in to the Country to stay for any time or for one Night only, the Friseur has a Horse provided for him, and accompanies her.'[26]

Yet Mary found, as so many who strive for celebrity often do, that there was a dark side to her glittering life. She had enjoyed fame thanks to her career on the stage, but the adoration of her peers and audiences did as much for her confidence as it did for her coffers. Apart from the occasional less-than-fabulous review, Mary was a popular girl. Becoming mistress to the Prince of Wales changed all that. Suddenly the press and caricaturists targeted Mary with laser precision, mercilessly shredding her connections with the prince and his circle. She became referred to more and more frequently as *Perdita*, no longer Mary or the respectable Mrs Robinson, but the embodiment of the fictional shepherdess who discovered that she was, in fact, a secret princess.

Mary could no longer enjoy her jaunts to Ranelagh and found herself disturbed by the other patrons who assembled to stare at her, making trips out in her carriage a nightmare. Frequently she was besieged in shops by the crowds that gathered outside, waiting to catch a glimpse of the prince's infamous mistress. She had flown too high and press and public alike were ready to cut her down to size. Once upon a time the media had adored her, now they decided that she had climbed way, way above her station.

Under the title, *The Tablets of Perdita*, the 1780 pages of the *Whitehall Evening Post* gave a rather snarky account of the lady's daily routine in which she was more immoral queen than exclusive mistress!

> 'Ten o'clock in the morning.]— Waked.— The most pleasant dreams!— Thought I was in Kensington Palace— had a

levee— all the Nobility paying their court to me— Made Lord
— a Duke. […]

Lord — tapped gently at my bed-chamber door — *Waked*
— He is let in, and *politely* left alone with me.

We embrace!— the deed is done— my wishes are
accomplished.'[27]

And who, might we ask, is the mysterious unnamed lord who appears to
enjoy such favour from our fair Perdita? None other than Lord Malden,
the prince's trusted friend and the very man who delivered those early love
notes and assisted in the clandestine midnight meetings between the couple.
Mary, you see, hadn't been entirely faithful to her royal lover and had, on
occasion, tumbled into Malden's embrace.

Wales, it must be said, hadn't been an angel either. By now established in
his own residence, he was gambling and wenching all over town, pursuing
the courtesan, Elizabeth Armistead, with gleeful and unrestrained abandon.
He didn't want to be tied down and as he would show time and again
throughout his life, nothing made a woman more boring than knowing
that she had capitulated to him. He was all about the thrill of the chase
and Mary might have been the first woman to fall for his charms but she
certainly wasn't the last. Now he was free and single, there was no shortage
of admirers beating a path to his door.

Florizel ended the relationship little more than twelve months after that
heady evening when he first set eyes on *Perdita* on the Drury Lane stage.
Wales would never be one for breaking up kindly and he ended things with
Mary by the means of a note that said simply, 'we must meet no more.'

Mary's world collapsed. The prince ignored her pleas to meet and just as
she had feared might happen, she had indeed fled from the certainty of her
career to pursue the phantom disappointment of princely romance.

Although Wales ignored Mary's impassioned requests for a meeting for
some time, he did eventually capitulate. At this liaison he told her that he
still loved her but that shadowy enemies were conspiring to destroy their
romance. After many hours of conversation, the couple parted as friends.
Imagine Mary's heartbreak when she and the prince happened upon one
another in Hyde Park the next day and he turned away, pretending not to
know who she was.

Mary had lost everything. With no rich lover to support her and no career
of her own, she soon incurred eye-watering debts simply by continuing to
live in the manner to which she had become accustomed. She lived in Park
Street, in a house that had been refurbished for the Countess of Derby,

and she travelled everywhere in a brand new carriage. From being the public darling she was now its laughing stock. She daren't even return to the stage, for fear of the catcalls and humiliations she would have to endure. With that £20,000 nowhere to be seen, Mary went into crisis mode. The only thing for it, she decided, was to publish the love letters that the Prince of Wales had sent to her.

'A certain *amour royal* is now totally at an end; a separation has taken place a *thoro* for more than three weeks, and a *settlement* worthy of such *a sultana* is the only thing now wanting to break off all intercourse whatever. Mrs R—n thinking the adjustment of this part of the *divorce* too essential to be trifled with, has roundly written to her once *ardent lover*, "that if her establishment is not duly arranged within the space of fourteen days from the commencement of the new year, his — — must not be surprized if he sees a full publication of all those *seductory epistles* which alone estranged her from *virtue* and the *marriage vow*!"'[28]

There are two ways of looking at this. It was either an act of desperation by a lady in dire straits or one of revenge by a woman scorned. Either way, Mary knew that those red hot letters would set the bookshops alight and make her a fortune.

When George III heard of her plans, he was mortified. He immediately instructed that quintessential negotiator, Colonel George Hotham, to enter into talks with Mary's representative, Lord Malden, with an aim to keeping the lid on the letters. During their meetings, Hotham ascertained that Mary, who was still spending as though she had no limits, owed somewhere in the region of £5000. Accordingly Hotham wrote to the monarch and made a request of this sum in return for full and final settlement of the matter of the letters and the promise made by the prince in his IOU. This should be regarded as a gesture of goodwill, Hotham clarified, because the young prince had been underage when he made his promise to Mary and there was no legal requirement for them to honour it *at all*.

'In obedience to Your Commands, I take the earliest Opportunity in My Power of informing Your Lordship, that I have Authority to say that in consideration of a past Connexion, which never more can be renewed, Mrs Robinson has it in Her Power to receive the Sum of five Thousand Pounds; which, on Her

Restitution of such Papers as passed during its continuance, will instantly be paid Her.

This Sum, on a strict Retrospect into every Part of Mrs Robinson's conduct during the Time the Attachment subsisted, is deemed as proper and Sufficient Reward; & I am command to acquaint Your Lordship, as I will beg the favour of You to inform Mrs Robinson,) that nothing farther will be offer'd; that this Proposal is Final; & in case of that Lady's Non-Acceptance of this Sum, Your Lordship will receive no farther Trouble on this Unpleasant Subject.'[29]

The newspapers revelled in the fall of the woman who had seemingly had it all. She had staked her future and her reputation, the most precious thing she had, on a teenage prince and lost it all. And the press *loved* it. Alas, there was to be no happy ending for Perdita. Even now, rumours abounded that she was motivated only by greed and would not accept the more than generous payment that she had been offered. Hardly surprisingly, they proclaimed, for she had always been a schemer, a manipulator, a woman of the very worst sort. After all, asked the gentlemen of the press, what kind of woman demands money after sex? The inference was vicious. For Perdita, the fallout from her far from fairytale romance was brutal.

'The Perdita, it is very confidently reported, has lately had an offer from the parents of *Florizel* of 600l. per annum, and a douceur of 6000l. provided she will give up the originals of all Florizel's letters; but the avaricious *Thais* is determined to hold fast the r— *amorous budget*, unless she is granted double the above annuity, as well as douceur; and without a speedy compliance she threatens to publish them to the world.

When such eminent persons as the parents of *Florizel* can be *threatened* into a compliance with the demand of a pr—te, what a defect is there in the laws of Britain? Surely it cannot escape the observation of those concerned in this ridiculous negotiation, that in case a sum was given to this woman in order to get possession of the original letters, that she would certainly preserve copies, and every use might be made of them that can possibly be made of the original.

It is certain had *Florizel* debauched *Perdita*, he ought to have made her an ample settlement for the loss of her honour; but as it is notorious that was not the case; his family ought to treat her menaces with silent contempt. To negotiate with her on any terms is only to make her impertinent, and if in consequence of a disappointment, she dare to publish the letters of a noble youth, betrayed into an indiscretion by an artful woman, we may fairly say that her very existence would be apocryphal.'[30]

Mary was furious and though rebuttals appeared in the editions that followed, the prevailing sense was that the unfortunate actress had got what she deserved.

On 29 August 1781 Lord North wrote to the king to tell him that he had enjoyed further discussions with Hotham and the agreement was made. Mary would receive her £5000, later amended to include an additional annuity of £500 per year for life.

'Lord North received yesterday the honour of his Majesty's command to meet Lieutenant Colonel Hotham & settle the payment of the £5000 stipulated for the recovery of his Royal Highness's letters. He has seen the Lieutenant Colonel this morning, & has given orders for a warrant to be made out for that sum on account of Special Service. This method appears to Lord North the most convenient as Col Hotham will be obliged to account for the disposal of it to his Majesty only. Lord North had heard of this unhappy affair and indebted as he is to his majesty's goodness must feel for every event which gives uneasiness to his Royal Breast. He cannot but admire & applaud his Majesty's paternal tenderness and wisdom in delivering even a large sum to withdraw the Prince's letters from the hands in which they are now.'[31]

With the letters handed over and destroyed, the love affair of Perdita and Florizel was well and truly over. Though the prince would go on to enjoy decades worth of amorous and notorious adventures, Mary did her best to gather up the shreds of her previous life. Entirely fraudulent collections of letters purporting to be from the couple were published and Mary fled the public gaze to what she hoped would be a new life in France.

In the years that followed Mary endured illness and heartbreak yet through it all, she took up her ink and kept on writing. Memoirs, poems, opinions flowed from her pen. She died in 1800, forever *Perdita*.

Let us return now to Mrs Jordan, whom we last saw happy and content with her lover, Richard Ford. Together the couple had three children to go with that one she had been carrying courtesy of Daly when she arrived from Ireland. Of course, Ford was hardly Dora's first affair in England but he was the one that stuck, even if he never got round to making things official. Far be it for me to cast doubt on Dora's motives for her progression up through the ranks of callers from that hopeful young lieutenant, via landowners, minor politicians and lawyers, but Wilkinson does affectionately note that she always liked the finer things in life, and perhaps that extended to gentlemen too.

> 'But now, dear Mrs. Jordan, you do like the cash, and I believe
> and hope you take care of it; that you love to receive it I know,
> and so does every other manager; you *have* made us all know
> that: you will excuse my being jocular.'[32]

She would end up wishing that she had taken better care of the cash than she did!

In 1790 Dora took on the fateful role of Little Pickle in *The Spoil'd Child* at the Theatre Royal, Drury Lane. Thanks to what came afterwards she would be forever known as *Pickle* in the press, and the role of the naughty little boy who indulged in all manner of pranks became indelibly associated with her. Let us not downplay the importance of costume in the appeal of the role either, for 'the exquisite symmetry of Mrs. Jordan's form in male attire,'[33] did much to enhance her appeal. In her *breeches* roles, those famed and forbidden legs could be shown off at their very best and audiences flocked to snap up tickets for the show.

Among those who crowded into the theatre to pay tribute to Mrs Jordan's shapely limbs was Prince William, the Duke of Clarence and St Andrews, brother to George, the Prince of Wales. Known as the *Sailor Duke*, Clarence enjoyed a life on the ocean waves and had done so since the age of just 13. He had, by leaving his family at such a young age, been *almost* protected from following the Prince of Wales into trouble. Yet, like his brother, he had a troublesome eye for the ladies. He had already fathered a son in Halifax, Nova Scotia, in 1788[34], and seemed to have no inclination to make a dynastic marriage.

Yet just as Wales became smitten on that fateful first meeting with Mary, William was bewitched as soon as he set eyes on Dora. Unlike Wales,

Clarence wasn't *quite* as notorious for his amours as his brother, and his entanglement with Dora would outlast anything that Wales ever attempted.

It would not, alas, survive his realisation that he was destined to be the king.

Dora and Ford split up. Behind the scenes they bickered over the fates of their two surviving children and in the press speculation began to grow about the cause of the division. Typical for the Georgian fourth estate, there was no delicacy when it came to the wording, and we find the *Morning Post and Daily Advertiser* taking gleeful and, it must be said, rather obscene delight in dropping some very indelicate hints indeed.

> 'Mrs. JORDAN [...] may be complimented on never wanting the Prompter - for a certain illustrious character is ever behind the scenes with her part in his hand!'[35]

Incorrigible, weren't they?

Yet Dora had misjudged the public mood. When she missed several performances due to illness, her audiences became restless and asked if she had already begun shirking her duties as a professional for the sake of spending time with her rumoured lover. Soon Little Pickle's shine was beginning to tarnish. When she moved to a rich new neighbourhood and began gadding about in the Georgian equivalent of a big, flashy car, the backlash was inevitable.

> 'The velvet sopha on Mrs. JORDAN'S new carriage is an emblem of the luxuriant meretriciousness from which some people amount from *piety in pattens* to *wickedness in a coach*.'[36]

Still, wickedness in a coach seemed to suit Dora and the Duke of Clarence and it wasn't long before they were out and about together, shamelessly revelling in their new-found love. Knowing that George III would disapprove of his entanglement, Clarence wasn't about to seek his father's approval under the Royal Marriages Act and Dora was perfectly happy to be her duke's significant other whether or not they were legally bound. Yet this was a scandalous attachment regardless of how the parties felt and speculation grew about how long the couple would remain childless, so devoted to one another were they.

'Mrs. JORDAN has of late grown thin; but there is great prospect, that, in the Spring, she may get *round* a little,'[37] wrote the *Star* in January 1792. Sadly Dora lost the baby she was carrying and it was another year before Dora grew *round* again. By that time she had secured her lover's commitment in the shape of a gold and diamond ring, which George III decided to turn a blind eye to. Dora was nothing but a mistress, he told himself. She wasn't a wife, she would never be queen, so let them have their fun, immoral though that fun was.

In fact, one might speculate that in this case at least, the king might have had some measure of sympathy. Although William *did* eventually reign, at the time of his burgeoning affair with Dora the chance of him one day becoming sovereign was remote at best. He wished happiness for his son and if that happiness was to be achieved by living an admittedly unmarried life of domestic bliss with Dora, then so be it. In a show of how accepted she became as the duke's unofficial consort, Dora was awarded an annuity of £1200 per year and her children were to be provided for, regardless of the identity of their father. Yet at first the press and public were not nearly so understanding, and the actress and the duke became the punchlines to a hundred jokes.

In what is probably the most notorious example of mockery the couple endured, *Lubber's hole, - alias - the crack's Jordan,* was a cartoon by James Gillray that showed a half-dressed sailor thrusting his head and upper body into an enormous cracked chamber pot with female legs. The sailor, merrily trilling a sea shanty, was the Duke of Clarence. The chamber pot, otherwise known as a *Jordan*, was Dora. It was crass, cruel and, if you were a Georgian, hilarious. In a convenient gift to the cartoonist, the shanty that Clarence is singing just happens to be that which she performed whilst dressed in a natty sailor suit as Little Pickle, the role that had won the duke's heart.

'What girl but loves the merry tar
We o'er the ocean roam sir,
In every clime we find a port,
In every port a home, sir
Yeo, yeo, yeo, yeo, yeo, yeo.'

What girl but loves the merry tar indeed?

Though it might be tempting to recall that promised £20,000 that Mary never received from Wales and wonder what similar arrangement existed between Dora and Clarence, it would be wrong to do so. In fact, more often than not it was *he* who benefitted financially from the relationship. She was used to working and supporting not only herself, but her two daughters, so when her lover fell into debt, it was second nature for Dora to leap to his aid. He told his banker, 'Mrs. Jordan is getting both fame and money; to her I owe very much, and lately she has insisted on my accepting four and twenty hundred pounds which I am to repay as I think proper.'[38] Hardly a woman out to make a quick pound, as popular songs noted!

'As Jordan's high and mighty squire
Her playhouse profits deigns to skim
Some folks audaciously enquire:
If *he* keeps her or *she* keeps him.'

Mrs Jordan let them mock, for she was robust enough to withstand joshing about her children's fathers, her living arrangements and even her name. Dora could afford to be thick-skinned, secure in the devotion of the Duke of Clarence. She hardly cared if the press sneered when she 'took her *seat* (certainly not her *place*) with the Duke of Clarence in the Prince's Box,'[39] for she knew full well what her place was, and for twenty years, it was at the side of Clarence.

When the couple moved to Bushy Park, Dora assumed the role of hostess there as though she was the legitimate Duchess of Clarence, which she certainly was *not*. Yet as the years rolled by, one might be forgiven for forgetting that Dora was anything other than an official wife. She bore the duke ten children, all of whom took the name Fitzclarence, and continued to be the perfect hostess to guests at the family home on the occasions when she wasn't working and she also carried on ploughing her income into the family. The scandal of their romance subsided as they always do and for a time all was well. In terms of sheer time and devotion, Mary and Wales came nowhere close to Dora and Clarence but the ending, sadly, was similarly unhappy.

By 1810 King George III's wits had been almost entirely claimed by the madness which has become synonymous with his name. The Prince of Wales was set to become Regent and with only a broken marriage and one daughter to his name, suddenly Clarence had moved unexpectedly to within touching distance of the throne. That meant things had to change.

He needed a wife, an heir and a legal marriage, and he could have none of those things with the woman who had shared his bed and his life, not to mention *her* considerable earnings, for the last two decades.

On 23 December 1811 Clarence had a deed of separation drawn up. Without warning, he summoned Dora from her theatrical engagement at Cheltenham to a meeting in Maidenhead. No longer young, no longer pretty and no longer bringing in the money she had once commanded, Dora found herself dumped. Once again the names of Little Pickle and the Sailor Prince became synonymous with scandal. This time it was not the woman who bore the brunt of derision, but the man who had broken her heart.

The public was shocked and called for Clarence to think again and clasp Dora to his bosom once more. He had wasted no time in moving on and was already searching for the perfect royal bride, tirelessly pursuing the much sought-after heiress, Catherine Tylney-Long[40]. When his pursuit ended in disappointment he cast his net again, and he had no time to be admonished by poets!

For shame, your *G—ce*, a man like you
Should scorn so base an act so do;
And in a person of your years
The action ten times worse appears.
[…]
Return to Mistress J....n's arms
Soothe her, and quiet her alarms;
Your present differences o'er,
Be wise, and play the fool no more.

Dora's heart was broken, for she could not imagine what beyond money might have occasioned the duke's change of heart. She wrote that they never argued in all the long years of their affair and though Clarence told Dora that he longed to keep her friendship, her nerves were left in tatters. Even in her fury she couldn't help but credit him with kindness, and her devastated letters in the aftermath of her desertion are filled with angry confusion. One can feel her conflict as she does battle with her own conscience and tries not to speak too ill of the man who had left her high and dry.

'[…] we never had, for twenty years, the *semblance* of a QUARREL. But this is so well known in our domestic circle, that the astonishment is the *greater!* MONEY, money, my good friend, or the *want* of it, has, I am convinced, made HIM, at this moment, the most wretched of men; but having done *wrong*, he does not like to retract. But with all his excellent qualities, his domestic *virtues*, his love for his *lovely* children, what must he not at this moment *suffer!*

[…] do not hear the D. of C. unfairly abused; he has done *wrong*, and he is *suffering* for it; but, as far as he has left it in his *own power*, he is doing every thing KIND and NOBLE, even to the *distressing* HIMSELF.'[41]

Clarence negotiated a settlement for his former partner and their children. It included £1500 a year for Dora, £1500 for their daughters, who would remain in her custody, and an amount to ensure their ongoing comfort. The agreement also stipulated that should Dora ever return to the stage, she would forfeit not only the custody of her daughters, but also the £1500 set aside for their care. Clarence was a caring father though and was determined that whoever would eventually become his bride *must* agree to his seeing his children whenever he so wished. This was not negotiable.

Yet the amount provided for Dora's comfort simply wasn't enough. Having incurred debts not through her own extravagance but that of the duke whose creditors she had paid off throughout their long relationship, she began to consider the possibility of resuming her career.

What else *could* she do?

When the newspapers rallied their fury to mount fresh attacks on Clarence, blaming him for Dora's financial situation, she wrote to them in strong terms to defend him, loyal at every turn. Yet even as she put pen to paper he was still seeking for a rich, ideally royal bride who would satisfy his debts and provide him with the all-important heir. Dora passionately assured the public that she had not been subject to any cruelty and that Clarence would never stand between her and her ability to return to her profession. Yet when she did go back to the stage he was as good as his word. She was forced to forfeit the girls and a large portion of the allowance that she had been awarded.

Dora's triumphant return to the limelight was anything but a resounding success and her debts mounted, forcing her to flee to France to escape her creditors. Perhaps mercifully she didn't live long enough to witness the

Duke of Clarence's marriage to Adelaide of Saxe-Meiningen, who would eventually become his queen[42]. Let us not leave this tale without giving the duke his due though, for in the early years of his reign, he commissioned a very singular piece of statuary.

William wept freely as he told the sculptor, Francis Chantrey, exactly what he wanted to be carved from marble. He wished for a life-size depiction of Mrs Jordan, *Little Pickle*, and two of her children. Eventually, that is exactly what Chantrey produced. The king intended that the sculpture would be housed in Westminster Abbey as a mark of his undying affection and respect for Dora. In fact the statue enjoyed a long and rather tangled life before it found a permanent home. Today it is on display in Buckingham Palace, a lasting memory of the remarkable Mrs Jordan.

Chapter 6

An Unfatherly Act

The Royal Marriages Act was not popular. It cast a long shadow over the lives of those members of the royal household who had fallen foul of it, even if it didn't end the marriages that had come before it. For Cumberland and Gloucester, it might have meant domestic upheaval but at least their marriages were safe. Because those unions took place before the Act was passed they could not be annulled, leaving the couples free to live as husband and wife. How the Act was regarded within the royal family we cannot be entirely certain. Certainly George III and Queen Charlotte were great champions of it, and certainly the king's brothers were not. What of his children, though?

One of them was about to be brave enough to test the mettle of the Royal Marriages Act and he would soon be met by a full broadside. Yet this was not George, Prince of Wales, who having made his own secret marriage to Maria Fitzherbert, was never brave enough to admit that he had taken a Catholic bride. He was content to be known only as the prince with a Catholic mistress and a prince with a mistress was not as scandalous as all *that*. Besides, the scandals of the Prince of Wales could command a volume all of their own. Those of his brother, the Duke of Sussex, on the other hand, were on a rather smaller scale.

But they were no less deliciously appealing to the Georgian public, though!

Prince Augustus Frederick, the eventual Duke of Sussex, was born in 1773. He was the sixth son of the king and queen and the only one who didn't pursue a career in the armed forces thanks to a rather severe case of asthma that destroyed his hopes of naval glory. Sent to the University of Göttingen in 1786, he seemed destined to become unremarkable and but for his love life, he would have been very ordinary. Perhaps the king hoped that the drama of secret and unsuitable marriages wouldn't contaminate this new generation but if that was the case, he was about to be disappointed.

Augustus Frederick, 'an amiable and dutiful youth, tenderly beloved by his august parents, and dear to all who have the happiness of knowing him'[1], was not possessed of a strong constitution and whilst he was in Hanover, his health began to fail. In fact, he grew so ill that the newspapers were soon ringing with dire warnings about his condition, suggesting that the young Augustus Frederick was lingering on the threshold of death. With Germany growing colder as winter approached, it was decided that the young prince would benefit from a move to warmer climes so, in 1792, Augustus Frederick travelled to Rome.

In his new surroundings the young man flourished. Yet considering he was a member of a ruling house which had risen to power at the expense of more than fifty Roman Catholic pretenders to the throne[2], his next move might have suggested that he had a rather more inquiring mind than his family would have liked. As a known Catholic sympathiser, he took advantage of being in Rome to pay a visit to Pope Pius VI and followed up this worrying development with a social call on Cardinal Henry Benedict Stuart. You might well raise an eyebrow at the Cardinal's name and you'd be right to do so, for according to the Jacobites, who still gritted their teeth at the thought of King George III being on the British throne, the cardinal was the rightful heir to the crown. Rather than worshipping in Rome, the Jacobites thought, he should have been ruling in Britain.

The young Augustus Frederick had no interest in placing a Stuart on the throne though, and his business in Rome soon took a rather more romantic turn. It was here that he met Lady Augusta Murray. Though not of royal birth, Lady Augusta was of impeccable stock as daughter of John Murray, 4th Earl of Dunmore; her maternal grandfather was the 6th Earl of Galloway. Augustus Frederick became so deeply enamoured with Lady Augusta that he was determined to make her his own. At five years his senior, she was a little worldlier than her suitor but she wasn't willing to compromise her morals or her reputation. In fact, she decided, she would not consort with the prince until they were married, although she unquestionably knew of the risks involved in getting married without the king's consent. She wrote to Augustus Frederick to assure him that, 'all promises, though sacred in our eyes and in those of Heaven, shall not oblige you to do anything towards me that can in the least prejudice your future interests.'[3]

Years later the prince remembered their courtship in a letter to Lord Erskine[4]. He wrote, 'After four months intimacy, by which I got more particularly acquainted with all her endearing qualities, I offered her my hand unknown to her family [...] The candour and generosity my wife showed on this occasion by refusing the proposal and showing the personal disadvantage I should draw upon myself, instead of shaking my endeavours, served only to add new fuel to a passion which no earthly power could evermore have extinguished at length: after having convinced Augusta of the impossibility of my living without her I found an English clergyman and we were married.'[5]

The couple might have thought themselves hidden from public scrutiny but they were mistaken. The young man's infatuation hadn't gone unnoticed, albeit with a case of mistaken identity that must have given Augustus Frederick's brother, Prince Ernest Augustus a shock!

'The Lady to whom Prince ERNEST AUGUSTUS is said to have given very decisive symptoms of attachment is Lady AUGUSTA MURRAY, the eldest daughter of the Earl of DUNMORE.'[6]

The lady was right even if the gentleman wasn't and for a short time at least it was Prince Ernest Augustus to whom the press yoked Lady Augusta, hinting at 'a singular complexion'[7] between the two. That singular attachment was one of marriage, for the lady was not about to sacrifice her reputation.

Others were quick to warn the prince to take care and Sir William Hamilton, British ambassador to the Neapolitan Court, remarked wryly that Lady Augusta was 'by no means worthy of the regard [Augustus Frederick] seems to have for her'. He warned the prince 'never to push matters to the extremity, so as to lose the countenance of the King and Queen when, as the Queen of Naples told him, he would lose those honours and attentions which he now enjoys'[8]. Yet Augustus Frederick dismissed such concerns, leaving Sir William to impotently hope that Lady Augusta might involve herself in another intrigue, thus freeing her royal paramour from her spell.

It was not to be, and the couple was determined to see the marriage through, none more so than Augustus Frederick. Under the strict terms of the Royal Marriages Act, Augustus Frederick should at this point have withdrawn and made the official marriage request to his father, George III, before he proposed to Lady Augusta. Of course, it would have been incredibly unlikely that the king would have sanctioned such a marriage, given Augusta's relatively low birth. But instead of seeking permission, Augustus went ahead and enlisted the services of a Church of England clergyman, Rev William Gunn, who just happened to be touring Rome, and asked if he would be willing to join the two in matrimony.

Even now, Augusta held firm to her moral stance, convinced that the clergyman appointed to officiate the secret ceremony would simply assume that she had been Augustus Frederick's mistress. She begged her groom to tell Rev Gunn that they had not been intimate, and to assure him that her honour had remained intact and above all, 'don't let him imagine that I have been vile. Do this, my only love; but pray take care of the character of your wife, of your Augusta.'[9]

The very private ceremony took place at the Hotel Sarmiento on 4 April 1793 and was, at the time, a closely guarded secret. Yet in the world of the Georgian press secrets were hard to keep. Gossip began to seep out just as Augustus Frederick and his wife headed home to England, and the unforgiving glare of his father's court.

There was no keeping the marriage out of the public eye now, for the society gossip mill had already begun churning. As Augustus Frederick awaited a response from his father on whether he might be allowed to return home to Great Britain, the *Evening Mail* confidently published a report on the not-so-secret wedding, declaring it balderdash. It was a spectacular journalistic misstep, so certain in tone, so wrong in content, but surely George III suspected the truth of the matter, for he had been around this block plenty of times before.

> 'The marriage of Prince AUGUSTUS with Lady AUGUSTA MURRAY has been very confidently reported in several fashionable circles, and in all the daily papers; we have hitherto taken no notice of these reports, - but, having made it our business to enquire into the fact, we are enable to say, from the best authority, that the report is wholly unfounded.
>
> The report originated in a letter received by a young lady of fashion from her brother abroad, who mentioned that Prince AUGUSTUS had very often frequented the house of Lady DUNMORE: this has been construed into a proposal of marriage, - and a significant shrug from a few ladies who pretend to be in the secret, has made it to be believed that the parties in question are actually married.'[10]

And what must father and son both have been thinking? Perhaps we should be generous and believe that the king still didn't believe what his son had done but Augustus Frederick must certainly have been anxious. Once

George discovered the marriage, he knew that both men would be placed in a most invidious position, and it was one from which neither could retreat. Yet George doted on the young man, so maybe Augustus Frederick believed his father's affection would be enough to secure his own happy ever after.

Sadly, he was mistaken, for the king was to remain true to the furious declaration made to Cumberland all those years ago. Back then, he had stated that he could give even his brother no quarter and show no understanding for, 'I have children who must know what they have to expect if they could follow so infamous an example.'

There was to be no forgiveness.

Upon their arrival in England, Augustus Frederick and Augusta underwent a second marriage. On 5 December 1793, with the blushing bride clearly so pregnant that she was almost ready to give birth[11], the couple attended St George's in Hanover Square and were married again by the Rev John Downes under the not very cunning pseudonyms of Augusta Murray and Augustus Frederick (not quite a criminal mastermind, our Augustus). The initial Roman marriage had now been supplanted by a British one, leaving no doubt about the state of their union. Of course, there was more at stake here than simple family pride for any son of the king stood in line as an heir to the throne and their own children likewise. A matter of the heart was now a matter of the constitution.[12]

When Augusta gave birth, the press celebrated that 'this Lady is as well as can be, and that the son of Prince AUGUSTUS is in perfect health!'[13], but still there was no official recognition of the marriage, even though apartments were allegedly being prepared for mother and baby at Windsor. Although Augusta had satisfied her own moral requirements by marrying her price before she became his lover, considering the dates in question, as far as the world knew, she was just one more royal mistress.

All of that was about to change.

> 'To Day the king told me that the Lord Chancellor had acquainted him yesterday after the levé [sic] with the disagreeable news of Augustus's marriage with the Lady Augusta Murray, eldest daughter of Earl Dunmore on Thursday the 5th December 1793 at St Georges Hannover [sic] Square, that the Register was found, and that he had given orders to the Chancellor, the Archbishop of Canterbury and the other ministers to proceed

in the unpleasant business as the law directs, Augustus having married under age being against the Marriage Act. Also orders are given to stop Lady Dunmore and her daughter joining him, or leaving England.'[14]

Queen Charlotte's diary entry of 25 January 1794 was followed three days later in the same journal by a report on the opening of an investigation into the marriage. Here, the Rev James Trebeck, Clerk in Orders of the Parish of St George, Hanover Square, produced the appropriate register and there in black and white, recorded first on the day in question, was evidence of the marriage. The witnesses had been John and Mary Jones, a coal merchant and his mantua maker wife. Lady Augusta had lodged temporarily in the couple's home on South Molton Street, and Mrs Jones had been a favoured dressmaker to her family for years, so the couple was a natural choice to serve as witnesses. The matter was now in the hands of the king, who also happened to be the father of the groom.

He would not be merciful.

Just as the king had once warned Cumberland that he would not hesitate to wield the full force of the Act against his own children, now he did just that. So it was that the prince who had visited not only the pope in Rome but also the supposed Jacobite heir to the throne, was now hauled into the full glare of the court for something so simple as marrying without the permission of his father.

As Augustus Frederick boarded the *Aquilon* bound for Italy at his father's insistence, the validity of his marriage was being considered by the Privy Council and on 22 January, *The Times* broke the story. Names weren't mentioned, but it wasn't hard to fill in the gaps.

> 'A marriage *ceremony* has very lately been performed, which is likely to furnish the sea-tables, at the west end of the town, with a topic of conversation for the winter. One of the parties is a young gentleman of very high rank, who has just gone abroad - the other is the daughter of a northern Peer, who, it is whispered, has already given an *unequivocal proof* of her attachment to the gentleman alluded to - but as it is yet *nameless*, we are under the necessity of leaving our fair readers to *guess* the nature of it.'[15]

Within the space of a week, the names of the bride and groom had been published along with the history of their courtship, their marriage and the fact that the couple had a child together. All of this would have been perfectly unremarkable and of little interest to the public if the groom had been anyone other than the offspring of the sovereign. That not-so-simple fact rendered the marriage illegal and George III moved to have the union of his own son and Lady Augusta annulled.

The Privy Council questioned the mother of the bride as well as the two witnesses and the clergyman who had performed the service, but none were prosecuted as a party to the illegal marriage. Lady Dunmore had known nothing of the wedding in Rome, she claimed, and though she was aware of the English ceremony, she had not been present. Mr and Mrs Jones, meanwhile, admitted that they had witnessed a wedding but swore that they hadn't known the groom was a Prince of the Blood Royal. After all, just like the gentleman of the cloth who read the service, they had simply assumed that Augustus Frederick was just one more groom, with nothing to make him stand out as remarkable. Queen Charlotte's diaries reveal that Augustus Frederick was in fact posing as a *Devonshire gentleman* who had been sure to take lodgings in the parish served by St George's. The Joneses were at pains to point out that all was right and proper as far as they knew at the time and that, at no point until after the wedding were Augustus Frederick and Lady Augusta left alone together in their home on South Molton Street.

The press and public rallied behind the couple. Lady Augusta was of good stock and the pair were genuinely in love, so why shouldn't they be happy? Indeed, far from live without the benefit of marriage the couple had at least attempted to make their partnership legally, morally and religiously binding, it was only the tyrannical actions of George III and his damned Royal Marriages Act that was keeping them from making a happy family.

With his son safely stuck overseas and Lady Augusta forbidden from joining him, King George provided her with an annuity to support the child that he knew without a doubt was his grandson (there was no evidence to suggest that either Augustus or Augusta had ever had a previous relationship.) Though on different continents, Augustus Frederick assured his wife that he loved her as much as ever and would not allow anyone to enter their home who did not acknowledge her as his wife. His mind was made up, but in July 1794 the couple felt the full weight of the Royal Marriages Act when Henry Stevens, the registrar of the Arches Court of Canterbury, declared 'that the said pretended marriage, or shew [sic] or effigy of marriage [...] was and is absolutely null and void to all intents and purposes whatsoever.

[…] Royal Highness Prince Augustus Frederick was and is free from all bond of marriage with the said Right Honourable Lady Augusta Murray.'[16]

The verdict, read by William Wynne, was hardly a victory for anyone, though the king was doubtless pleased at the outcome. The public looked darkly on their monarch for his actions, especially the fact that he had instigated the scandalous proceedings when Lady Augusta was recovering from the birth of her child. Not only that, but he had sent that child's father far away, tearing the family apart at the moment of their greatest trial. Unsurprisingly Augustus Frederick and his wife refused to accept the ruling of the court. As far as they were concerned they were married, no matter *what* the Arches Court might care to tell the world.

The prince was plunged into misery and his sisters, who had for so long been his confidantes and friends, were forbidden by their parents to write to their errant sibling. Once more in Rome, the place where he had known such happiness, Augustus Frederick found himself isolated and unhappy. For weeks he was barely seen, becoming a recluse in his home and when he finally did step outside, he shunned society. Deep in his misery Augustus Frederick remained a solitary figure who could be glimpsed roaming the ancient ruins, always alone. In London, Lady Augusta refused to be cowed and, buoyed by her husband's words of love and support, she continued to be a small but sharp thorn in the royal side.

> 'Lady AUGUSTA MURRAY has of late sported a crimson and green livery, similar to that of the minor branches of the Royal Family. Thus decorated she appeared a few days since in the Ride in Hyde Park, and alighting from her carriage to walk with a noble relative, attracted much attention.
>
> The circumstance of a certain AUGUST LADY having lately appeared with a Royal livery in the Ride, is said to have caused an order to be issued for enforcing more strictly the regulations of the Park.'[17]

Yet for all his protestations of love, the prince was soon filling his continental days with what the king called *lamentable* company. His debts began to climb and his fidelity to his wife was likely questionable at best. His reclusive ways eventually gave way to a whirlwind of engagements and visits from senior European royals, so he clearly wasn't suffering *too* much without his wife.

Looking back now with the benefit of modern hindsight, it's all too easy for us to ask why Augustus Frederick didn't just stand up to his father and say, *enough is enough*. After all, didn't a bona fide king later abdicate the throne for the sake of an American divorcee? Let's not judge Augustus Frederick by twenty-first or even twentieth century standards though, for he was not a twenty-first century man. He had been raised by a mother and father who held duty and piety above all things, and had been taught that sin and temptation lurked around every corner and that succumbing to these things was the worst possible turn a soul might take. Yet at the same time he watched his father tussle with the responsibility of his role, not to mention the health problems that would later claim his sanity. Unlike his brother, the tearaway Prince of Wales, Augustus Frederick lacked the streak of narcissism that would have allowed him to let his father go hang whilst he pleased himself.

Don't misunderstand this favoured son though because he certainly *tried* to please himself, and that second wedding in Hanover Square was more than proof of that. It was his best effort to ensure that the marriage in Rome could not be thrown into doubt despite it being an Anglican ceremony, yet it shows a dizzying lack of forethought or realism. No matter how many wedding ceremonies he and Lady Augusta underwent they would never be able to ignore the existence of the Royal Marriages Act. Due to the groom's absolute insistence that his original marriage was valid and binding, Augustus Frederick would not have approached the Privy Council for permission to marry when he reached the age of 25, even though the Act gave him every right to do so.

So, having defied law, convention and the will of his crowned father, it seemed as though Augustus Frederick's claims of everlasting love might actually be true. What man would go through so much for the woman in his life if he wasn't devoted to her, if their bond wasn't one that could transcend any challenge that the world threw at it? Alas not, but who can tell when the seeds of doubt began to take root? But more of this later. For now though there were more pressing concerns because Lady Augusta was united with her husband in a 'very strange and improper meeting in Berlin'[18], a reunion which according to the correspondence between the king and his ministers was a most unusual state of affairs.

Travelling under the assumed name of *Ford*, Lady Augusta turned up unexpectedly in Berlin, claiming that she had been told her husband was dying. Although Augustus Frederick was unwell, he certainly wasn't in danger of death, and her sudden appearance threw everyone into panic. She immediately appealed to the Prussian king for protection and began living the high life, despite the fact that neither she nor her husband had money to spare for such things. To make matters worse, she quickly left her hotel and moved in with Augustus Frederick. Both claimed that she intended to stay a week or so, which nobody believed for a moment. Once Augusta was settled, Augustus Frederick wrote to his father to explain that his wife was ill in mind and body as a result of the journey and anxiety over his health, and that she could not possibly be asked to move on before she had a proper chance to rest. He was at pains to point out that he had advised Augusta to return to Britain as soon as she was able though, as he knew this would be the king's wish. It was a brave and naive bit of damage limitation.

There was more to his correspondence than that though. In a letter to his brother, the Prince of Wales, Augustus Frederick floated the possibility that he might be allowed to travel home too. When Wales approached the king, George was shocked by Augustus Frederick's cunning. Wales had hoped that having his brother home might allow him to be convinced of the error of his actions, George saw it as a sly way of returning with Lady Augusta on his arm, as though he had every right to do so. All of this concern from the Prince of Wales was somewhat ironic of course, considering the fact that he had contracted his own illegal and clandestine marriage just a few years earlier!

On the matter of acknowledging Lady Augusta as anything more than a mistress, the king was immovable. He saw no point in opening further discussions with his son, for he had no intention of recognising Lady Augusta as any sort of official consort. The prince, fired with passion and indignation, would not be silenced. He wrote to Henry Dundas, 1st Viscount Melville[19], informing him that Lady Augusta had sailed for Britain once more in the interests of keeping the peace with the king. In return for this thoughtfulness, he hoped that she might be allowed to share in her husband's allowance, pitiful though it was, and enjoy some measure of comfort when the two were separated. Not only that, cried Augustus Frederick, but promises to settle his wife's debts had not been kept and those promises had even been snatched back from beneath her very nose, leaving her helpless and near destitute!

Augustus Frederick, once so quiet and unassuming and gentle, had grown rather more steely during his years on the continent. He certainly wasn't above the odd pointed comment when it came to getting the matter of his beloved's allowance raised in the Houses of Parliament. The prince had been ill during his time in Berlin and the couple claimed that Lady Augusta had hastened to his side to wish him a tearful and final farewell. Augustus Frederick knew how unpopular the king's decision to pursue the annulment had made his father and he fired a sharp little arrow into this letter to Dundas, no doubt certain that George III would see it one way or the other.

> 'The world knows, or will know with time, [...] that if those who have advised his Majesty in the whole of this transaction, had spoken with that freedom which their situation both required and ordered them to do, and which would have been becoming of men of honour, [Augusta] would have been amply provided for. Perhaps time may disclose many truths, and though Lord Loughborough[20] thinks that having got back his letter from Augusta [...] in which he promised her debts should be paid, and which were contracted by her having been left pennyless [sic] for three years, yet I would have his Lordship to know that an attested copy of that very letter is now in my possession, and will be even produced by me for the amusement of the public whenever such a measure for our mutual advantage will render it necessary.'[21]

Dundas replied in coolly respectful terms, assuring the prince that his letter would certainly be passed to the Lord Chancellor for attention. Yet he also stated that, without the king's express permission, no member of either House could raise the matter of either Augustus Frederick's allowance or that of Lady Augusta. By this point even Queen Charlotte, that bastion of piety, was of the opinion that this had gone on long enough. She wrote to the Prince of Wales, 'in my oppinion [sic] Augustus's return to England, & one Conversation between Him & the Kg might do more than Millions of letters [...] but at Present H. M. is so averse to this step, that I could not with any Propriety press it any further.'[22]

Yet the couple was together once more, for richer or poorer. This was the time for them to prove that, even in matters of royal penury, love might finally conquer all.

It was not to be.

In 1800 Augustus Frederick returned to England, travelling under the pseudonym of *Ford*, which his not-quite-wife also employed for her continental travels. At first there were reports that the couple had set up house together in Grosvenor Square and soon they were preparing to welcome a daughter to the household, seemingly perfectly happy despite the ructions the marriage and annulment had caused within the royal family. Yet George III always knew the quickest route to his sons' hearts. Enforced exile from his father's kingdoms had left the young prince with mounting debts so, when his father offered to pay them off and Parliament granted him a fat allowance of £12,000 if he gave up Augusta, Augustus Frederick accepted.

The reason behind the end of the relationship between Augustus Frederick and Lady Augusta has never been fully explained. Perhaps, having been apart for so long, they simply found that their love had cooled. Perhaps one or the other was less faithful than they had promised they would be (maybe even that *lamentable company* that Augustus Frederick so enjoyed in Europe played its part), perhaps the lure of money and title was too great to resist. Yet whatever the motive, the relationship sputtered to a halt sometime before the birth of Augusta Emma in 1801.

With his creditors satisfied, Augustus Frederick moved into Kensington Palace. He was awarded the title of Duke of Sussex, confirming once and for all that he was back in his father's favour. Even so, as an avowed Whig, their very different political opinions would keep them at arm's length for some time yet. The saga of Augustus Frederick and Lady Augusta didn't end there though, for Lady Augusta began to use the title Duchess of Sussex, much to the chagrin of the royal family. Let us not forget that this was the woman who had travelled from Britain to Berlin against the wishes of the king himself, so she was never going to simply fade into the background.

In 1802 *The Morning Post and Gazetteer* wrongly reported that the couple was on the verge of reconciliation, stating that the prince was planning to move to Hanover with Lady Augusta. There, the mistaken journalist wrote, the marriage 'is valid according to German laws: so much so, in deed, that his son would be Elector of Hanover were all the other children of his present MAJESTY to die without male issue'[23]. Regardless of the dubious legalities of this supposition and the marriage itself there was no real hope of a reconciliation and when Lady Augusta pursued her royal sometime husband to Lisbon in the Spring of 1802, he refused to see her. In fact, this is hardly surprising considering that there was some speculation over the possibility of an Anglo-Portuguese union through an official marriage. That marriage never came about and given the small issue of the Portuguese royal daughters being Roman Catholic, it's hardly surprising. Imagine the humiliation of Lady Augusta, turned away on her arrival in the country and shunned by the man who had once gone against the will of the king himself to wed her.

With no chance of reconciliation, Lady Augusta turned to the courts for redress. She filed a suit in the Court of Chancery alleging that she was rightly owed £4,000 a year from the prince's £12,000 allowance, not to mention 'an establishment suited to her rank and dignity'. To this she added the costs to educate and support their two children, among numerous other sums that the lady believed were her rightful due. She stated that she had not received a single penny from Augustus Frederick and requested that his annual allowance of £12,000 be frozen until she had received all the arrears that were owing to her.

Lady Augusta duly received her £4,000 and for some time, everything seemed calm. Her appearances in the news became limited to her occasional social engagements and a few column inches were given over to the king's agreement in 1806 that she could change her name and title to become known as Baroness D'Ameland.

'We understand', wrote the *Hereford Journal* on 29 October, 'the name of D'Ameland belongs to a Sovereignty of the House of Nassau, from which her Ladyship is lineally descended.'[24] This also meant that Lady Augusta got to keep her royal connection without using the disputed title of the Duchess of Sussex - no wonder George III was happy to agree to her request!

There was to be one final unhappy twist in the tale of the marriage of Augustus Frederick and Lady Augusta Murray. Unlike some royal gentlemen, the Duke of Sussex was a loving and involved father and at first he was more than happy for his children to remain in the custody of their mother. As the years passed though he became increasingly concerned by reports that the pair was being raised by Lady Augusta to believe that they were rightfully a prince and princess. Of course, as soon as Augustus Frederick chose to accept the decision of the court that annulled his marriage, his children lost any right to take a royal title. Even before the annulment, their right to use the title of prince or princess was dubious at best and certainly not legally binding in any way. Lady Augusta wasn't going to let the matter rest and even made enquiries about the possibility of a marriage between Princess Charlotte of Wales, the only *legitimate* child of George, Prince of Wales, and her son. It was never a viable option, as it would have made him husband to the heir to the throne.

That was a step too far for the now dutiful Augustus Frederick, whose father was by now battling with ill health again. In 1809 he filed a case to have his children removed from the custody of Lady Augusta and placed in the care of court-appointed guardians. The press and the public were hungry for the next chapter in the saga of the baroness and the duke. It was so unexpected, a resurgence in a story that they thought had concluded years ago.

The case was heard by the Lord Chancellor, John Scott, 1st Earl of Eldon. He listened to arguments from the legal teams of both parties and much to the annoyance of journalists, decided to declare his verdict in private. His hand-picked audience consisted of Augustus Frederick, Lady Augusta and their lawyers. Into the room they all traipsed and, a little later, the door opened and the Lord Chancellor emerged, followed by Lady Augusta. Though no one outside of that select group knew then what had been decided, it was soon confirmed that Augustus Frederick had been successful. The children were taken from Lady Augusta's care and placed in the custody of Francis Rawdon-Hastings, the Earl of Moira, where they were to become the responsibility of their royal father. It was only now that their surname was changed to reflect their new circumstances and the pair became known as Augustus and Augusta Emma d'Este. The bloodlines of both Augustus Frederick and Lady Augusta could be traced back to the House of Este, so it made sense to use this name, which recognised both sides of the family.

It was a sad end to what had started as a whirlwind love story. Lady Augusta did not marry again and we might fancy that she still considered herself to be already married to the Duke of Sussex, regardless of what the law might say. Augustus Frederick remained unmarried for decades until the death of Lady Augusta on 5 March 1830. Just over a year after his first wife died he married Lady Cecilia Letitia Buggin, a woman twenty years his junior and the respectable daughter of the Earl of Arran. Although this wedding was also undertaken in contravention of the Royal Marriages Act, this time there was little drama, for now the possibility of Augustus Frederick or his child assuming the throne was remote. In the event, no children were born of the marriage anyway.

Though Lady Cecilia and Augustus Frederick did not have any children, they were a happy couple. Lady Cecilia was made Duchess of Inverness in 1840 by Queen Victoria, as a gesture of the affection she felt for her by now elderly uncle[25] and his wife. The duke died in 1843 and was greatly mourned by the public and his family alike. When his second wife passed away thirty years later, she was laid to rest beside her husband.

Though Augustus Frederick's early romantic days might have been scandalous and full of the sort of drama that made him the talk of the town and the thorn in his father's side, by the time of his death, all of that had been forgiven and mostly forgotten. Augustus Frederick had outlived a scandal which paled in comparison to the behaviour of his loathed brother, the Prince Regent. Instead the elderly Duke of Sussex had gone full circle and was, once again, bookish, beloved and a generally solid sort of chap!

How's that for a happy ending? Too convenient by half.

There is an elephant in this particular room.

Not literally, one would never be so cruel, but there was more than one secret wedding amongst the royal children. Most notorious was probably that of the capricious Prince of Wales and a Roman Catholic widow from Shropshire. She was the infamous Mrs Fitzherbert, and her name is inextricably linked to George IV.

Maria Fitzherbert's fame has eclipsed that of Lady Augusta Murray and in the consciousness of royal scandal watchers, it continues to do so. There are likely a few reasons for this, yet chief amongst them must be the fact that *her* secret groom wasn't Prince Augustus Frederick, Duke of Sussex, but the Prince of Wales, heir to the throne. After all, what stakes could possibly be higher than the crown?

Yet that tale, with its abandoned bride, parliamentary questions and frankly appalling behaviour from the groom, is widely known, so let us content ourselves with a brief recap here.

Maria Fitzherbert was a twice-widowed woman of almost 30 when she met the pretty Prince of Wales. Wealthy, connected and realistic, she resisted Wales despite threats of suicide and promises of everlasting love, but not for long. The couple was secretly married in 1785 and remained so for the rest of their lives, but it wasn't a happy connection. At first all was well but Wales' love of women and gambling soon blighted their marriage, and though the world saw Maria as nothing more than the prince's mistress, when George III heard rumours of the clandestine union, he was furious. Under the strict terms of the Act of Settlement that had brought George I to the British throne marriage to a Roman Catholic would cost the Prince of Wales his eventual crown and the king wasn't about to see his son throw away his duty in the name of love.

With that in mind, it was decided the rumours had to be quashed. The king didn't want to know if they were true, he simply wanted them silenced. The gossip was dismissed in Parliament in return for a massive payout for the debt-ridden prince and he agreed to an official marriage to Caroline of Brunswick, whom he would quickly come to hate.

George and Maria's relationship was on and off for years but the denial and official marriage drove a stake through the heart of their love and the couple parted forever. Maria never remarried and when Wales, now King George IV, died in 1830, he was buried with her miniature around his neck. He had been through a vast collection of rich, beautiful and titled lovers but it seems that none of them eclipsed the memory of the enchanting Mrs Fitzherbert.

Less well-repeated than the yarn of Mrs Fitzherbert is that of Princess Elizabeth of the United Kingdom, so let us give centre stage to a royal lady, and one who had a couple of rumoured secrets of her own. This wasn't a widely-known scandal, of course, for it wasn't public knowledge, but it would be a royal crime *not* to delve into the story of Princess Elizabeth and the mysterious George Ramus.

Elizabeth was born in 1770 as the seventh child of George III and Charlotte of Mecklenburg-Strelitz. Among her father's household staff was a number of chaps named Ramus, chief among them Billy, who had been a senior page of George III for decades. In all of the various gentlemen named Ramus on the royal payroll at various times, however, none of them appeared to be the rumoured *George*. Of this mystery, more later.

The princess was a frail and often sickly girl, suffering from a seemingly endless round of chest complaints and unexplained spasms. Her life might have seemed rather uneventful, yet in his biography of her sister, Amelia, William Childe-Pemberton threw out a very casual mention of something that could be very scandalous indeed. He wrote that Elizabeth 'in her early youth had made a secret marriage with a Mr Ramus, by whom she had children. But the circumstances were unromantic.'[26]

As was the reporting of it. Isn't this a scandal of pure gold though? One of the most sheltered princesses in Europe supposedly having a baby by a royal page then going on to secretly marry him is hardly a regular occurrence in the court circular!

Where the rumours of a marriage and child first originated is hard to say, but over the years, historians have been utterly unable to substantiate them. Elizabeth's biographer, Dorothy Margaret Stuart, was intrigued by the fact that the Marriage Registers for the years 1783 to 1845 were missing from Kew Church, and wondered if the key to the secret might be found within, but it would seem unlikely. After all, there would be little to gain from spiriting away more than sixty years' worth of registers for the sake of one clandestine marriage.

Over the years the waters around the rumoured marriage grew muddier still until some spurious works began to state that Ramus was a page to George III - he *wasn't* - and even that the sovereign had attended the wedding. We can't say for sure that the king didn't, because we can't say for sure that there was a wedding, but is that *really* likely given his piety and unswerving focus on duty? George certainly wouldn't have given permission for the marriage to be contracted, for no Princess of the Blood Royal would be permitted to wed the son of a page, so to imagine the king might actually be present at such a union seems like a step too far, even in a time when royal affairs were hardly unusual.

The first mention of the scandal in print appears to have been in Crisp and Howard's multi-volume *Visitation of England and Wales*, which surveys the heraldic history of the nation. In the fifth volume the editors record the genealogy of the Battye family of Frognal, Chelston, County Devon and right there, in the very opening pages, there is something quite unexpected. Without any ceremony or explanation there is a simple, casual note that appears to be the first print appearance of this most unusual rumour.

> 'Marian Martha, daughter of James Money, by Eliza his wife, dau. of George Ramus, Page to George III., by the Princess Elizabeth his wife, dau. of George III.'[27]

Eliza, it was later rumoured, had been spirited away to India by one of the mysterious George Ramus' relatives, an employee of the East India Company. Unlike other supposed illegitimate royal children, she made no effort to pursue a claim to any title and that seemed to be that. The years rolled on, the rumoured parties grew older but the story never quite faded away.

This is one of those stories that grew larger and more convoluted with each passing year. We can confidently ascertain that George Ramus never worked for the royal family yet as the years sped by and the rumours were repeated, a little bit of embroidery began to occur. According to hearsay, Ramus appeared to have lived a number of lives both as a lifelong loyal retainer and at the same time, a page who had been fired for dishonesty. In fact he had not been a page at all if the household records are to be trusted. The facts, such as they ever were, began to sink into scandal.

So with no George Ramus in the royal service, we are left with three distinct possibilities. The first is that George has been confused with one of the several other men named Ramus who worked for the royal household. Secondly, we might wonder if it is a pseudonym for another candidate. Thirdly and finally, we must consider the possibility that the story has been fabricated.

Eliza, the supposed daughter of the marriage, was apparently and conveniently raised by another member of the Ramus family. Of course, a royal princess having an illegitimate baby and marriage is quite a different matter to a prince doing the same thing. The mistresses of princes were ten a'penny but clandestine marriages were less so. Elizabeth wasn't the only princess rumoured to have had a secret baby, but it was a baby that seemed to have been born and spirited away without a single witness, all done under the cover of a reoccurring attack of ill health.

In fact, might the reason for the rumour have been good old-fashioned revenge? A page named Billy Ramus was fired from the king's service in 1789 for mocking George III during an episode of madness. Perhaps it was a disgruntled Ramus or a member of his family who pointed the finger at Elizabeth's chastity out of revenge. When we consider the circumstances of his sacking and the king's efforts to make sure that the unemployed Ramus didn't suffer as a result of his losing his job, this becomes somewhat less likely.

Thanks to his ill-judged mockery of the ailing sovereign, William Ramus was dismissed after spending twenty-one years in the service of the king. Until that day he 'was the gentleman to whom the Monarch was indebted for every piece of chit-chat.[28]' So far, so much motive for revenge, but that's about to change. Once George III began to recover he forgave his former retainer for his cruel jibes, showing a merciful streak that he often displayed to those in need[29]. As a mark of gratitude and affection for Ramus' years in the harness, the king awarded his faithful retainer an annuity and recommendation so that he could go to India and join the staff of Charles Cornwallis, the Governor-General. We must then consider the intriguing claim that Princess Elizabeth's child with her secret husband was supposedly raised by a member of the Ramus family in India and wonder if there was more at play in George's actions than simple mercy. Though Ramus' departure was delayed by ill health, when he recovered and resumed his travels, there was frustratingly no mention of a child in his custody. So was Billy Ramus the true groom and father of Princess Elizabeth's illegitimate child who went to India to be with his daughter or was the entire story a fabrication?

I am minded to say the latter, yet there is a small and intriguing coda to this unusual tale.

Years later George IV's estranged and wildly gossipy wife, Caroline of Brunswick, threatened to drop a proverbial bombshell. She muttered darkly about a prospective speech in which she would not only lift the lid on her hated husband's behaviour but could promise, 'not to confine herself to that alone but to give a little historical narrative of the behaviour of each member of the Royal Family, not forgetting the offspring of the unmarried princesses. She is quite capable of telling the whole story.'[30]

If only she had!

Chapter 7

The Seaside Stranger

'Thomas Ward, a stranger, adopted by Samuel and Charlotte Sharland. Born 5 August 1800. Baptised 14 August 1800.'

The pages of this book, just like the history of George III's family, are filled with scandal and most of it came courtesy of the gentlemen of the household. In the hothouse world of the Georgian court it was not easy for a princess to break out and live a riotous life, but a prince might gad about and consort with whomsoever he pleased. Yet that didn't mean that the girls *couldn't* make a little bit of scandal of their own, just that it wasn't half so common for them as it was for the boys.

Born in 1777, Princess Sophia of the United Kingdom was one of the six daughters of George III and Queen Charlotte. Perhaps her very name was a portent of what was to come as she was christened Sophia Matilda, and her middle name was intended to honour the memory of Caroline Matilda, whose foray into Denmark was to end in one hell of a scandal.

It must have been difficult to be one of the daughters of George and Charlotte, for those troublesome sons did tend to steal the limelight. As Sophia was growing into a young woman, the Prince of Wales was firing the opening salvos in what would become a very prolonged war of attrition with his wife, Caroline of Brunswick, and there was only so much attention to go round. As is so often the case, the quieter, younger child received only a marginal share of the limelight. Worse still, as Sophia's childhood progressed, the king's mental health deteriorated alarmingly and he experienced a prolonged bout of what would become his infamous madness.

Young Sophia didn't realise as she enjoyed her ladylike education, but her father's illness would eventually have an enormous impact on the lives of her and her sisters. While the eldest, Charlotte, Princess Royal, managed to escape the family bosom and marry[1], the others were not so fortunate. George was tormented by the unhappy fate that had befallen his sister, Caroline Matilda, in Denmark, and the sicker he got, the more he worried that one of his daughters might suffer a similarly dreadful experience if she left the safety of the British court to go abroad.

Well, you might ask, why not just marry an Englishman and remain safely at home? To this the royal family would no doubt clutch their diamonds and swoon. A Princess of the Blood Royal married to a mere noble? Perish the thought! No, a royal princess absolutely must marry a gentleman of the same status or greater, nothing less would possibly do.

Quite apart from concerns about what might wait for them overseas, there was always the prescient matter of politics. A royal marriage entailed a vast amount of negotiation not to mention diplomatic wrangling and the prospect of overseas trips. All of this would come at a time when George was already politically and mentally pushed to his limits. The thought that he might be strong enough to enter into marriage discussions was absurd. On top of all that, Queen Charlotte would not even entertain the thought of it, for she relied on her daughters more than anyone else in her intimate circle. They were her only confidantes and, as her husband's health grew more frail, she held them more tightly than ever. In their circle, the sisters referred to themselves as *the nunnery* yet to the world outside, 'never, in tale or fable, were there six sister princesses more lovely.'[2]

To our modern sensibilities it's all too easy to imagine the Georgian princesses as girls who had everything from wealth to education to comfort, but they enjoyed little freedom. George always doted on his younger children and Princess Sophia became his favourite in times of mental illness, spending long hours at his side as he battled invisible demons. Imagine then the love and distress that must have tangled in her youthful breast when she was sent to sit with her father during his periods of mania. He recalled one of these to Fanny Burney, a mere throwaway recollection but when witnessed by a mere child, these incidents must have made their mark on the young princess Sophia.

> 'I have had the honour [the king said] of about an hour's conversation with [Sophia], in the old style; though I have given up my mad frolics now. To be sure, I had a few in that style formerly; upon my word I am almost ashamed; — Ha! ha! ha!'[3]

Sophia watched as suitor after suitor came calling in the hope of securing the hand of her sisters and suitor after suitor was sent away unsatisfied. No doubt she soon began to realise that her own future would not involve marriage and without that, the options for a princess were limited. In fact, the absence of a husband meant that Sophia was destined to face exactly the fate her mother intended: the role of lifelong confidante for a wife whose husband was crumbling, taking the very foundations of her world with him. There was to be no discussion or debate and Charlotte, for all her piety and gentle manner, was as hard as iron on the subject. The girls would stay at home.

Yet sometimes, home is precisely where scandal can find you.

As the Princess Royal left Britain for her new life overseas, Sophia remained at home. Intelligent, witty and gentle in nature, she was popular with her tutors and siblings alike and longed for a freedom she would never know. As the princess grew older, she grew bored, and longed to know more of the world outside the palace windows.

Just before she turned 20, Sophia found a friend in Frances Garth, who was assistant governess to Princess Charlotte, the newborn daughter of the bitterly estranged Prince and Princess of Wales[4]. Befitting a lady in such a position, Miss Garth could point to an immaculate heritage and she was not the only member of her family in the royal employ. As Queen Charlotte wrote in a letter of recommendation to the Prince of Wales, Frances was 'niece to the colonel of that name who I have seen several times last year[5]'. Indeed, it was among the personal staff of King George III that the *other* Garth could be found, and he was to become an important figure in Sophia's life.

The fellow in question was Colonel Thomas Garth[6], equerry to George III[7], and he was a gentleman of pedigree. Small of stature and thirty-three years older than young Princess Sophia, the trusted royal retainer was instantly recognisable by the large purple birthmark that coloured his forehead and the skin around one of his eyes. This unmissable feature of the equerry was recorded by Sophia's sister, Princess Mary, in a letter to the Prince of Wales in 1798. With her tongue either mischievously or even spitefully lodged in her cheek she wrote, 'as for General Garth, the purple light of love *toujours le même*'. She goes no further and just a couple of lines along coyly dismisses any discussion of her siblings, writing, 'as to the sisterhood, that is too near to make any observations upon.' One can almost hear a certain wry smile and shrug accompanying her words.

Yet the attachment of Princess Sophia to Thomas Garth was the worst kept secret at court. Charles Greville[8], that inveterate recorder of his life and times, not to mention other people's business, gleefully recorded in his memoirs the gossip surrounding the couple. They were the talk of the household and in the Georgian world, scandal was a real currency. Greville heard on the gossip grapevine that Sophia was 'so in love with [Garth] that everyone saw it. She could not contain herself in his presence.' And, being Greville, he recorded it for posterity. No doubt Sophia would been delighted to know that her business had been the talk of the court.

For those who would ask why a young princess, celebrated for her intelligence, wit and beauty, might fall for a man more than twice her age who had a large facial birthmark, one might gently point out that there is more to a chap than his looks. Garth was renowned for being a gentleman in every sense of the word. Well-travelled, cultured, urbane and, one suspects rather alluring for a girl who was forbidden to meet men beyond those of her own household. It is not impossible to imagine that Garth might well have held some attractions for the young princess. Greville makes it sound rather more predatory, but it's worth noting he always did have an eye for purple prose.

> 'The only reason why people doubted Garth's being the father was that he was a hideous old devil, old enough to be her father, and with a great claret mark on his face which is no argument at all, for women fall in love with anything and opportunity and the accidents of the passions are of more importance than any positive merit either of mind or body. There they [the princesses] were secluded from the world, mixing with few people, their passions boiling over, and ready to fall into the hands of the first man whom circumstances enabled to get at them.'[9]

Boiling over isn't the half of it.

For several years Sophia had endured recurring stomach problems and in 1799 they returned, rendering her so unwell that she became housebound for some time. Bored and frustrated by her invalid state, she heard reports of the Prince and Princess of Wales' ongoing war of attrition; little might she know, given the gossip that later began to circulate, how the side she chose to support might come back to haunt her. For gossip has to start somewhere, even if that is with one's own family.

George and Caroline had married in 1795. From their very first meeting, the omens were terrible and when Wales turned up to the ceremony drunk as a newt, the die was cast. He spent the wedding night in a paralytic stupor and, when he had recovered his wits, could only complain about his new bride's lack of personal hygiene. For her part, Caroline was no more impressed by her groom and later commented that, if she could go back to the altar and be given a choice of death or marriage, she would certainly choose death. Somehow this mismatched couple managed to produce a child, Princess Charlotte of Wales, but they barely made it past their first anniversary before they went their separate ways.

Caroline set up home in Blackheath and aggravated her estranged husband simply by getting on and living her life. As popular with the British people as her husband was unpopular, she held salons and gatherings for Wales' political opponents, but he was convinced that there was more to it than that. He was certain that she was committing adultery. If the prince could prove it, then he might achieve the almost impossible: a divorce.

In fact, the prince's desperate search for something to end their marriage would go on fruitlessly until Caroline's dying day in 1821. For now though, as the eighteenth century drew to a close, it was time for the royal siblings to declare which side of the battle lines they stood.

Miss Frances Garth, friend to Sophia, went to Blackheath with Caroline to serve as a woman of the bedchamber. Though her elder brother would have been furious had he known that his sister and Frances had kept in touch, Sophia continued to write to her friend, sending her letters via a trusted member of the household. When gossip began to seep out about the princess just a few years later, it will come as no surprise to learn that it originated with Caroline, who despite getting on well with Sophia, liked to use negative family gossip to get back at Wales.

In March 1801 a concerned Princess Elizabeth approached Dr Thomas Willis, who was one of the doctors caring for the unwell king in his episodes of madness, and asked to speak to him on 'a very delicate subject'. This was 'the cruelty of a fabricated and most scandalous and base report concerning P.S. [Princess Sophia]'[10]. That scandalous and base report was the rumour that, when laid up at Weymouth with illness in 1800, Sophia had given birth to an illegitimate son fathered by Thomas Garth. Willis, of course, did not go into the substance of the rumours in writing but unequivocally rejected the very thought of it out of hand, noting that 'such a report must in its nature be false as those who are acquainted with the interior of the King's houses must testify.'[11]

George III. William Wynne, after
Allan Ramsay. 1791.

Queen Charlotte. Thomas
Gainsborough.

THE ROYAL FAMILY OF ENGLAND IN THE YEAR 1787.

The ROYAL FAMILY of GEORGE III

Above: The royal family of England in the year 1787. Thomas Stothard. 1800.

Left: The royal family of George III: George, Prince of Wales, Frederick, Duke of York, W. Henry, Duke of Clarence, Prince Edward. 1795.

The royal family of George III:
Princess Royal, Princess Augusta
Sophia, Princess Elizabeth,
Princess Mary. 1795.

Princess Caroline Matilda, Queen
of Denmark. James Watson, after
Francis Cotes. 1771.

The Prince of Wales and the Duke of York. Valentine Green, after Benjamin West.

Prince Henry, Duke of Cumberland. Thomas Watson, after Joshua Reynolds.

Her Royal Highness the Princess Elizabeth. William Ward, after Johann Heinrich Ramberg. 1801.

Princess Sophia of the United Kingdom. Anonymous.

Maria, Countess of Waldegrave. James McArdell, after Joshua Reynolds.

Prince William Henry, Duke of Gloucester. Anonymous.

Mrs Robinson. Joshua
Reynolds. 1784.

George the Fourth when
Prince of Wales. After
Sir Joshua Reynolds.

Left: Mrs Fitzherbert. John Condé,
after Richard Cosway. 1792.

Below: The modern paradise,
or Adam and Eve regenerated,
showing the Prince of Wales
and Maria Fitzherbert. William
Humphrey. 1786.

Right: Prince Frederick
Henry, Duke of Cumberland.
Anonymous.

Below: Florizel and Perdita.
Anonymous. 1783.

Prince Augustus Frederick, Duke of Sussex. After William Skelton.

A BOY
Said to be Sir Augustus Frederick d'Esté (1794–1848)
by Richard Cosway: signed and dated 1799

Miniature in the Victoria and Albert Museum

Augustus d'Este. Richard Cosway. 1799.

Mrs. Jordan in the Character of
the Comic Muse. Thomas Park,
after John Hoppner. 1787.

King William IV when Duke of
Clarence. Henry Dawe. 1827.

Above: The humbug or an attempt at tragedy, with the Jordan [struck through and replaced by] Joram Upsett, showing Mrs Jordan and the Duke of Clarence. 1791.

Left: Ernest Augustus, King of Hanover. H R Cook, after G Saunders.

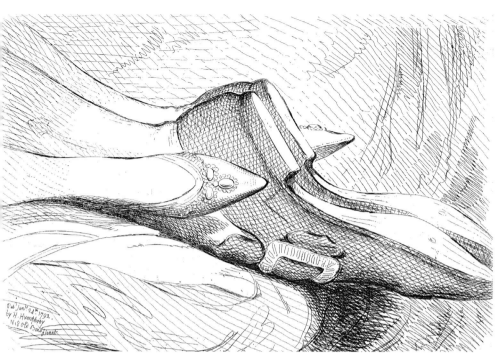

Above: Fashionable Contrasts
- or The Duchess's little shoe
yielding to the magnitude
of the Duke's foot. James
Gillray.1792.

Right: His Royal Highness
the Duke of Kent. Thomas
Cheesman, after Muller.

His Royal Highness
Frederick, Duke of York.
John Jackson. 1822.

The Modern Circe or a
Sequel to the Petticoat,
showing Mary Anne
Clarke and Wardle. Isaac
Cruikshank. 1809.

Fanny Burney. Charles
Turner. 1840.

A man disappearing
into a cracked chamber
pot which has the legs
of woman; implying
the illicit relationship
between the Duke
of Clarence and
Mrs. Jordan. James
Gillray. 1791.

HORATIO WALPOLE, EARL of ORFORD.
From an original Drawing by T.LAWRENCE ESQ.R.A. in the Possession of
SAMUEL LYSONS, ESQ.
Drawn by W.Evans. Engraved by H.Meyer.

PUBLISHED NOV.24.1811. BY T.CADELL & W.DAVIES, STRAND, LONDON.

Horatio Walpole, Earl of Orford. W Evans. 1811.

George III as he was in his final illness. Charles Turner. 1820.

But must it really, or was Willis simply unwilling to consider that it might, just *might*, be true?

In the winter of 1799, just before Sophia fell victim to one of the attacks of ill health to which she seemed so vulnerable, she spent time at Windsor Castle with her favourite equerry, Thomas Garth. Although she usually resided at the Lower Lodge, during a period of sickness Sophia moved to the Upper Lodge, the home of the king and queen. With her parents away in London it was left for Garth to serve as attendant to the young lady. It would appear that he attended her very well indeed.

During the months that followed Sophia began to gain weight at a rate of knots and her ailing father, George, asked what might be the cause of his daughter's changing form. Though the king was well at the time of the supposed pregnancy, his family was aware of the constant threat of a relapse. It seems inconceivable that Queen Charlotte wouldn't have suspected their daughter's condition[12] but if she did, she chose not to disclose it to her husband for fear that news of an illegitimate pregnancy might tip him over the edge into another episode of mania. Instead Charlotte placated George with the news that Sophia was suffering with dropsy and would soon be quite well again.

It was left to the courtiers to give whispered voice to what everyone suspected, that the princess was in fact heavy with child. As the intelligence seemed to originate with Elizabeth Thynne, Marchioness of Bath and Mistress of the Robes to Queen Charlotte, one might confidently claim that it came straight from the top.

A suspicious number of months later (round about nine, in fact), Sophia was bed bound at Weymouth under the care of the esteemed doctor, Sir Francis Milman. It was here, according to society gossip overheard by Lady Bath, that the princess gave birth to a little boy on 5 August 1800. The child was christened Thomas and he was recorded in the parish church on 11 August as a foundling, who would be cared for by Samuel and Charlotte Sharland. As the infant slumbered in the home of the tailor who had taken him in, the courtly rumour mill ground into life.

Turning the millstone was Lord Glenbervie, the sort of chap who would probably describe himself as a well-meaning soul of discretion. No doubt Sophia would disagree with that assessment. Glenbervie and his wife were good friends with Caroline of Brunswick and it was from Caroline that they received all the most outrageous gossip in town. Sophia was well aware of what people were saying about her and wrote to her friend, Lady Harcourt, thanking her for being a supportive confidante. There are, of course, two ways to interpret the passage below. One might be that Sophia *had* intrigued with Garth and that the 'little trifle' she describes is the manner in which gossip has taken a few imprudent embraces and spun them into a tale of an illegitimate baby. Another is that the 'little trifle' is the child itself, but one suspects that Sophia would hardly dismiss such a monumental occurrence so lightly. An unmarried Georgian princess giving birth to a son by an equerry was no 'little trifle' by any means!

> '[…] the excessive kindness of your manner has, I assure you, greatly soothed my distressed and unhappy days and hours. Be assured my dearest Lady Harcourt, that I will do all in my power to prove I am not ungrateful for all your kind concern about me, by the prudence of my conduct; but you will allow, I am sure, that I require time to recover my spirits, which have met with so severe a blow.
>
> I have no doubt that I was originally to blame, therefore I must bear the reports, however unjust they are, as I have partially myself to thank for them… It is grievous to think what *a little trifle will slur a young woman's character for ever* [sic].'[13]

Let us imagine though that Sophia really did view her son as a *trifle*. Could that be because, as some have suggested, she had actually undergone a secret marriage to Garth? In that case, the birth of a child, though scandalous to those who thought him illegitimate, would be less of a moral issue to Sophia. In the eyes of God, after all, she would have been a wife, making her son entirely legitimate. Thanks to the Royal Marriages Act, that union would *not* be legal in the eyes of British law but for a young lady of faith like Sophia, it's not impossible to think that this might have been a secondary concern.

Glenbervie recalled that Caroline, the estranged Princess of Wales, wondered whether Sophia might have not realised she was pregnant until she went into labour. This may seem absurd given her intelligence but she was sheltered and had suffered from episodes of ill health throughout her youth. Was it likely that Sophia had put the weight gain and other symptoms down to another bout of her many and varied ailments?

Although we should keep in mind the fact that Glenbervie's information was mostly gleaned from the Princess of Wales, how much weight should we lend the rumours? Caroline certainly had good reason to smear the royal family, for she and her husband were constantly engaged in a bitter game of one-upmanship. Yet Sophia had friends in Caroline's household and was not an enemy of the Princess of Wales, so it would seem odd for Caroline to attack her sister-in-law with such sordid gossip if it was entirely unfounded.

Add to this the fact that Thomas Garth became the young foundling Tom's guardian and the evidence for the prosecution begins to mount. If Sophia really did have a child with the equerry who later raised the little boy, Caroline's claims that Sophia didn't know she was pregnant suddenly seem a lot less far-fetched. Not only that, but Garth's star in the royal household continued to ascend undimmed, a far cry from the fate one might expect of a man who, to paraphrase Greville, had simply been the first man to get his hands on the princess.

With the possibility of marriage denied to them by their father's illness and their mother's obsession with keeping her daughters close by, Caroline suggested that the royal family had reached an understanding with the girls. According to Glenbervie's recollections, it was an unwritten rule that the princesses could 'indulge themselves in the gratifications of matrimony,' provided that they 'manage matters with prudence and decorum, and form attachments as near to conjugal connection as the restriction imposed on them will admit of.'[14]

Little Tom remained in the care of the Sharlands for some time, with the tailor and his wife seemingly ignorant of the baby's real parentage. He had been delivered to them swaddled in an ornate and clearly expensive silk skirt on which was embroidered a coronet, and all his upkeep was paid for by, surprise, surprise, Garth, but there was no hints as to who his mother might be. The modest Sharland household began to improve and the tailor became rather too sure of his own importance. Soon all of Weymouth knew that he was caring for a foundling of mysterious but illustrious birth, and the Sharlands became desperate to know the secret of the infant who had been placed in their care.

As soon as Samuel and Charlotte made enquiries regarding Tom's parentage with Garth, the die was cast. Tom was taken out of the couple's care and entrusted to Major Herbert Taylor who was, at the time, private secretary to the Duke of York[15]. *Tommy Garth*, as he became known following his adoption, was soon indulged and spoiled. His every wish was met, his every command obeyed and he was sent to Harrow to enjoy the best education that could be purchased. Though he and virtually all of Weymouth and polite society decided Garth was his father, the identity of his mother was rather more closely guarded.

Yet the story, already quite scandalous enough, was to assume a somewhat darker edge with another rumour that began to circulate regarding not Tom's mother, but his *father*.

> 'The King and Queen had stepped over the carpeted plank and ascended the steps in due form, when the Duke of Cumberland, who had not been of the sailing party, darted into the boat, seized on the Princess Sophia and kissed her, and then drew her arm through his and conducted her on shore.'[16]

Ernest Augustus, Duke of Cumberland and Teviotdale, later to be accused of murder, election meddling and jumping into bed with anything that moved, had always been fond of his little sister. But he soon found himself facing a rumour that he had raped Sophia and was in fact the father of the *foundling*, Tommy Garth. This unthinkable state of affairs would have been the monstrous scandal to end all scandals but I can't subscribe to the belief that Cumberland fathered a child by Sophia. Just as we will see when we relive his blood-drenched encounter with his valet, Cumberland was a useful Hanoverian bogeyman. Disfigured, somewhat odd in manner and politically unpopular, he was an easy scapegoat. Sophia's own letters mention that though kind he could be imprudent yet one can hardly hold this as proof of incest.

We must decide then whether we think there is adequate evidence to find Cumberland guilty of this most heinous of crimes. It is quite a thing to sit as judge and jury on a case such as this but I don't think I can convict Cumberland of the charge against him. It is always difficult when faced with an allegation for which virtually no proof exists but in this case, not only is there a lack of evidence against Cumberland, but there is a wealth of it against Garth. Of course, all of this is circumstantial and one might argue that perhaps, if Cumberland was indeed the father of his own sister's child, then it would be in the interests of the royal family to cover up the crime by providing a figure who would selflessly pose as the *real* parent. Yet if this is the case, would they really have chosen a man so very close to the king, an equerry whose very involvement in the life of Tommy Garth only served to give even more circumstantial proof that Sophia was the mother of an illegitimate baby? Would they not simply have placed the infant in the care of a trusted family, rather than muddy the waters by involving an unmarried equerry who could easily be linked to the princess?

The rumour appears, surprise, surprise, to have originated with the always imaginative Princess Caroline of Brunswick in another of her many salvoes against her estranged husband's family. She had probably just observed the very close relationship between the brother and sister and had come to her own wild conclusions. Glenbervie recorded the allegation with wide-eyed horror, writing:

> 'The Princess of Wales told Lady Sheffield the other day, that there is great reason to suspect the father to be the Duke of Cumberland. How strange and how disgusting. But it is a very strange family, at least the children – sons and daughters.'[17]

Caroline and Sophia had never quarrelled though. Quite to the contrary, the young princess was always kind to her sister-in-law, so such gossip might seem surprising. Yet Caroline was never happier than when she was the centre of attention and she was given to what she would no doubt think of as harmless fun and tale-telling. She once joked that a child she was caring for out of charity was her own illegitimate baby and she ended up under investigation as a result, so bad taste jokes and gossip were right up Caroline's street. Those who the tales concerned might, of course, have had a different view. One person's *harmless fun is* another's malicious gossip, and in the battle between the Prince and Princess of Wales, nothing was off limits.

If Cumberland and Sophia had had a child, either as the result of an incestuous relationship or assault, then giving responsibility for him to Thomas Garth made precious little sense. Instead the child would surely have been given into the custody of someone a little less close to home. One thing is certain though. In that case, the boy's guardian wouldn't have paraded Tommy around with quite the enthusiasm that Thomas Garth did. He took great delight in showing the boy off and made no real efforts to pretend that he wasn't Tommy's father.

Of course, there's always the possibility that Garth was given custody of Sophia and Cumberland's son *because* he was willing to agree to such a pretence and could be relied on not to spill the rather sordid beans. Again though, giving the boy's care to a bachelor was *bound* to cause gossip. Then there is the third possibility beyond Garth or Cumberland, that Sophia's relationship was with someone of lower birth. The name most often associated with this rumour is that of a page called *Papendyck*, though even Greville wasn't too sure about that bit of gossip. All of this wilfully ignores those reports of Sophia being unable to contain herself in Garth's presence. There is also the matter of a letter Sophia herself wrote to Garth, and it is not one that requires a great deal of imagination to interpret.

'Your dear ring has given me some tremendous pinches […]
I shall never forget you, my dear General, to whom I owe so
much. Your kind remembrance of me is a cordial. Your calling
me your S makes me as proud as Lucifer … I love you more
and more every day. God bless you, my dearest dear General.'[18]

This is a love letter, plain and simple, and its reference to a ring is both
tantalising and mysterious - the rumoured wedding, perhaps, but certainly a
token of romantic affection. The tone of the letter is not the polite indulgence
of a princess to a trusted old retainer, but a heartfelt note of love from a
young woman who was sheltered and lonely and had given her heart to a
man to who she could never marry.

As the years passed and Sophia returned to her sheltered life, Tommy
to his education at Harrow and Garth to his role of trusted royal equerry, it
might have seemed as though the drama regarding the Weymouth foundling
had blown over. Princess Charlotte, who Garth was charged with serving,
reported that young Tommy was an over-indulged young man who was
allowed frequent liberties by his by now elderly *adoptive* parent. He rode
out and about through Weymouth as though he were a young and beloved
member of the royal house itself. He courted the public and rejoiced in
being the centre of attention, which he was all too happy to snatch from his
guardian's charge. She was real royalty - Princess Charlotte of Wales, the
heiress to the throne.

So what became of little Tommy Garth?

Tommy followed his father into the military, but there the similarities end.
There was to be no *trusted royal retainer* label for him. He did not enjoy
much success but did indulge in a rather major scandal of his own. A bad
boy through and through, Tommy eloped with Lady Georgiana Astley,
wife of Sir Jacob Astley and a daughter of the famed Dashwoods of West
Wycombe[19]. The result was a messy and scandalous trial involving that
Georgian favourite, *criminal conversation*, with claim and counter-claim
keeping the public and press enthralled[20]. It was Tommy's return to the
spotlight, and he was determined to linger on the stage[21]. As we have already
seen, criminal conversation, better known as 'crim con,' was a suit, usually
brought by a husband against his wife, in which he sued her for committing
adultery. Though some countries still hear criminal conversation cases, it
was abolished in the United Kingdom over 150 years ago.

The elderly Garth was by now in declining health and he believed that his days were numbered. A year before his death he supposedly gave Tommy a locked box containing a number of letters that told the truth behind his parentage and, we might assume, named Princess Sophia as his mother. In desperate need of money Tommy wrote to his former guardian, Sir Herbert Taylor, and told him that, loathe though he was to upset anyone, he had no choice but to ask Princess Sophia for a financial bailout. Taylor, by now private secretary to the ailing King George IV, was determined that Tommy should do no such thing.

Sir Herbert made an offer to the young soldier. If Tommy was to deposit the box of letters his father had given him in a bank then he would be given an annuity of £3,000. Tommy complied and no sooner had the box been deposited then it duly disappeared, taking the contents of the letters with it. Tommy was furious for those papers were undoubtedly of huge blackmail value to him. He responded by issuing an affidavit in which he claimed he had been robbed of a valuable cache of correspondence. Once again, the scandal was fizzing.

> 'Thomas Garth [was] in possession of, and rightfully entitled to, certain documents, papers, and correspondence, of very great value and importance, relating immediately to his fortune, station, and affairs, and to the claims which he had upon certain persons named in such documents and correspondence, and to the mode by which such claim could be substantiated and enforced.
>
> [Sir Herbert Taylor] was very desirous of obtaining possession of the above-mentioned documents and correspondence, or, at any rate, of having the same so securely deposited in safe custody, that neither this deponent nor any other person should without his, the said Sir Herbert Taylor's, assent, obtain access thereto, and that the said Herbert Taylor entered into a negotiation with this deponent for that purpose.
>
> [It was agreed] that all the then outstanding debts of this deponent should be discharged by or by the direction of the said Sir Herbert Taylor, and that an annuity of 3,000l. per annum should be effectually secured to this deponent for his life; and that by and on the part of this deponent, that the box containing all the above-mentioned documents, letters, and correspondence, should be sealed with the respective seals of

this deponent and the said Sir Herbert Taylor, and, so sealed, should be deposited [and] remain in the hands of some banker or bankers to be mutually agreed upon.

[…] But this deponent saith, that no sum of money whatever hath in fact been paid to this deponent since the said deposit so obtained [and that sir Herbert intends to] prevent this deponent from regaining possession [of the box and its contents].'[22]

And just like that, the scandal was ignited all over again. The press wondered what could possibly be hidden in that tantalising box, locked, secured and now spirited away. There had been no explanation to justify the payment Tommy requested, nor any reason that the press could see for him thinking himself entitled to any sort of payment unless it was in return for the preservation of a most marvellous secret.

'*What secret was to be kept*? Tell that, or say nothing,"[23] demanded *The Times*. Although the writer mused that perhaps the secret was already out there, walking around in public and making a nuisance of himself. Was that secret Tommy Garth? Those who wondered what information Tommy might have should not look for the box, argued the columnists, but for the mysterious character who now had possession of it. As *The Times* delicately put it, 'the point to which these clumsy advocates should direct themselves is not, *what* is Captain GARTH, but *who* he is.'[24]

Who indeed?

'Capt. Garth is the son of General Garth. General Garth is, by a marriage fulfilling all the moral and religious conditions of such a contract, the husband of an illustrious lady. The union, however, though such as must satisfy the most unscrupulous and delicate consequence is, by a law affecting one family, and only one, in the realm *politically* invalid.'[25]

Sophia stayed silent on the matter of the locked box and as far as we know, never saw Tommy in later life. Hints in her letters suggest that she had a fear of promenading in Weymouth in case she encountered a certain unnamed person and it's not a stretch to imagine that the person in question might be Tommy. Whilst it's not improbable that she feared bumping into him simply because of the way their names had been linked as mother and son, it's just as if not far more likely that she *was* his mother, and that's why she was so anxious about the two of them being seen together.

In the light of Tommy's return to the public eye all those old rumours began to resurface, along with fresh speculation about the marriage that may or may not have happened; the marriage that would have rendered Tommy Garth legitimate. So were Garth and Sophia married? It's possible though by no means definitely proven. The truth is, we'll never know.

> 'General Garth, whose name has been so much mentioned,
> died last Monday at his house in town, aged 85.'[26]

Thomas Garth died on 18 November 1829. He divided his possessions between his nephew and Tommy Garth, the foundling who was probably his son. All of this came too late for Tommy, who ended up languishing in debtors' prison. His lover, Georgiana, stayed true to the man she had eloped with and went to prison with him. It was here that she died, falling victim to scarlet fever just days after giving birth to their only child, Georgiana Rosamond.

Sir Herbert Taylor engineered a lump sum of £10,000 from the late Thomas Garth's estate to secure Tommy's release. He and little Georgiana eventually secured an annuity of £300 - a long way from the £3,000 he had once demanded but better than nothing to a man in dire straits. Time was ticking away and the players in the drama, once so scandalous and shocking, were dwindling. General Garth was the first to go, but Princess Sophia was soon to follow.

> 'Her Royal Highness the Princess Sophia, daughter of his
> late Majesty George III, and aunt to the Queen, expired at
> half-past 6 o'clock, on Sunday afternoon, at her residence at
> Kensington.'[27]

Twenty-seven years after the death of the princess, Tommy Garth, foundling, soldier, rake, prisoner and possible son of the royal House of Hanover, died too. Georgiana alone was left to pursue in vain the claims her father had made. She died in 1912, the last of the supposed descendants of Sophia.

The tale of the princess and the equerry is one of the most tantalising mysteries of the court of George III. It's likely now that we shall never know the truth yet the memory of Tommy Garth lingers over the house of Charlotte and George, a motherless spectre that has never really faded away.

Chapter 8

A Grand Old Scandal

'[…] The copyright of Milton's Paradise Lost sold for only 15/.
Mrs. Mary-Ann [sic] Clarke, the courtesan, obtained for the
copy of her Memoirs, from the Earl of Chichester, 10,000/.!!!'[1]

Like so many courtesans and royal mistresses throughout history, Mary
Anne Clarke's origins were obscure. In fact, it was probably the lady herself
who obscured them, scrubbing out her past so that she might be known only
by her illustrious present. Once infamous, in the modern consciousness
Mary Anne's fame has been eclipsed by her great-great-granddaughter, the
novelist, Daphne Du Maurier[2], yet in her day Mary Anne Clarke was the
name on everybody's lips.

According to popular belief, Mary Anne Clarke's story began around
1776 in a grimy back lane of London[3]. What little we do know of her life
can be taken from an 1809 work entitled *Authentic And Interesting Memoirs
of Mrs Clarke, From Her Infamy To The Present Time*, which purports to tell
a true and unvarnished story. We can probably be very dubious indeed about
her involvement in the work and it might be wise to take the contents with
a grain of salt. Being that this book is the text from which all biographical
information about Mary Anne seems to stem, let us take it as our tentative
guide to these hidden years.

Sadly the identity of Mary Anne's mother has not been accurately
recorded yet her father, it seems, was a tradesman named Thompson. Here
in the gloom Mary Anne was a rare ray of brightness in an otherwise dull
and unhappy world, yet she was to know sadness at an early age. Mary
Anne's father, the mysterious Thompson, died when she was still a child
and her mother swiftly married again, this time to a Mr Farquhar, who was
employed by a printing house. Yet Mary Anne had no intention of remaining
in the forgotten lanes of London forever, she was determined to make it big.

As she grew, Mary Anne soon proved to be a smart, savvy sort of gal. The
sort who was destined for *something*. Taught to read and write by Farquhar,

she was soon a regular sight around Fleet Street, running errands for her stepfather and even doing the occasional bit of proofreading and correction, all of which brought more money into the far from stuffed family coffers. Mary Anne's good looks and ready wit soon endeared her to the gentleman of the area and at the age of 17 she married Joseph Clarke, the son of a wealthy man.

Joseph, however, was *not* destined to be Mary Anne's handsome prince. A cheating drunkard, he squandered his money and went bankrupt. By this time he and Mary Anne had two children, Ellen and George[4], and she wasn't about to fall back into destitution. Mary Anne left Joseph behind and it's here that the narrative of our heroine's life becomes intriguingly muddy. That very fanciful *memoir* claims that she immediately and improbably became a celebrated actress but this seemed to be a rather generous interpretation of a career path that might have been rather more *earthy* than Mary Anne or the authors wished to acknowledge.

However whether on the stage or in the bed, Mary Anne slowly began to make her way through the ranks of ever more illustrious lovers. Whatever the career path, by 1803 Mary Anne was a courtesan and a well-known one too, not for her the alleyways and backstreets of London. It was now that she flounced into the path of a man with whom she became intrinsically linked, Prince Frederick, Duke of York and Albany.

The Duke of York was the second son of George III and Queen Charlotte. He was close friends with his profligate brother, George, Prince of Wales, and the two men shared the same fun-loving, spendthrift approach to life. Born in 1763, he filled his days with wine, women and gambling, plunging headlong into debt. Just as his older brother did, York agreed to an official marriage only on the understanding that his considerable debts would be settled if he *did*, and on 29 September 1791, he married his cousin, Princess Frederica Charlotte of Prussia[5], in Berlin. She was the only child of the dismally unhappy marriage between Frederick William II of Prussia and Elisabeth Christine of Brunswick-Lüneburg and when she arrived in Britain for a second marriage ceremony at Buckingham House on 23 November, the public and royal family instantly warmed to her.

Sadly the marriage was not happy and the couple soon parted ways, although their separation was at least amicable. The Duchess of York took up residence at Oatlands Park in Weybridge, where she remained until her death. Her husband, meanwhile, continued with his military career, though it did not *quite* glitter. Still, being the son of the king had its benefits and in 1795, the Duke of York was appointed commander-in-chief of the armed forces. Years later, of course, this illustrious office would come back and bite him. Hard.

The Duke of York might have presided over defeats and concessions, none of which did his reputation as a commander any favours, but he did have an undeniable zeal for military reform. His appointment marked the end of 'the time at which everything […] was rotten in the British Army.'[6] He would not suffer incompetent or self-serving officers and took an interest in the welfare of common soldiers that led the distinguished military scholar, Sir John Fortescue, to claim that the Duke of York did 'more for the army than any one man has done for it in the whole of its history.'[7]

A man, particularly a royal duke, cannot be *all* army and reform, and the Duke of York had never been a chap who found the company of soldiers adequate replacement for the company of women. When he fell for Mary Anne, he fell hard and took her as his official mistress. Mary Anne rather liked being the belle of the prince and the gossipy and irresistible Captain Rees Howell Gronow[8] related a particularly shocking occasion on which, attending the theatre with her lover, Mary Anne was mistaken for the Duchess of York and addressed as 'Her Royal Highness'. Far from being embarrassed, she revelled in the infamy. The girl from the gloomy and crime-ridden back alleys had left all that behind and now, as the lover of the Duke of York, she was living large.

> 'Though she is not a perfect beauty[9], she has many agreeable attractions; one in particular from a well-turned arm. Lively and gay in conversation. […] Her face is oval, but not long; small nose, dazzling dark eyes, beaming with the most irresistable [sic] archness, and captivating intelligence; her mouth is small, and presents good even teeth; her skin is delicately fair, without being of a dead white; a sufficient colour adorns her cheeks, and we have no hesitation in saying, that, without being regularly handsome, she is second to none in those attractions that please the opposite sex.'[10]

The duke provided Mary Anne with an eye-wateringly opulent home at 18 Gloucester Place[11] and here, with literally dozens of staff at her disposal, she was the queen of the courtesans[12]. All of this was paid for by the duke, but his gifts of a few thousand pounds each year were not enough to keep Mary Anne in the style to which she wished to become accustomed. She had agreed to become York's mistress on the understanding that he would pay her an allowance every month but the money was sporadic at best, and her debts kept on mounting. It was time, the lady decided, to get a little part-time job on the side.

Mary Anne knew that one of York's duties was signing off the lists of soldiers who were due a promotion. These soldiers had purchased a commission, meaning they paid a set amount of money to be promoted. The practice was completely above board and existed as part of army life for more than two centuries. Never keen on paperwork, York would often simply add his signature without reading the lists and he certainly never scrutinised them. Shrewd and savvy, Mary Anne realised that these lists could easily be amended. A gentleman's name might be added to the end of the list before it was signed off, and nobody would ever be any the wiser. As she often took dictation for her lover, there would conveniently be no discrepancy in handwriting and no hint that anything nefarious was afoot. Mary Anne's scheme was simple, those who wanted a promotion would pay her a fee and she would add their name to the list, securing them the leg-up that they so desired.

Mary Anne's relationship with the Duke of York ended in 1806 but her lifestyle continued unabated. At first the duke seemed reluctant to fund her extravagances but when she threatened to publish memoirs of their affair as well as their sauciest letters[13], he caved in and provided her with an annuity paid from his own allowance. Once again the payments were slow and when the debt-ridden duke cut off Mary Anne's cash flow altogether in 1808, the foundations were laid for trouble. Mary Anne could never keep quiet about her escapades and in 1808 Major Denis Hogan published a personal memoir in which he stated that he had been denied promotion because he refused to deal with Mary Anne Clarke. The wheels of scandal were turning, and the gossip mill was gathering pace once more.

'It has been often observed to me by *connoisseurs*, that I should have had no reason to complain, if I had proceeded in the *proper way* to seek promotion. But what is meant by the *proper way?* I applied to the Duke of York, because he was commander-in-chief. To his royal highness I was directed by the king's orders to apply; and with these orders alone I felt it consistent with my duty as an officer, and my honour as a gentleman, to comply. But if any other person had been the substitute of the Duke of York, I should have made my application to that person. If a [...] Clarke [...] had been invested by his majesty with the office of commander-in-chief, to that person I should have applied; nay, if it had pleased his majesty to confer upon a female the *direct command* of the army, I should have done my duty, in applying to the legal depositary of power: but to none other should I condescend to apply; for I scorn undue influence, and feel incapable of enjoying any object, however intrinsically valuable, that should be procured by such means.'[14]

The cat was almost out of the bag. It would take a politician's farcical dive for cover from the arms of a courtesan to free it completely.

'The way in which Colonel Wardle first obtained information of the sale of commissions was singular enough. He was paying a clandestine visit to Mrs Clarke, when a carriage with the royal livery drove up to the door, and the gallant officer was compelled to take refuge under the sofa; but instead of the royal duke, there appeared one of his aide-de-camps, who entered into conversation in so mysterious a manner as to excite the attention of the gentleman under the sofa, and led him to believe that the sale of a commission was authorised by the Commander-in-Chief; though it afterwards appeared that it was a private arrangement of the unwelcome visitor. At the Horse-Guards, it had often been suspected that there was a mystery connected with commissions that could not be fathomed; as it frequently happened that the list of promotions agreed on was surreptitiously increased by the addition of new names. This was the crafty handiwork of the accomplished dame; the duke having employed her as his amanuensis, and being accustomed to sign her autograph lists without examination.'[15]

Captain Gronow's reminiscences are at times rather fanciful, but his recounting of the beginning of the fall of the Duke of York is irresistibly amusing. It is also, considering Mary Anne's love of gentlemen friends, drama and opulence, entirely believable.

Mary Anne went on spending cash she didn't have and enjoying the society of gentleman callers at her home. Among them was Colonel Gwyllym Lloyd Wardle, a radical politician. Wardle and Mary Anne were enjoying an *interlude* when a royal carriage drove up to the house and out stepped one of the Duke of York's aides-de-camp. Fearing discovery, Wardle hid beneath the sofa and there listened as the aide and Mary Anne discussed her selling of commissions to men who wished to advance at a discount. Wardle could scarcely believe what he was hearing and he determined that this could *not* go unpunished, or unknown – showing a particularly Georgian lack of loyalty to his mistress.

> 'Mr. Wardle rose to move for an inquiry into the conduct of H.R.H. the Duke of York. Mentioned several instances of gross abuse of power [and claimed that] Mrs Clarke, a lady with whom the Duke of York was intimate, sold commissions and promotions at less than held the emulated terms, as appeared by a written scale that was sent to an officer:
>
> | | Mrs Clarke's Prices | Regulated Prices |
> | --- | --- | --- |
> | A Majority, | £900 - - - - | £2,000 |
> | A Company, | 700 - - - - - | 1,500 |
> | A Lieutenant, | 400 - - - - - | 550 |
> | An Ensigncy, | 200 - - - - - | 400 |
>
> Money has been lodged in the hands of a third person till the promotion of an officer was Gazetted; then the money was paid to Mrs. Clarke, and by her to the Duke of York's silversmith, in part for a debt contacted by the Duke of York for the lady's service of plate.'[16]

Wardle took his intelligence to the House of Commons. On 20 January 1809, he introduced a motion calling for an inquest into the behaviour of the duke. His wish was granted and a public enquiry began, causing consternation among Members of Parliament. After all, the Duke of York was the favourite brother of the Prince of Wales and with the king's health in crisis, to risk upsetting the famously capricious Wales was dangerous indeed. He might be king or regent in a matter of months[17] and few if any wanted him as an enemy. This was London's hottest ticket and once the enquiry opened, it was clear that the star witness was certainly Miss Mary Anne Clark. The outcome would be damning for the Duke of York.

Over a period of two weeks the conduct of the duke and Mary Anne was systematically picked apart at the bar of the House. It became the city's main topic of conversation and Mary Anne's name was on everyone's lips from the moment she glided into proceedings on 1 February 1809. Not only was York aware of her commission sales, she told the committee, but he profited from them too. Quick-witted, composed and basking in the limelight, Mary Anne was utterly unfazed by the questions thrown at her. Perhaps York should have listened to that old saying about a woman scorned!

Though the king's failing mental and physical health had placed him in dire straits, it had also become a rallying point for the British people. Laid low by war, they focused on the old king as a bastion of morality and all that a British monarch should be. The scandalous events in the House of Commons did much to enforce the impression that his sons were anything but his spiritual heirs. It seemed as though not a day went past without some new and shocking revelation but this, the sale of commissions in the army by a courtesan, was beyond the pale. If Mary Anne was to be believed then loyalty, honour and valour counted for nothing in the consciousness of the supposedly reforming duke. Instead, should a soldier wish to progress, the only qualification was a very deep pocket from which to produce the asking price.

It might come as a surprise to learn that the duke himself did not have to testify. As a royal prince, he was given leave to defend himself in a letter, leaving his former mistress to face Parliament. Perhaps he thought that she might crumble, that she was the epitome of the weak and feeble woman. If so, he was mistaken, for Mary Anne took to the task with aplomb.

> '[Mary Anne] with apparent self-composure curtsied to the House - she wore a light blue silk pelisse bordered with deep lace, a lilac coloured velvet bonnet, partially concealed beneath the foldings of a veil which hung over her forehead, and carried upon her arm a large swan down muff.'[18]

Resplendent in her fashionable getup, Mary Anne positively sang. She was happy to spill the beans about the fact that she had taken money in return for intervening in promotions. This was hardly news, for Wardle had been an eyewitness to such an exchange from beneath that opulent sofa. It wasn't the admission that *Mary Anne* was guilty that sent the public into a frenzy though; it was her recollection that the duke knew *exactly* what she was up to.

Far from adding names to the lists without York's knowledge, Mary Anne claimed she had openly discussed the matter with her lover at dinner. When asked if the duke knew that Mary Anne received a payment for facilitating the promotion she answered in the affirmative, casually stating, 'I mentioned it to his Royal Highness on that day'[19]. Mary Anne wasn't intimidated by the massed ranks of the Houses of Parliament and, at the end of two hours of questioning, she was as cool and collected as she had been at the start. William Wilberforce noted with admiration that Mary Anne 'was elegantly dressed, consummately impudent, and very clever; [she] clearly got the better in the tussle.'[20]

This, of course, was a game changer. Now the Duke of York wasn't just a fool for a pretty face or someone whose lackadaisical attitude to paperwork had fallen victim to the schemes of Mary Anne. Her testimony meant that the commander-in-chief himself, the man responsible for the British army, could be bought. He was no longer an innocent if unprofessional dupe, but the sort of character who would let his mistress decide who gained promotion and when. If this was true, it brought the honour of the duke and the very institution of the army itself into question. The names of those who had procured favours were dragged through the mud and the public as one was disgusted. Anonymous letters accused those who had paid for promotion of being little better than pimps, with the duke happy to take their money for a favour. In the House, meanwhile, Lord Temple observed that loving naivety was no defence for 'surely a person of the Duke's talents and education must have known that the mistresses of princes have always been the sources of corruption. They had always established a kind of shop to sell the favours of the court.'[21]

Yet other witnesses were quick to paint a somewhat different picture. Doctor Andrew Thynne, a highly respected physician who had attended Mary Anne for a number of years, was soon revealed as one of the men who acted as a go-between for the lady and those seeking advancement. Although he freely agreed that Mary Anne's closeness to the duke was the reason for his involvement with her, he refuted the suggestion that the duke knew that money was changing hands. In fact, when asked whether Mary Anne was open with the duke about her payments he told the members that Mary Anne 'desired him to conceal the fact of the money she was to receive from the world, and from his Royal Highness most particularly.'[22]

The matter of the duke's honour, then, rested on who was to be believed. At best he was a trusting fool, at worst, he was corruption incarnate. Lord Folkestone, a radical Whig who opposed York's control of the armed forces, was determined to bring the duke to justice and raised the matter of York attempting to secure a loan of £40,000 from Robert Kennett, an upholsterer, in return for influential government office. Although this was not part of his army duties, it showed that the duke was not above seeking cash for favours. It looked as though the case was all tied up. In his letter to the House, the duke did not lower himself to the matter of facts, but relied instead on the red stuff that flowed in his veins. He was a Prince of the Blood Royal, he reminded his persecutors, and his honour was enough. The letter was read out in Parliament before a hushed crowd, an all-or-nothing attempt to shut things down once and for all.

> 'I have waited with the greatest anxiety until the Committee of Inquiry had closed its examination, and I now hope it will not be deemed improper in me to address a letter to the House of Commons, through you, on the subject. I observe, with the deepest concern, that in the course of the inquiry that has been gone into, my name has been coupled with transactions of the most criminal and disgraceful nature; and I must always lament a connection that has exposed my honour and my character to such unmerited animadversions. With respect to any concern in such transactions, I now, ON THE HONOUR OF A PRINCE, most solemnly assert MY ENTIRE INNOCENCE. I deny, not only any participation in, or connivance at, those transactions, but also the least knowledge or consciousness of their existence.
>
> I hope that the House of Commons will not, upon such evidence as has been produced, adopt any proceeding prejudicial to my character and honour; but if upon such testimony, the House of Commons should think my innocence questionable, I claim from them the justice of not being condemned without a trial, nor tried without those sanctions, the benefit of which is enjoyed by every British subject; I also require permission to give evidence, as in other cases under the ordinary administration of the law.'

A prince he may be, the public agreed, but he was no gentleman. Things looked dire for the duke and all that was left was for Parliament to pronounce him guilty. Yet, when the House divided to vote on the matter of the duke's corruption, not to mention whether he should resign as commander-in-chief, Folkestone and Wardle were in for a surprise.

The division came out in favour of the duke and acquitted him of accepting bribes by a margin of 278 to 196. Unsurprisingly, the ailing king was delighted that his son had been exonerated, yet the Duke of York did not revel in his victory. He had been humiliated, his private business dragged out into the public arena and his integrity challenged. Rather than celebrate, he chose instead to resign. This put a stop to any further enquiries and finally let the matter and the Duke of York, rest.

> 'Last night the Chancellor of the Exchequer communicated to the House of Commons the substance of a letter from his royal highness the Duke of York to his Majesty, tendering his resignation of the office of commander-in-chief […] his royal highness having resigned his situation of Commander-in-Chief, the house did not now think it necessary to proceed further in the business.'[23]

The duke's reputation was ruined despite his exoneration at Westminster. Nowadays cash for questions and cash for access are regular scandals in the press, making this seem like a particularly modern affair. And, like all the best tabloid tales, it came with an unexpected encore.

Mary Anne received a payment of £10,000 and an annuity of £400 from the government on the understanding that she would not publish her memoirs and would surrender all the letters that the duke had sent her. Meanwhile Wardle, the man who had started the ball rolling when he requested an inquiry into the conduct of the Duke of York, became a hero of the people. Yet he did not have long to bask in the glow of the public's admiration for mere months later, Wardle was sued by Francis Wright, an upholsterer. Colonel Wardle, it transpired, had offered to pay to furnish Mary Anne's entire house if she would testify against her former lover. When the furniture bills went unpaid, Mary Anne encouraged Wright to sue, thus quietly bringing Wardle's *own* corruption out into the public eye. Not so much cash for commissions as furniture for a favour.

When the court found in Wright's favour, Wardle declared himself a patsy. It was all to nothing and he was ordered to pay Wright's bill for Mary Anne's furniture and all associated costs. Yet Wardle wouldn't go quietly. He threatened to counter sue Mary Anne and Wright, alleging a conspiracy against him.

It was not the only alleged conspiracy involving Mary Anne and York. The loudest whispers of all levelled the blame for the sorry affair at the door of Prince Edward Augustus, Duke of Kent and Strathearn, the fourth son of George III. As far back as 1808, Kent's secretary, Thomas Dodd, had made the acquaintance of Mary Anne, and there were some who believed that

Kent had engineered the end of his brother's career, motivated by jealousy of York's achievements and rank. His aim, it was alleged, was to take York's place as commander-in-chief. If Kent managed to achieve this shady goal, he promised his co-conspirators that their loyalty would be rewarded with 'a *lucrative* situation in the government when the duke of Kent [became] commander in chief of the army!'[24]. In return, all the conspirators had to do was to secure the testimony of the not-so innocent, wide-eyed Mary Anne Clarke and bring down the Duke of York.

This was a scheme, said Mary Anne, borne out of a seething envy that had reached a head when Kent was appointed Governor of Gibraltar by the War Office in 1802. It was a Georgian Cain and Abel.

Above all else, Kent's instructions in this new post were to restore discipline to a garrison that was running out of control. In fact, he clamped down with such force that the troops mutinied. The three leaders of the rebellion were shot and a fourth was flogged to death, resulting in Kent's swift recall to Britain scarcely more than twelve months after his appointment. Left to his own devices the garrison descended into chaos once more. In her ghostwritten[25] take on the case, Mary Anne alleged that York had to intervene to save his brother from facing a court martial and this stung Kent's pride so badly that he swore revenge against his sibling. Yet did Kent, embarrassed by events in Gibraltar, *really* conspire to bring down his brother so that he might take his place as commander-in-chief?

> 'I believe there is scarcely a military man in the kingdom, who was at Gibraltar during the duke of Kent's command of that fortress, but is satisfied that the duke of York's refusal of a Court Martial to his Royal brother, *afforded an incontestible [sic] proof* of his *regard* for the *military* character, and honor of the duke of Kent; for if a Court Martial had been granted to the governor of Gibraltar, I always understood there was but *one* opinion, as to what would have been *the result;* and then, the duke of Kent would have lost several thousands a year, and incurred such public reflections, that would, most probably, have been painful to his *honorable* and *acute* feelings. It was however, this *act of affection* for the duke of Kent, that laid the foundation of that *hatred* which has followed the commander in chief up to the present moment; - and to this *unnatural feeling*, he is solely indebted for all the misfortunes and disgrace to which he has been introduced.'[26]

During the ensuing case between Mary Anne and Wardle these allegations were aired in the light of day. Wardle was asked if he was in the pay of Kent, and if he had bought Mary Anne's testimony in order to ruin the Duke of York. The politician dismissed such an idea as preposterous but the court found against him. Once the darling of the people, Wardle's popularity was beginning to wane. Mary Anne even repeated her allegations in print in 1810, claiming that she had been duped by Kent's aides in return for assurances that were not kept. At first, wrote Mary Anne, they had promised her as much money as she might need to become entirely independent, with figures as high as £5,000 a year thrown about. Naturally, Mary Anne assured the reader, she would never have betrayed her lover for something as base as money. Only when she was assured that the gentlemen who were conspiring against York were honest, honourable and genuine did she deign to lend them her assistance.

Money was important *too*, of course.

Mary Anne, rather refreshingly, was surprisingly sanguine about her motives for appearing as a witness against the Duke of York. She quite openly acknowledged that any claim that she had been motivated purely by a patriotic zeal to serve the public would rightly have been met with incredulity. Instead she came clean, and admitted in her memoirs that, 'If I had not been well satisfied of receiving the remuneration agreed upon, not all the jacobinical parties in Europe should have introduced my letter and person to the notice of Parliament.'[27] In fact, when Mary Anne spilled the beans, the overriding theme of her book wasn't truth or scandal or revenge, but the fact that every single person seemed to be on the make. From doctors to courtesans to politicians and dukes, everyone had an angle.

Mary Anne negotiated a payment of £7,000 and the promise of an annuity as well as the assurance that her son with her husband, Joseph, would receive an excellent education and a military commission. In return she handed over the Duke of York's letters to Herbert Taylor and promised never to disclose what the missives contained. She was a celebrity, beloved of printmakers and gossipmongers alike, and she revelled in it.

For Wardle, the man who had, for a brief period, been a hero, the glory was nothing but a distant memory. Once, not so long before, the public had mounted a collection to meet his legal bills, raising more than £4,000 and awarding him the freedom of the City of London. Now his reputation lay in tatters, and all thanks to a courtesan who came from nowhere to pen 'the most disgusting proof of infamy and conspiracy on the part of all the detestable nest of Wardellites.'[28]

Wardle's career limped along and in 1810, when it was proposed in Parliament that the Duke of York return to his former office of commander-in-chief of the armed forces (a position that had been overseen by Sir David Dundas in the intervening years), Wardle, a radical Whig, naturally, voted against him[29]. It was not enough. In 1811 York was returned to the position from which he had been toppled by scandal[30]. His father, in the grip of the madness that had propelled the Prince Regent to power that same year, likely knew little of his son's late, far from celebrated, triumph.

So what became of the leading lady? What did history have in store for Mary Anne Clarke?

This sort of story generally goes one of two ways: ruin or triumph.

Mary Anne initially appeared to be hurtling towards the former when a libel suit against her saw her flung into prison. On her release she travelled to Europe and eventually made her home in France. Here she received an endless stream of callers, keen to hear all the gossip that she was more than happy to share. She lived in France until her death in 1852, content, healthy and merrily notorious to the end of her days.

Chapter 9

The Bloody Triangle

'Neale! Neale! I am murdered!' And with that horror struck cry began one of the most bizarre royal scandals of the Georgian era.

The controversies that touched the royal House of Hanover were often saucy, sometimes financial but, thankfully, rarely scaled the bloody heights of the murder of Count von Königsmarck back in the dark, dying days of the seventeenth century. In 1810, fresh blood was once again spilled and some said it flowed all the way to the feet of the future King of Hanover. As the fifth son of George III and Charlotte of Mecklenburg-Strelitz, Ernest, otherwise known as the Duke of Cumberland (not to be confused with the *other* Duke of Cumberland, his uncle who had so embarrassed his family with Lady Grosvenor) had an impeccable pedigree and, of course, an impeccable collection of rogues amongst his siblings. He was also the rather shady character suspected by some of fathering a son by Princess Sophia, his own sister!

Some of those siblings had a weakness for the ladies but when the Grim Reaper came calling at St James's Palace in the early hours of 31 May 1810, some gossips whispered that the Duke of Cumberland's weakness was not for the fairer sex at all.

But did Ernest Augustus, Duke of Cumberland and Teviotdale, and future King of Hanover, *really* have a penchant for the chaps, and would he have stooped to cold-blooded murder to cover it up?

The Duke of Cumberland had been sleeping - *alone*, despite the rumours that followed - in his room at St James's Palace. As the world slumbered, one man remained awake, and this man had murder on his fevered mind. At some point between 2.00 am and 3.00 am, an assailant slipped into the duke's bedroom, either from the hallway beyond or having lain concealed within a closet. He set down the dark lantern that he carried and prepared to perform a grisly task.

The intruder, moving swiftly through the dark, silently retrieved a sabre and approached the duke. There was no doubt that this was an inside job, for how else would a villain with murder on his mind know that the duke kept a sabre in a particular drawer in his room and make his way to that exact place? One cannot guess what went through this imposter's head as he stood there, looking down at the nightcap clad head of the king's 38-year-old son, but he screwed his courage (or at least his fury) to the sticking place and brought down the blade with a skull-splitting ferocity.

As soon as the first blow landed the duke, quite understandably, awoke. Luckily for him when the second strike of the sabre hit, it was the flat of the blade that made contact, rather than the razor-sharp edge. Even so, he was grievously injured from the four wounds to his skull that he received and when we read the report of his surgeon, Sir Everard Home, it seems miraculous that he survived at all. Cumberland's injuries were so bad that his brain became exposed, yet adrenaline prevented him from realising the true extent of his wounds and instead of collapsing or going into shock, he sprang into action.

Home later gave a grisly report of the Duke of Cumberland's condition. If you're of a squeamish disposition, look away now.

> 'I visited the Duke of Cumberland upon his being wounded, and found my way from the great hall to his apartment by the traces of blood, which were left on the passages and staircase, and found him on the bed, still bleeding, his shirt deluged with blood, and the coloured drapery above the pillow sprinkled with blood from a wounded artery, and which puts on an appearance that cannot be mistaken by those who have seen it. This could not have happened, had not the head been lying on the pillow when it was wounded; the night ribbon, which was wadded, the cap, scalp, and scull [sic], were obliquely divided, so that the pulsations of the arteries of the brain were distinguished.'[1]

At first Cumberland didn't realise how bad the injuries that had been inflicted on his royal skull were. In fact, he reported hearing a mysterious hissing sound in between the first pair of blows and the second and recalled later that he thought it was a bat, wondering momentarily if it had flown into his chamber and collided with his head as it lay upon the pillow.

When the sabre landed again, of course, Cumberland knew that he was under attack. He struggled out of bed, injured, disoriented and unable to see who was slashing at him despite the light of a lamp that was burning in the bedchamber. Alone and vulnerable, the instinct to fight or take flight kicked in. The Duke of Cumberland was a born scrapper and this was his chance to finally see a bit of action. Unarmed, clad in his nightgown and with his skull split down to the brain, he wasn't about to fall to his own sabre.

Cumberland wisely didn't try to go one-on-one with the sword-wielding maniac, but instead made for a door and his one hope of survival. The distance between the bed and that escape route must have seemed like the longest on earth and before he could reach the door the sabre struck again, this time inflicting a deep wound on the duke's right thigh. Only then did he call for help. That horrified cry of, 'Neale! Neale! I am murdered!' brought his page, Cornelius Neale, running.

As the duke staggered from his chambers with blood pouring from his scalp, he was quickly joined by the stunned Neale. Despite his injuries and, no doubt by now beginning to feel the impact of shock, Cumberland warned the page that the would-be killer was still in his bedroom. Bravely stealing himself for a fight to the death, the valiant Neale stepped into the scene of the crime. He snatched up a poker as soon as he crossed the threshold. In fact, the danger had passed and there was no one in the bedroom at all, least of all a sabre-wielding madman. Neale did find the abandoned sword thrown down at the open doorway that led to the neighbouring Yellow Room and from there, escape into the palace would be the attacker's only option.

By now possessed of the fire of righteous indignation, Neale was keen to give chase but the duke wouldn't hear of it. Instead he asked his page to assist him in reaching the porter's room and it was there that he summoned the household staff and ordered that the palace be secured as a matter of urgency. This, Cumberland hoped, would stop the would-be assassin from escaping.

Growing faint and increasingly weaker due to loss of blood, the duke finally consented to rest. He was receiving medical attention when he was informed that Joseph Sellis, one of his valets, could not be located. Although this no doubt gave Cumberland pause, he was far more intrigued when he heard what had been found in his own room. In one of the three closets that were attached to the Duke of Cumberland's bedroom was quite a collection of very - some would say *conveniently* - incriminating evidence.

> In the closet where he supposed the assassin was concealed, informant found a pair of black leather slippers, with the name Sellis written in each slipper, which informant believes to be of the hand-writing of Joseph Sellis, an Italian[2], one of the

valets of his Royal Highness the Duke of Cumberland; there was also a dark lantern, a bottle of water, and the scabbard of the sword which was found upon the floor in the bed room; there was also two bolsters, which are used in the day time for ornamenting the bed of his Royal Highness, and the key of the closet was in the inside of the door, which was not usual, and could have been of no use but for the purpose of locking the door, where he supposes the assassin had concealed himself.'[3]

The evidence against Joseph Sellis was swiftly mounting and as Cumberland's injuries were catalogued[4], the household rallied to find Sellis.

With Neale occupied in the care of the duke, his wife, Ann, summoned a porter and together they went to Joseph Sellis's room. Though they knocked on the locked door loud enough to wake the dead, Sellis didn't answer. Eventually, the intrepid duo was forced to make their way through the palace to another door that they hoped would afford them access.

As they hurried through the darkened hallways it became apparent that all was not as it should be. A door that should be unlocked was bolted from the other side whilst other doors, specifically those that would mark the escape route from the Duke of Cumberland's bedroom to that of the missing valet, stood open. Had someone come through them in a rush, perhaps?

Upon reaching Sellis's room, Mrs Neale was horrified to hear a sound like gurgling coming from within. It was quickly followed by the sound of liquid splashing onto the floor. With one eye on the lady's finer feelings, her companion peeked into the room and recoiled in horror.

Joseph Sellis was dead, his throat slashed; but had he taken his own life, or was he another victim of the madman roaming St James's Palace that night?

The inquest into the attack opened promptly on 1 June under the auspices of Samuel Thomas Adams, Coroner of the King's Household. Since the reign of Henry VIII, a statute[5] decreed that every inquest into a violent death in a royal palace or any other building in which the monarch was residing must be undertaken by the holder of this illustrious station. (Actually the king hadn't been in residence on the night of the attack, as he was never very keen on St James's Palace.) Previously the jury had been assembled by yeoman officers but this time, after some confusion over who should serve, the eventual jury was made up of local householders[6]. The inquest was assembled in the Kitchen-Court at St James's and there Adams was charged with resolving this most serious and unpleasant matter.

THE BLOODY TRIANGLE

Could Adams and his jury unpick this mystery?

More to the point, just who was Joseph Sellis, and why might he have wanted his employer dead?

Joseph Sellis had been born in Corsica but his job as a gentleman's valet had taken him all over the world. He was a man with friends in high places and had served the Duke of Cumberland for five years. Quarrelsome, opinionated and full of his own importance or inoffensive, gentle and shy, depending on whose opinion you chose to believe, the one thing all were agreed on was that Sellis was a valued member of the royal household. He was so well thought of that he had received personal gifts from Queen Charlotte. Indeed, he was said to have been one of just two people to have a key to the queen's personal chambers, the other being Charlotte herself!

Sellis had been with the duke for some years but the two men were as headstrong as one another, so disagreements weren't uncommon. There had even been occasions when Sellis had left his royal master and had taken up a station elsewhere. In the end he had always returned to Cumberland, to whom he had seemed unflinchingly loyal despite their occasional run-ins.

Yet at the inquest into the attack a different side of the trusted royal employee emerged. The jury heard that Sellis has once been a valet to a gentleman named Mr Church and had lived in New York whilst in his service. It was here that Church's desk had been burgled by an unknown member of the household, who broke open a chest with a hammer and stole a large sum of money, a gold watch and a diamond pin. Determined to discover who was responsible, Church questioned all his staff and eventually concluded that Sellis must have committed the crime. He had enjoyed easy access to Church's private apartments and rather worryingly, possessed a hammer which precisely fitted the marks on the burgled chest.

Though the lack of anything more than circumstantial evidence meant that no formal charges could be brought, Sellis lost his position in Church's household. Luckily for him Church wasn't a vengeful man. He dismissed Sellis but gave his former employee a payment to ensure he would not fall into penury as he sought another position. If rumours of burglary weren't enough to prove he had been a thoroughly bad sort, Sellis had been loud and proud in his opposition to the British crown whilst in America, frequently damning not only the king and his family but the Almighty too!

Martha Perkins, who had worked with Sellis during his time in Church's employ, went one step further. Not only had he damned the king, she said, but Sellis hadn't been averse to a bit of mischievous stone-throwing.

'[Martha Perkins] very frequently heard Joseph Sellis say, Damn the King and all the Royal Family of England, and she once heard him say that he was the man who had thrown the stone at the King in going to the House of Commons.'[7]

A thoroughly bad lot indeed, even if the claims of hurling stones were fabricated by a boastful Sellis or a mischievous Martha.[8]

Sellis was not tainted by his run-in with the American law and soon after his return to Britain, he had found himself a job with the Earl of Mount Edgcumbe. It was whilst in the service of Lord Mount Edgcumbe that he had met Cumberland and had secured his royal posting. So was Sellis an innocent who had been given a second chance, or was he a villain intent on social advancement and scalping his employers - literally?

The press and public were sure that the answer was resoundingly the latter and as the inquest continued, a steady stream of witnesses came forward in the wake of the scandal to throw more doubt on Sellis's character. Sarah Varley, a housemaid who had previously been in the duke's employ, detailed the search for a missing poker that was later discovered concealed behind the Corsican's bed. Intriguingly, when she found a pistol in the rooms used by the valets, she had assumed that it belonged to Cornelius Neale until his wife had told her that it was actually owned by none other than Joseph Sellis.

It is at this point that things take a decidedly bizarre turn. The pistol turned up again in the depositions of Cumberland's domestic staff and, quite out of nowhere, Neale himself claimed ownership of it. He explained that he had been verbally attacked by Sellis the year before the attack on the duke. Sellis had called him a thief and, though all investigations to discover if he *was* a thief found the charges groundless, Neale was shaken.

Neale became so convinced that Sellis intended to do him harm that he purchased a pistol and kept it with him in the room he shared with the other valets. When one of his roommates told him that he wasn't happy with having a loaded firearm in the bedroom, Neale claimed that he had locked the gun away. He said that he had then simply forgotten about it, never having any cause to retrieve the firearm from that safely locked cupboard where it had been stored. Indeed, Neale was absolutely convinced that it had been Sellis's plan to murder Cumberland and saddle *him* with the blame, as payback for the argument that had led him to purchase the gun in the first place. Sellis, it seemed, was a man with a curiously murky past and an equally cloudy present. This bad-tempered, truculent character had also been a husband and father of four, all aged under 10. Those children now found themselves fatherless.

The jury heard that Joseph Sellis had slashed his own throat with a razor, inflicting a wound so deep that only his spine had stopped the blade. As one witness wrote, 'the blood which evidently issued from his own wound, exhibited one continued stream, and formed one condensed mass or sheet of blood, which covered him from his neck to his knees'[9]. It was a night on which blood seemed to be flowing and spattering rather freely in St James's. During the visit of the jury to the palace they found blood splashed seemingly everywhere between the duke's apartment and that in which Sellis' still-warm corpse was discovered. Of course, the duke had made his way from his bedroom to Neale's and Neale had even trodden on the bloody sabre. Even worse, given that the weapon had been abandoned at a crime scene, Neale had picked up the sabre and taken it with him when he and Cumberland had gone to seek the assistance of the porter. That sabre, the household was quick to point out, had been sharpened by Sellis himself just days before. Its edge was rendered as keen and deadly as a razor, which few besides Sellis would have known about. There was no reliable trail to follow, as Neale had paddled through the gore and gone from room to room with the duke, so it's hardly surprising that the blood had been spread to different parts of the palace.

Sellis's room had been preserved intact. His body still lay upon the butcher's slab of a bed, covered in his own blood. The records of the trial described the gruesome scene with no small amount of relish.

> 'The Jury then proceeded to the room where the corpse of the departed villain remained. They found it, with the whole of the body (except the head and feet) covered with blood; the razor which did the deed in a very bloody state. The deceased's neckcloth was cut through in several places. The drawers, wash-hand bason-stand [sic] and the bason were bloody.'[10]

Despite the initial investigations of Ann Neale and the household staff, it was Private Thomas Creedy of the Coldstream Guards who was reported to have been the first person to actually enter Sellis's chambers. He was so horrified by the sight that had greeted him that he'd almost panicked but, gathering himself, he had checked the room for the presence of any concealed assailant who might have attacked Sellis *and* the duke. He found nobody.

Creedy had then left the room and his place had been taken by Sergeant Joseph Creighton, who was later reported to have been the first man on the scene. Perhaps this was a question of rank, perhaps a question of confusion, it hardly matters in the grand scheme of things. What *does* matter is that Creighton admitted to having picked up the bloodied razor from the floor, where he found it about 2 ft from the bed. For some unexplained reason, he had put the razor down elsewhere, far from the body. The question of where exactly the razor had originally been found would later give rise to all sorts of nasty rumours.

Cumberland, meanwhile, recovered from his injuries with admirable speed. Henry Halford, who was physician extraordinary to George III, George IV, William IV and the princess who later became Queen Victoria, was at his beck and call and the Prince Regent was the first family member to visit his brother after news of the attack was sent to Carlton House.

As soon as the reports of the gruesome crime at St James's reached the public, they were hungry to know more. As we've already learned several times in the pages of this book, nobody loved a scandal like the Georgians. As the dawn broke, callers began to arrive at the palace in the hope of seeing the scene of the dastardly deed and, of course, they weren't disappointed.

> 'The numerous inquirers, yesterday, at the Duke of CUMBERLAND'S were admitted to see the Duke's bed-room, and the room in which *Sellis* put a period to his existence. They were both in the same state as when the deeds were done. The sheets and white satin pillows, that were on the Duke's bed when he was attacked were put on the bed again, to satisfy the curiosity of the Public.- The bed and room remain in the same state.'[11]

By this point the late Mr Sellis was no longer in residence. Long before the curiosity seekers arrived and without the presence of his widow and fatherless children, the dead man's remains had been spirited away for burial in a rude, unmarked pit.

> '*Sellis's* remains were taken from the Duke of CUMBERLAND'S on Sunday noon, in a hearse, to the neighbourhood of Oxford-street. It was a matter of doubt whose duty is was to perform the unpleasant task of burying the body in a cross-road. The Board of Green Cloath sat upon the subject till nine o'clock on Sunday evening. About one o'clock the body was removed to Scotland-yard, by four

men, and interred in a hole nearly opposite the egg warehouse, and the lime wharf. Notwithstanding so much secrecy was observed, and it being midnight, about thirty people were collected.'[12]

As Sellis, branded a would-be assassin, a motiveless murderer who couldn't even lay the blame at the door of madness, was hurled into that unhappy grave, he had already been tried and convicted in the public consciousness. Likewise and unsurprisingly, the jury at the inquest into the attack was soon gearing up to legally confirm this verdict and have it enshrined in the records of royal and criminal history forever. Whatever lay behind the assault was a mystery, as was the true reason for Sellis's reported suicide. Perhaps it was guilt or even a fear of punishment that caused him to take his own life.

However one person remained convinced that Joseph Sellis was an innocent man, and this was his wife, Mary Ann. She had been left as a widow with four young children and a husband whose name was forever blackened, but it was a name that she was determined to clear. In her statement to John Read, chief police magistrate, Mary Ann told the inquest that her spouse had been in good spirits on that fateful day, though he had been suffering from the lingering remnants of what had been a nasty cold. Still, there was nothing about the day that might render a man murderous or cause him to lose his reason. Although he wasn't on duty that night, she explained that Joseph had told her that the duke had expressed a desire to go to Windsor on the following morning, which would have meant an early start for his valets. Intriguingly, the duke later confirmed that there was no truth in this. He had never voiced any intention to go to Windsor, yet the innocent Mrs Sellis knew of no reason for her husband to tell such a lie. Because one of the Sellis children was ill and not sleeping well, in order to ensure that his own rest was undisturbed before his early morning call, Sellis had decided to spend the night in his room at St James's. Then he'd returned to the very chamber in which he had met his death.

Mrs Sellis explained that her husband had never spoken ill of the duke nor the royal family, regardless of what people who claimed to have known him in America were saying. Mary Ann closed by stating that, before he departed for bed that night, Sellis had asked her to collect his dirty linen the following morning and to prepare a dinner of veal for him once the duke had left for Windsor. The implication was clear, no man planning to take his own life would make such plans. Of course, the enquiry simply interpreted this as the behaviour of a chap who had no intention of taking his own life, because he had no intention of being caught. Had Sellis got his way Ernest Augustus, Duke of Cumberland and Teviotdale, would have been dead and Joseph Sellis would have escaped without detection.

Yet there was one thing in Mary Ann's testimony that suggested she might like to point the finger elsewhere. Neale had already stated that he believed Sellis intended to lay the blame for the attack at *his* door, but what if that weren't actually the case? What if the truth was the opposite; that Neale had intended to see *Sellis* hanged for a crime that he hadn't actually committed?

Surely a simple personality clash couldn't possibly be the motive for such a dreadful plot though?

Twelve months earlier, Sellis certainly *had* gone after Neale, attempting to have him removed from his place in Cumberland's service. If he was indeed the same man who had stolen from his employer, Mr Church, then Sellis was by then clearly a totally reformed character and wasn't about to let his colleague get away with any wrongdoings of his own. In a letter dated 9 July 1809, sent to the duke's secretary and confidante, Sir Benjamin Stephenson, Sellis warned that Neale was a cheat, and had been fiddling his expenses and those of the household for his own benefit. Sellis could offer no evidence to back up his claims other than alluding to a mysterious third party who had told him of Neale's dodgy dealings, but he was up in arms nevertheless. He wrote that he would rather be redeployed than be forced to continue to work alongside Neale. Intriguingly, given the comments others made about Sellis's own lack of good manners, Sellis found Neale 'a rogue [...] with whom no human being is able to live upon friendly terms [...] no longer can I live with this monster'[13]. Indeed, so extensive and costly were Neale's supposed tricks and backhanders that, 'had this business [been heard by] a Court of Justice, the man would have been transported for at least seven years'[14].

Nothing came of this correspondence, but it seems that those who claimed Sellis was intending to frame Neale might equally argue that Neale would have had equally good reason to frame Sellis. But while it might seem strange that Sellis had attacked the duke and then attempted suicide, it seems stranger still that Neale might have attacked the duke, hot-footed it through the palace, murdered Sellis in a way that is more bloody then most, and then been back at his rooms to look after the wounded duke without missing a beat and without a drop of blood on him.

What, though, if there had been another party involved?

The official inquiry into the incident didn't much care for fanciful conspiracy theories and concluded that Joseph Sellis had acted alone. The position of his body, the locked doors that made the escape of any intruder impossible and the discovery of the valet's slippers in the duke's closet where the assailant had hidden himself made for an open and shut case in the eyes of the jury. They concluded that, upon returning to his chambers after the attack, Sellis had attempted to wash the evidence from his hands. The basin full of clean water was soon clouded with blood and the nailbrush found in the valet's locked room was stained red. The jurors surmised that when he realised that the trail of blood would lead the search parties directly to him, regardless of how well he cleaned his hands, Sellis had panicked. Rather than face the courts he chose death by razor. His first efforts to cut his throat were hampered by the intricately folded cravat he wore and this bore multiple blade cuts to prove the theory.

Then, no doubt in a mania of guilt and terror, Sellis tore off his cravat, threw himself down on his bed and slashed his throat with so much force that he almost severed his own head from his body. It was a hideous end for a man who had been much respected by the duke. Sellis' motive for all of this had simply been hatred of Cornelius Neale, who appeared to be intent on usurping his place in the duke's affections. Neale's wife was a royal housekeeper, Sellis's was not, Neale had an apartment in St James's Palace long before Sellis was afforded the honour, and slowly this jealousy gnawed at him until it had become blind hatred. Hungry for advancement and influence and positively desperate to see Neale lose his place at the duke's side, Sellis fixed on a dastardly plan to frame his imagined adversary for his own heinous crime.

Joseph Sellis was vilified as a stone-cold villain, utterly without any redeeming features. When an account of the crime and trial was made publicly available, it didn't flinch from levelling an accusing finger directly at Joseph Sellis, an apparent devil amongst men.

The inquest lasted for less than a day. The jury of seventeen men was convinced by the evidence and fifteen members found Sellis guilty of the attack and concluded that he had indeed committed suicide. Two of the jury abstained because they could not declare themselves confident that Sellis was sane at the time of the crime, though they believed him to have committed it, regardless of his mental state.

And as far as the official verdict of *fell de se*[15] went, that was that. Life moved on and the players in this unfortunate drama tripped off to the next scene. Mary Ann Sellis, widow of the supposed assailant, was even rumoured to have benefited from the famed philanthropy of the ever-generous Queen Charlotte.

> 'Mrs. Sellis, the unfortunate widow of the wretched man who is supposed to have made an attack on the life of the Duke of Cumberland, set up a haberdasher's shop in the Haymarket, soon after the shocking event. She has, however, lately given up that business, as the Queen has settled a pension on her life.'[16]

There was no truth in this rumour as Mrs Sellis was quick to point out in a letter to *The Morning Chronicle*. Not only was the gossip of the queen's charitable support of the widow untrue, it was doing nothing to help the grieving Mrs Sellis pick up the pieces of her life.

> 'MR. EDITOR,
> The erroneous statement in *The Morning Chronicle* and other papers, respecting the Widow of Sellis having received a pension from the Queen, from whatever motive it was inserted, has done me a great disservice, not only with persons inclined to employ me, but also with the Parish Officers, who positively deny me any relief until that mis-statement is contradicted, which I request you will have the goodness to do, and you'll oblige,
>
> Your's [sic], &c.
> M A SELLIS'[17]

And that wasn't the only rumour that attached itself to the sorry matter of Sellis and the Duke of Cumberland.

Cumberland was not liked by the British people. He'd had a reputation for savagery during his army days and, as a committed hardline Tory, he never showed any inclination to take a liberal stance on *anything*. Seen as stern, unbending and rather sinister, he was just the sort of chap that one could imagine being involved in some very dark deeds.

The first suggestion in print that the duke might have played a role in Sellis's death came in 1812 when Henry White's *The Independent Whig* accused Cumberland of being party to the valet's murder. Yet what could possibly have driven the Duke of Cumberland to be involved in such a bloody, brutal attack on a man who had shown him nothing but loyalty?

There were plenty of theories and rumours circulating in the streets of London and, as one might expect, the majority of them ended in one conclusion. It all came down to sex. Over the course of six months or so *The Independent Whig* published a series of letters from the so-called *Philo Junius*[18] that put into print all of the rumours that had been doing the rounds in the city since that fateful night in 1810.

Some claimed that Cumberland had fathered a child with Sellis' wife, whilst others stated that Cumberland and Sellis had been lovers until Neale appeared on the scene and stole the duke's affection. Another theory was that Cumberland had been blackmailed by Sellis over an affair with another male domestic. It was all a bit much for the duke and he instigated proceedings against publisher Henry White for libel. The case opened on 5 March 1813 and was focussed on one letter in particular, in which *Philo Junius* sought clarification on eight questions.

'First, was not the report well founded, that it was not till after repeated attempts had been made, that a jury could be found sufficiently hardy to say that Sellis was his own executioner?

Secondly, was not the razor, with which it was concluded the business was done, found at a great distance from the body?

Thirdly, was not the coat of the domestic, drenched with blood, found on a chair at a considerable distance from the body?

Fourthly, whether the basin was not placed deliberately at the side of the bed, evidently for the purpose of catching the blood?

Fifthly, whether the body was not nearly cold when found?

Sixthly, whether Sellis was not troubled with such an asthmatic cough, that it would have been impossible for him to conceal himself for more than half an hour, without betraying himself?

Seventhly, as to the situation of the slippers in the closet in which it was supposed that he concealed himself?

Eighthly, was not the neck cloth cut in pieces in such a way as to militate strongly against the idea of the deceased having cut his own throat?'[19]

In case there could be any doubt as to what was being suggested, replies to the letter were published in which correspondents openly agreed on Sellis having been the victim of a murderer who was referred to only as 'the ——————'. The inference was clear, just fill in the blank.

The case against White was prosecuted by the famed barrister, Sir William Garrow[20]. In his short speech, Garrow pointed out that the jury was not there to consider how Sellis died, but only whether the publication of the letters constituted a libel. In his defence, conducted by James Scarlett[21], White argued that the article he had published couldn't possibly be interpreted as blaming Cumberland for murder. Besides, White went on, he was merely printing the rumours that had already been the talk of the town for years. Quite apart from that, he added, the paper had printed a good many pieces that one might consider to be *pro*-Cumberland alongside the letters that had seen him dragged into the dock to defend his reputation before Edward Law, Lord Ellenborough. Regardless of his defence, White was found guilty so quickly that the jury didn't even need to retire. He was sentenced to fifteen months in Newgate and a £200 fine.

The eight questions went unanswered.

And so, it seemed, Joseph Sellis was finally laid to rest.

Not a bit of it.

The years wore on and Cumberland continued to attract scandal and rumour in equal measure, never rising much in the opinion of the public. At least Sellis's ghost no longer tormented him and as a raft of new gossip blighted the House of Hanover, that dead valet eventually faded into the mists of history.

The duke married his cousin, Frederica of Mecklenburg-Strelitz, in 1815. He was her third husband and when the couple met, she was already married to Prince Frederick William of Solms-Braunfels, by whom she had fallen pregnant after the death of her first husband. Frederica and Cumberland fell head over heels and, just as she was in the middle of divorce discussions with Prince Frederick William, he died. Aged only 43, his death struck some as just a little bit *too* convenient. It was one more sinister shred of gossip attaching itself to the coattails of the Duke of Cumberland.

Regardless of marriage, Cumberland continued to take lovers and as an unbending Tory, his Whig opponents were always quick to fan the flames of scandal. It was a gift to them when in 1830, another slashed throat brought Joseph Sellis screaming out of the grave on a tide of blood.

> '[The] Right Hon. Thos. North, Lord Graves, aged 54, who destroyed himself by cutting his throat with a razor [...] the body of the noble lord presented a most frightful spectacle; his head was nearly severed from his body.'[22]

Thomas Graves, 2nd Baron Graves, married Lady Mary Paget in 1803. By 1830, rumour had it that Lady Graves was a regular fixture in the Duke of Cumberland's no longer blood-soaked bed. On 7 February of that year, Lord Graves wrote a letter to his wife in which he declared his belief that she had not betrayed their marriage vows. He handed the note to his messenger, went to his bedroom, and cut his own throat from ear to ear with such force that he nearly decapitated himself.

Lord Graves was 54 and a father to a dozen children. He had served in Parliament for fifteen years before becoming Cumberland's Lord of the Bedchamber, and before the sun had risen in the sky on the day Graves' body was discovered, the jury had been called and the inquiry was underway. This sudden death struck no less a paper than *The Times* as most irregular, not to mention downright suspicious. That august organ was quick to raise the red flag of suspicion and point out the similarity between the two violent deaths that had occurred in the Cumberland household, twenty years apart.

> 'The jury must have been called out of bed to receive their summonses and groped about ere day broke for the dress which they quitted the night before! Is this usual, we ask? Is it decent? Does not nature revolt at it? We again say, then, that a fresh inquisition must be held.
>
> It is impossible not to connect this fearful act with a rumour which has been for some time in circulation; and to recall the public attention, however painfully, to another suicide, - an inexplicable and mysterious suicide. - with which a name that has been so often mentioned of late was also connected.'[23]

And so a whole new generation of gossip-mongers was once again privy to the rumours that the Duke of Cumberland was a man given to cutting the throats of his rivals. Just to spoil their scandalous fun, a raft of witnesses confirmed that Graves had been suffering with all manner of maladies for some time and one struggles to find a motive for this supposed murder. Those who claimed that Sellis had been slain to silence revelations of the duke's supposed homosexuality might well have been able to build a circumstantial case but it's a stretch to believe that a royal prince might cut a man's throat just to cover up a love affair. After all, mistresses were a fact of royal life.

No doubt rumours of Lady Graves' intriguing with the duke did nothing to lift the sorrowful spirits of her husband but there was no evidence, circumstantial or otherwise, to suggest that Cumberland had any larger part to play in the melancholy death of Lord Graves than that of a player in the supporting cast.

But Sellis would not go quietly back to the grave. In 1832, more than two decades after his death, his unquiet ghost made one final tormenting play.

A gentleman named Josiah Phillips published a book entitled *Authentic Records of the Court of England for the Last 70 Years*, and he didn't mince his words. After all, 'the general opinion was that the Duke was the murderer', and the author went on to outline an alternative explanation for the unhappy events at St James's Palace twenty years earlier.

'A short period before this dreadful catastrophe, [the attack on Cumberland and the death of Sellis], the Duke had been surprised in an improper and unnatural situation with this Neale by the other servant, Sellis, and exposure was expected.'[24]

The book went on to describe the dramatic events of the evening:

'A razor covered with blood was lying at a distance from his body, but too far off to have been used by himself, or to have been thrown there by him in such a mutilated condition, as it was very apparent death must have been immediate after such an act [the throat-cutting].

[...]

During the time the Duke's wounds were being dressed, the deponent believes Neale was absent, in obedience to arrangement, and was employed in laying Sellis's body in the form in which it was discovered, as it was an utter impossibility that a self-murderer could have so disposed of himself.

Deponent further observes that Lord Ellenborough undertook to manage this affair by arranging the proceedings for the inquest and also that every witness was previously examined by him.'[25]

There was no effort to beat about the bush here, the allegation was clear. The Duke of Cumberland and Cornelius Neale were lovers; having disturbed them in a tryst, Joseph Sellis threatened to expose what he had seen. He paid for that threat with his life, either at the hands of Cumberland or by someone else acting on the duke's command. Neale falsified the crime scene to suggest suicide whilst Lord Ellenborough, the man at the head of the inquest, steered the investigation in exactly the direction that the establishment wished it to go.

This classic conspiracy theory had everything; sex, power and a rich man with the dark influence needed to cover up a murder.

The book further went on to describe the cuts to Sellis's cravat and its padding, which suggested someone had sawn at them. Phillips conjured up the grisly image of a wash basin filled with bloody water where his murderer had attempted to clean the evidence of violence from their hands, and other circumstantial evidence that suggested a third party had cut the valet's throat before positioning him on the gore-soaked bed. In the aftermath of the attack, claimed the author, Ellenborough chose a jury that would suit his ends, even going so far as to refuse to allow a particularly explosive testimony from an anonymous source that could supposedly have blown the lid off the whole conspiracy. Once the verdict had been recorded, said the book, Cumberland travelled to Ellenborough's every single day, no doubt to discuss what reward the law lord would receive for towing the party line.

Should there be any doubt whatsoever, everything that the libel case now sought to punish was succinctly summed up in the following incriminating lines:

> 'We certainly feel sure that there was much mystery in the affair, and we ought to inquire from whence that mystery originated. Had it been the case of a poor man he must have been hung, and his body given for dissection, merely upon circumstantial evidence! but [sic] the son of a reigning monarch has, by circumstantial evidence only, been acquitted.'[26]

The libel trial opened on 25 June 1833. Once again, the purpose was not to ascertain who had or hadn't committed suicide or hidden in private apartments wielding sabres, but whether Phillips had committed a libel by claiming that Cumberland had played a sordid role in the death of his late valet. Likewise, the trial had no interest in whether or not Phillips had written the article in question; he was the printer and publisher and that was enough to make him responsible for its content.

This time the case was presided over by Thomas Denman, Lord Chief Justice[27]. The defence argued that there could be no verdict of libel in this case because the rumours had been circulating for decades, so it was really nothing new. Indeed, even if Phillips was found guilty, the rumours would continue to be discussed by the public so there was little motive other than revenge in pursuing the case. Either way, as the defence noted, to believe that the duke would be wounded by the book was to 'believe that a gnat could sting through the skin of an elephant'[28] and Cumberland 'would have exercised a better judgment had he not instituted the prosecution'[29].

Perhaps unsurprisingly given his utter lack of remorse, Josiah Phillips was found guilty. Sentenced to just six months in prison, he fled the country and preserved his freedom.

The poor old Duke of Cumberland would be dogged by rumours of all manner of villainy to the end of his days. He didn't really deserve such a hatchet job but with his scarred face and authoritarian attitude, he was a handy ogre on which his opponents could pin all sorts of cruel rumours. When Cumberland became King of Hanover, he proved himself to be far from the monster that his political opponents had portrayed him as. He was a mostly benevolent and well-liked monarch, who preferred diplomacy over force.

Mud, sadly, stuck to Cumberland for 200 years and it lingers on today. He is still often thought of as the king who got away with murder.

Our thanks must go to the rabble-rousingly, teeth-gnashingly absurd George Merryweather for a paragraph which neatly lays bare all the worst and most fanciful claims that ever attached themselves to Cumberland.

> '[The Duke of Cumberland] is distinguished as a real or intentional Sodomite and an actual murderer and mangler of the dead; as a debaucher of other men's wives; as a hypocritical protector of religion and a real persecutor of religion, in the persons of the Roman Catholics; as a gratuitous insulter of modest ladies; as a dandified general without the qualifications of a corporal; as a founder of illegal clubs for treasonable purposes; and as a perjured and deliberate liar.'[30]

Who'd be a duke?

Afterword

'Adieu! I have told you all I know, and as much is scandal, very possibly more than is true.'

So we reach the end of this gazetteer of scandal and take our leave with the tantalising thought of what came next; of the saucy exploits of Caroline of Brunswick and the ever-changing lovers in the life of the Prince of Wales, not to mention yet more hair-curling tales of the Duke of Cumberland. All of these must wait for another time, for another king, as George III's reign dwindled away with his frail health. Where once the court had been ruled over by a pious monarch and his ever-faithful wife, in the world of the Regent there was to be drama, love affairs and scandal aplenty.

George III died in 1820 after six decades on the throne. His Royal Marriages Act lived on for much longer but the court that he had striven to create - a world where all was honour and fidelity - never did materialise during his reign. He presided over a changing world, full of wilful sons and confined daughters, not to mention having to deal with the fate of his sister, the former Queen of Denmark, living out her dwindling days in a lonely room.

No man, no king could hope to contain the raging passions and hidden secrets of the royal court but George III was not the first to try and do so. Nor, of course, would he be the last.

Bibliography

Adams, John. *The Flowers of Modern History.* Dublin: Grueber and McAllister, 1796.

Adolphus, John (ed.). *A Correct, Full and Impartial Report, of the Trial of Her Majesty, Caroline, Queen Consort of Great Britain, Before the House of Peers.* London: Jones and Co, 1820.

Adolphus, John. *Memoirs of John Bannister, Comedian, Vol. I.* London: Richard Bentley, 1839.

Allen, Julia. *Swimming with Dr Johnson and Mrs Thrale: Sport, Health and Exercise in Eighteenth-Century England.* London: James Clarke and Co Ltd, 2012.

Allen, Walter Gore. *King William IV.* London: The Cresset Press, 1960.

Andrew, Donna. *Aristocratic Vice.* New Haven: Yale University Press, 2013.

Angelo, Henry. *Reminiscences of Henry Angelo with Memoirs of His Late Father and Friends.* London: Henry Colburn, 1828.

Anonymous. *The Annual Register, or a View of the History and Politics of the Year 1794.* London: R Wilks, 1806.

Anonymous. *The Annual Register, or a View of the History and Politics of the Year 1844.* London: F&J Rivington, 1845.

Anonymous. *The Athenaeum, Part DLIII for the Month of January. 1874.* London: John Francis, 1874.

Anonymous. *The Black Book; An Exposition of Abuses in Church and State, Courts of Law, Municipal Corporations and Public Companies.* London: Effingham Wilson, 1835.

Anonymous. *A Brief Account of the Coronation of His Majesty, George IV.* London: D Walther, 1821.

Anonymous. *A Circumstantial Narrative of a Late Remarkable Trial.* London: M Love, 1770.

Anonymous. *Copies of the Depositions of the Witnesses Examined in the Cause of Divorce Now Depending in the Consistory Court of the Lord Bishop of London, at Doctor's-Commons.* London: J Russell, 1771.

BIBLIOGRAPHY

Anonymous. *The Eclectic Review: Vol XIX*. London: Thomas Ward & Co, 1846.

Anonymous. *The Edinburgh Annual Register for 1809, Vol Second — Part Second*. Edinburgh: John Ballantyne and Co, 1811.

Anonymous. *The Edinburgh Magazine, or Literary Miscellany. Vol. III*. London: James Symington, 1794.

Anonymous. *The Fashionable Cypriad, Part 1*. London: Mr Henderson, 1798.

Anonymous. *The Freemasons' Quarterly Review, 1843, Vol I*. London: Sherwood, Gilbert, and Piper, 1843.

Anonymous. *Free Thoughts on Seduction, Adultery and Divorce*. London: J. Bell, 1771.

Anonymous. *A Full and Complete History of His R—l H—ss the D— of C—d, and Lady G—r, the Fair Adulteress, Vol I*. London: J Porter and T Walker, 1770.

Anonymous. *The Genuine Copies of all the Love Letters and Cards which Passed Between an Illustrious Personage and a Noble Lady*. London: L. Browning.

Anonymous. *The Genuine Copies of Letters which Passed Between His Royal Highness the Duke of Cumberland and Lady Grosvenor*. London: J Wheble, 1770.

Anonymous. *George III: His Court and Family, Vol I*. London: Henry Colburn and Co, 1821.

Anonymous. *The Great Illegitimates!! Public and Private Life of that Celebrated Actress Mrs Jordan*. London: J Duncombe, 1795.

Anonymous. (June 22, 1867). *Hannah Lightfoot. The Spectator*, 10-12.

Anonymous. *An Historical Account of the Life and Reign of King George the Fourth*. London: G Smeeton, 1830.

Anonymous. *The Important and Eventful Trial of Queen Caroline, Consort of George IV*. London: Geo Smeeton, 1820.

Anonymous. *The Jurist: Vol. VIII - Part I*. London: S Sweet, 1845.

Anonymous. *La Belle Assemblée: or, Bell's Court and Fashionable Magazine, Volume 1*. London: John Bell, 1810.

Anonymous. *Letters from an Irish Student in England to his Father, Vol. I*. London: W Lewis, 1809.

Anonymous. *Letters on Literature by Photius, Junior. Volume I*. Brussels: Adolphe Wahlen, 1836.

Anonymous. *A Letter to Mrs Clarke on her Late Connection with the Duke of York*. London: J Bell, 1809.

Anonymous. *Masonic Offering to Prince Augustus Frederick.* London: Norris and Son, 1838.

Anonymous. *The Memoirs of Perdita.* London: G Lister, 1784.

Anonymous. *A Minute Detail of the Attempt to Assassinate High Royal Highness the Duke of Cumberland.* London: JJ Stockdale, 1810.

Anonymous. *The Monthly Magazine. Vol II, Part I for 1821.* London: Sir Richard Phillips and Co, 1821.

Anonymous. *The New Annual Register, of General Repository of History, Politics and Literature for the Year 1813.* London: John Stockdale, 1814.

Anonymous. *The New Prose Bath Guide, for the Year 1778.* London: Dodsley, 1778.

Anonymous. *Notes and Queries. Third Series - Vol Eleventh.* Oxford: Oxford University Press, 1867.

Anonymous. *The Parliamentary Debates from the Year 1803 to the Present Time, Vol XXVIII.* London: Longman, Hurst, Rees, Orme, and Brown, 1814.

Anonymous. *The Parliamentary History of England, Vol XVII.* London: Longman, Hurst, Rees, Orme, & Brown, 1813.

Anonymous. *The Percy Anecdotes, Vol. I.* New York: J&J Harper, 1832.

Anonymous. *A Political Epistle from Florizel to Perdita, with Perdita's Answer.* London: J Stockdale, 1781.

Anonymous. *Political Review of Edinburgh Periodical Publications.* Edinburgh: John Thomson, 1792.

Anonymous. *The R——l Register, Vol III.* London: J Bew, 1779.

Anonymous. *The Secret History of the Green Room, Vol. I.* London: J. Owen, 1795.

Anonymous. *The Trial of Count John Fred. Struensee.* London: Privately published, 1775.

Anonymous. *The Trial of His R H the D of C July 5th, 1770. For Criminal Conversation with Lady Harriet G—r.* London: John Walker, 1770.

Anonymous. *Trial: The King, on the Prosecution of Gwyllym Lloyd Wardle Esq MP against Francis Wright, Daniel Wright, and Mary Anne Clark, for Conspiracy.* London: Samuel Tipper, 1809.

Anonymous. *The Trial of Josiah Phillips for a Libel on The Duke of Cumberland.* London: J Hatchard and Son, 1833.

Anonymous. *The Whole Proceedings at Large.* London: J Wheble, 1770.

Anson, William (ed.). *Autobiography and Political Correspondence of Augustus Henry, Third Duke of Grafton.* London: John Murray, 1898.

Arnold, Catharine. *City of Sin.* London: Simon and Schuster, 2010.

Ashe, Geoffrey. *Do What You Will*. London: WH Allen, 1974.

Aspinall, Arthur (ed.). *The Correspondence of George, Prince of Wales, 1770-1812: Vol VII*. Oxford: Oxford University Press, 1971.

Aspinall, Arthur (ed.). *The Later Correspondence of George III*. Cambridge: Cambridge University Press, 1963.

Aspinall, Arthur. *The Later Correspondence of George III: December 1783 to January 1793, Vol II*. Cambridge: Cambridge University Press, 1962.

Aspinall, Arthur. *The Later Correspondence of George III: February 1793 to December 1797, Vol II*. Cambridge: Cambridge University Press, 1963.

Aspinall, Arthur (ed.). *Mrs Jordan and Her Family: Being the Unpublished Correspondence of Mrs Jordan and the Duke of Clarence, Later William IV*. London: Arthur Barker, 1951.

Baines, Edward. *History of the Reign of George III, Vol. I*. London: Longman, Hurst, and Co, 1820.

Baker, James. *The Business of Satirical Prints in Late-Georgian England*. London: Palgrave MacMillan, 2017.

Baker, Kenneth. *George III: A Life in Caricature*. London: Thames & Hudson, 2007.

Baker, Kenneth. *George IV: A Life in Caricature*. London: Thames & Hudson, 2005.

Bass, Robert D. *The Green Dragoon: The Lives of Banastre Tarleton and Mary Robinson*. Orangeburg: Sandlapper Publishing, 2003.

Bazalgette, Charles. *Prinny's Taylor: The Life and Times of Louis Bazalgette*. British Columbia: Tara Books, 2015.

Beacock Fryer, Mary, Bousfield, Arthur and Toffoli, Garry. *Lives of the Princesses of Wales*. Toronto: Dundurn Press, 1983.

Beatty, Michael A. *The English Royal Family of America, from Jamestown to the American Revolution*. Jefferson: McFarland & Co, 2003.

Bell, Robert. *The Life of the Rt. Hon. George Canning*. London: Harper, 1955.

Belsham, W. *Memoirs of the Kings of Great Britain of the House of Brunswic-Luneburg, Vol I*. London: C Dilly, 1793.

Benedict, Barbara M. *Eighteenth-Century British Erotica*. London: Pickering & Chatto, 2002.

Berkeley, Helen (ed). *Memoirs of Madame D'Arblay*. London: James Mowatt & Co, 1844.

Bisset, Robert. *The History of the Reign of George III. To the Termination of the Late War, Vol. II.* London: T. N. Longman and O. Rees, 1803.

Black, Jeremy. *George III: America's Last King.* New Haven: Yale University Press, 2008.

Black, Jeremy. *The Hanoverians: The History of a Dynasty.* London: Hambledon and London, 2007.

Boaden, James. *The Life of Mrs Jordan, Vol. I.* London: Edward Bull, 1831.

Boaden, James. *The Life of Mrs Jordan, Vol. II.* London: Edward Bull, 1831.

Borrow, George Henry. *Celebrated Trials and Remarkable Cases of Criminal Jurisprudence, from the Earliest Records to the Year 1825, Vol VI.* London: Knight and Lacey, 1825.

Bouce, Paul Gabriel. *Sexuality in Eighteenth-Century Britain.* Manchester: Manchester University Press, 1982.

Boulton, William. *In the Days of the Georges.* London: George Bell & Sons, 1909.

Bregnsbo, Michael. *Caroline Mathilde: Magt go Skæbne.* Lindhardt og Ringhof: Copenhagen, 2012.

Bregnsbo, Michael, Winton, Patrik and Ihalainen, Pasi (ed.). *Scandinavia in the Age of Revolution: Nordic Political Cultures, 1740–1820.* London: Routledge, 2011.

Brougham, Henry. *The Critical and Miscellaneous Writings of Henry Lord Brougham.* London: Lea & Blanchard, 1841.

Brougham, Henry. *Historical Sketches of Statesmen who Flourished in the Time of George III.* Paris: Baudry's European Library, 1839.

Brown, John. *Memoirs of the Courts of Sweden and Denmark, Vol I.* New York: The Grolier Society, 1818.

Brown, John. *The Northern Courts, Vol I.* London: Archibald Constable and Co, 1818.

Buckingham and Chandos, Duke of. *Memoirs of the Court of George IV, Vol I.* London: Hurst and Blackett, 1859.

Burke, Edmund (ed.). *Annual Register, Vol 56.* London: TC Hansard, 1815.

Burney, Frances. *The Diary and Letters of Frances Burney, Madame D'Arblay, Vol II.* Boston: Little, Brown and Company, 1910.

Burney, Frances. *Diary and Letters of Madame D'Arblay, Vol III.* London: Henry Colburn, 1854

Burney, Frances. *Diary and Letters of Madame D'Arblay, Vol V.* London: Henry Colburn, 1843.

BIBLIOGRAPHY

Bury, Lady Charlotte Campbell. *Diary Illustrative of the Times of George the Fourth: Vol I*. London: Carey, Lea and Blanchard, 1838.

Byrne, Paula. *Perdita: The Life of Mary Robinson*. London: Harper Press, 2012.

Campbell Orr, Clarissa. *Queenship in Europe 1660-1815: The Role of the Consort*. Cambridge: Cambridge University Press, 2004.

Carroll, Leslie. *Royal Romances*. New York: New American Library, 2012.

Chambers, James. *Charlotte & Leopold: The True Story of The Original People's Princess*. London: Old Street Publishing, 2008.

Chandler, David G and Beckett, Ian (eds.). *The Oxford History of the British Army*. Oxford: Oxford University Press, 1994.

Chapman, Frederic (trans.). *A Queen of Indiscretions, The Tragedy of Caroline of Brunswick, Queen of England*. London: John Lane, 1897.

Chapman, Hester W. *Caroline Matilda, Queen of Denmark, 1751-75*. London: Cape, 1971.

Chapman, Hester W. *Privileged Persons*. London: Reynal & Hitchcock, 1966.

Chauncey Woolsey, Sarah. *The Diary and Letters of Frances Burney, Vol II*. Boston: Little, Brown, and Company, 1910.

Childe-Pemberton, William. *The Romance of Princess Amelia*. London: G Bell & Sons, 1910.

Clark, Anna. *Scandal*. New Jersey: Princeton University Press, 2013.

Clarke, John, Godwin Ridley, Jasper and Fraser, Antonia. *The Houses of Hanover & Saxe-Coburg-Gotha*. Berkeley: University of California Press, 2000.

Clarke, Mary Anne. *Biographical Memoirs & Anecdotes of the Celebrated Mrs Clarke*. London: W Wilson, 1809.

Clarke, Mary Anne. *A Letter Addressed to the Right Honourable William Fitzgerald*. London: J Williams, 1813.

Clarke, Mary Anne. *Minutes of Evidence: Authentic and Interesting Memoirs of Mrs Clarke*. London: C Chapple, 1809.

Clarke, Mary Anne. *The Rival Princes*. New York: David Longworth, 1810.

Clarke, W. *The Authentic and Impartial Life of Mrs. Mary Anne Clarke*. London: T Kelly, 1809.

Cobbett, John M and Cobbett, James P. *Selections from Cobbett's Political Works, Vol III*. London: Anne Cobbett, 1811.

Cobbett, William. *Cobbett's Political Register, Vol XVII, From January to June 1810*. London: Richard Bagshaw, 1810.

Cobbett, William and Jardine, David. *Cobbett's Complete Collection of State Trials, Vol XXII*. London: Longman, Hurst, Rees, Orme and Brown, 1817.

Corrigan, Gordon. *Wellington: A Military Life*. Edinburgh: A&C Black, 2006.

Craig, William Marshall. *Memoir of Her Majesty Sophia Charlotte of Mecklenburg Strelitz, Queen of Great Britain*. Liverpool: Henry Fisher, 1818.

Craik, George Lillie. *The Pictorial History of England During the Reign of George the Third: 1792-1802, Vol III*. London: Charles Knight and Company, 1843.

Creevey, Thomas. *The Creevey Papers*. Cambridge: Cambridge University Press, 2012.

Crichton, Andrew. *Constable's Miscellany, Vol VI: Converts from Infidelity*. Edinburgh: Constable, 1827.

Crosby, B. *Crosby's Pocket Companion to the Playhouses*. London: B Crosby, 1796.

Cruikshank, George. *The Scourge; or, the Monthly Expositor of Imposture and Folly, Vol. IV*. London: W. N. Jones, 1812.

Curtis, Maurice. *To Hell or Monto: The Story of Dublin's Most Notorious Districts*. Stroud: The History Press, 2015.

Dabhoiwala, Faramerz. *The Origins of Sex*. Oxford: Oxford University Press, 2012.

Davenport, Hester. *The Prince's Mistress: Perdita*. Stroud: The History Press, 2011.

David, Saul. *Prince of Pleasure*. New York: Grove Press, 2000.

Delves Broughton, Vernon (ed.). *Court and Private Life in the Time of Queen Charlotte*. London: Richard Bentley, 1887.

Dillon, John Joseph and D'Este, Augustus Frederick. *The Case of the Children of the Duke of Sussex [Sir A and A d'Este] Elucidated*. London: James & Luke G Hansard & Sons, 1832.

Dodington, George Bubb. *The Diary of the Late George Bubb Dodington*. Salisbury: E. Easton, 1784.

Donne, W Bodham (ed.). *The Correspondence of King George the Third With Lord North from 1768 to 1783: Vol I*. London: John Murray, 1867.

Doran, John. *Lives of the Queens of England of the House of Hanover, Volume I*. New York: Redfield, 1855.

Durham, Samuel Astley. *History of Denmark, Sweden, and Norway, Volume III*. London: Longman, Orme, Brown, Green & Longmans and John Taylor, 1840.

Evans, Rev. John. *The New Guide, or Picture of Bristol*. Bristol: Lane.

Evans, Sir William David. *A Collection of Statutes Connected with the General Administration, Vol. V*. London: Saunders and Benning, 1829.

BIBLIOGRAPHY

Fitzgerald, Percy. *The Good Queen Charlotte*. London: Downey & Co, 1899.

Fortescue, Sir John (ed.). *The Correspondence of King George the Third from 1760 to December 1783, Vol II*. London: Macmillan and Company, 1927.

Fox, Charles James. *Speeches of the Right Honourable Charles James Fox in the House of Commons, Vol III*. London: Longman, Hurst, Orme, and Brown, 1815.

Fox, Charles James. *Speeches of the Right Honourable Charles James Fox, Vol V*. London: Longman, 1845.

Fraser, Flora. *Princesses: The Six Daughters of George III*. Edinburgh: A&C Black, 2012.

Fraser, Flora. *The Unruly Queen: The Life of Queen Caroline*. Edinburgh: A&C Black, 2012.

Galt, John. *George the Third His Court and Family, Vol. I*. London: Henry Colburn and Co, 1821.

George III. *The Correspondence of King George the Third with Lord North from 1768 to 1783*. London: John Murray, 1867.

Georgiana, Duchess of Devonshire. *Georgiana: Extracts from the Correspondence of Georgiana, Duchess of Devonshire*. London: John Murray, 1955.

Gillen, Mollie. *Royal Duke: Augustus Frederick, Duke of Sussex*. London: Sidgwick & Jackson, 1976.

Glover, Richard. *Peninsular Preparation: The Reform of the British Army 1795–1809*. Cambridge: Cambridge University Press, 1963.

Gold, Claudia. *The King's Mistress*. London: Quercus, 2012.

Gossip, Giles. *Coronation Anecdotes*. London: Robert Jennings, 1828.

Gough, John. *The History of the People Called Quakers, Vol I*. London: Darton and Harvey, 1799.

Graves, Charles. *Palace Extraordinary*. London: Cassell, 1963.

Gray, Denis. *Spencer Perceval: The Evangelical Prime Minister, 1762-1812*. Manchester: Manchester University Press, 1963.

Greenwood, William de Redman. *Love and Intrigues of Royal Courts*. London: T Werner Laurie, 1910.

Greville, Charles. *A Journal of the Reign of King George IV, King William IV and Queen Victoria, Vol I*. London: Longmans, Green, and Co, 1899.

Gristwood, Sarah, *Bird of Paradise*. London: Bantam, 2007.

Gronow, Rees Howell. *Reminiscences of Captain Gronow*. London: Smith, Elder and Co., 1862.

165

Gronow, Rees Howell. *The Reminiscences and Recollections of Captain Gronow, Volume the First*. London: John C Nimmo, 1892.

Gunn, Mark R. *History of the Clan Gunn*. Scotpress,1984.

Hadlow, Janice. *The Strangest Family: The Private Lives of George III, Queen Charlotte and the Hanoverians*. London: William Collins, 2014.

Haggard, John. *Reports of Cases Argued and Determined in the Ecclesiastical Courts at Doctors' Commons, Vol I*. London: W Benning, Law Books, 1829.

Ham, Elizabeth. *Elizabeth Ham, by Herself*. London: Faber & Faber, 1945.

Hamilton, Lady Anne. *The Authentic Records of the Court of England, for the Last Seventy Years*. London: J Phillips, 1832.

Hamilton, Lady Anne. *Secret History of the Court of England, from the Accession of George the Third to the Death of George the Fourth*. London: William Henry Stevenson, 1832.

Hampden Junr, John. *The Aristocracy of England*. London: Chapman, Brothers, 1846.

Hansard, TC (ed.). *The Parliamentary Debates from the Year 1803 to the Present Time, Vol XXXV*. London: Hansard, 1817.

Harris, James. *Diaries and Correspondence of James Harris, First Earl of Malmesbury: Vol III*. London: Richard Bentley, 1844.

Heard, Kate. *High Spirits: The Comic Art of Thomas Rowlandson*. London: Royal Collection Trust, 2013.

Hedley, Olwen. *Queen Charlotte*. London: J Murray, 1975.

Herman, Eleanor. *Sex with the Queen*. London: Harper Collins, 2009.

Hetherington Fitzgerald, Percy. *The Life of George the Fourth*. London: Tinsley Brothers, 1881.

Hewitt, Regina and Rogers, Pat (eds.). *Orthodoxy and Heresy*. Lewisburg: Bucknell University Press, 2002.

Hibbert, Christopher. *George III: A Personal History*. London: Viking, 1998.

Hibbert, Christopher. *George IV*. London: Penguin, 1998.

Hill, Constance. *Fanny Burney at the Court of Queen Charlotte*. London: John Lane, 1912.

Hobhouse, D. (May 19, 1939). *Hannah Lightfoot. The Spectator*, 34-36.

Hogan, Denis. *An Appeal to the Public, and a Farewell Address to the Army*. London: G Gorman, 1808.

Holland, Lord. *Memoirs of the Whig Party During My Time: Vol II*. London: Longman, Brown, Green and Longmans, 1854.

Holme, Thea. *Prinny's Daughter*. London: Hamish Hamilton, 1976.

Holt, Edward. *The Public and Domestic Life of His Late Most Gracious Majesty, George the Third, Vol I*. London: Sherwood, Neely and Jones, 1820.

Holt, Edward. *The Public and Domestic Life of His Late Most Gracious Majesty, George the Third, Vol II*. London: Sherwood, Neely and Jones, 1820.

Horrins, Johan. *Memoirs of a Trait in the Character of George III. of These United Kingdoms*. London: W Edwards, 1835.

Howard, John Jackson and Crisp, Frederick Arthur (eds.). *Visitation of England and Wales, Volume 5*. Privately published, 1897.

Howell, TB (ed.). *A Complete Collection of State Trials, Vol XV*. London: Longman, Hurst, Rees, Orme, and Brown, 1816.

Howitt, William. *Cassell's Illustrated History of England: Vol I*. London: Cassell, Petter, and Galpin, 1861.

Huch, Ronald K. *The Radical Lord Radnor*. Minneapolis: University of Minnesota Press, 1977.

Huish, Robert. *The History of the Life and Reign of William the Fourth*. London: William Emans, 1837.

Huish, Robert. *Memoirs of George the Fourth: Vol I*. London: Thomas Kelly, 1830.

Huish, Robert. *Memoirs of Her Late Majesty Caroline, Queen of Great Britain*. London: T Kelly, 1821.

Hunt, Margaret. *Women in Eighteenth-Century Europe*. New York: Routledge, 2010.

Hutton, James (ed.). *Selections from the Letters and Correspondence of Sir James Bland Burges, with Notices of his Life*. London: William Clowes and Sons Limited, 1885.

Ilchester, Countess of & Stavordale, Lord (eds.). *The Life and Letters of Lady Sarah Lennox*. London: John Murray, 1902.

Inglis, Lucy. *Georgian London: Into the Streets*. London: Viking, 2013.

Iremonger, Lucille. *Love and the Princesses*. New York: Thomas Y Crowell Company, 1958.

Irvine, Valerie. *The King's Wife: George IV and Mrs Fitzherbert*. London: Hambledon, 2007.

Jenkinson, Robert Banks. *The Speech of the Right Hon. The Earl of Liverpool in the House of Lords*. London: John Hatchard and Son, 1820.

Jerrold, Clare. *The Story of Dorothy Jordan*. London: Eveleigh Nash, 1914.

Jesse Heneage, J. *Memoirs of the Life and Reign of King George the Third, Vol II*. London: Tinsley Brothers, 1867.

Jesse Heneage, J. *Memoirs of the Life and Reign of King George the Third, Vol III*. London: Richard Bentley, 1843.

Johnson, Samuel. *The Lives of the Most Eminent English Poets, Vol II*. London: C Bathurst, J Buckland, W Strahan, J Rivington and Sons, 1781.

Junius. *The Letters of Junius: Vol I.* London: Privately published, 1774.

Kamm, Josephine. *Hope Deferred: Girls' Education in English History.* London: Methuen, 1965.

Kinservik, Matthew J. *Sex, Scandal, and Celebrity in Late Eighteenth-Century England.* London: Palgrave MacMillan, 2007.

Kiste, John van der. *The Georgian Princesses.* Stroud: The History Press, 2013.

Knight, Charles. *A History of England: Volume VI.* London: Bradbury, Evans, & Co. 1873.

Knight, Charles. *The Popular History of England: Volume VI.* London: Bradbury, 1860.

Langdale, Charles. *Memoirs of Mrs. Fitzherbert.* London: Richard Bentley, 1856.

Laquer, Thomas W. *The Queen Caroline Affair: Politics as Art in the Reign of George IV. The Journal of Modern History.* Vol. 54, No. 3 (Sep., 1982), pp. 417- 466

Laughton, Leonard George Carr, Anderson, Roger Charles and Perrin, William Gordon. *The Mariner's Mirror, Volume Forty-Four.* Cambridge: Society for Nautical Research, 1958.

Law, Susan. *Georgian Britain: Sex in High Places. BBC History Magazine,* March 2015.

Lecky, William Edward Hartpole. *A History of England in the Eighteenth Century, Vol IV.* London: Longmans, Green and Company, 1923.

Leslie, Anita. *Mrs Fitzherbert: A Biography.* York: Scribner, 1960.

Leslie, Shane. *Mrs. Fitzherbert: A Life Chiefly from Unpublished Sources.* New York: Benziger Brothers, 1939.

Lloyd, Alan. *The King Who Lost America.* New York: Doubleday: 1971.

Lloyd, Alan. *The Wickedest Age.* Newton Abbot: David and Charles: 1971.

Lloyd, Hannibal Evans. *George IV: Memoirs of His Life and Reign, Interspersed with Numerous Personal Anecdotes.* London: Treuttel and Würtz, 1830.

Longford, Elizabeth. *Wellington: Pillar of State.* London: Wiedenfeld & Nicolson, 1972.

Lovat-Fraser, JA. *John Stuart Earl of Bute.* Cambridge: Cambridge University Press, 1912.

Lyttleton, George Courtney. *The History of England, Vol. III.* London: J Stratford, 1803.

McCalman, Iain. *Radical Rogues and Blackmailers in the Regency Period. History Today.* Volume 28, Issue 5, 5 May 1988.

BIBLIOGRAPHY

McCalman, Iain. *Radical Underworld: Prophets, Revolutionaries and Pornographers in London, 1795-1840. Cambridge: Cambridge University Press, 1988.*

McLynn, Frank. *Crime and Punishment in Eighteenth-century England.* London: Routledge, 1989.

Melville, Lewis. *An Injured Queen, Caroline of Brunswick: Vol I.* London: Hutchinson & Co, 1912.

Melville, Lewis. *Farmer George: Vol II.* London: Sir Isaac Pitman and Sons, Ltd, 1907.

Merryweather, George (1838). *Kings, the Devil's Viceroys and Representatives on Earth.* New York: George Merryweather.

Minto, Emma Eleanor Elizabeth (ed.). *Life and Letters of Sir Gilbert Elliot First Earl of Minto from 1751 to 1806.* London: Longmans, 1874.

Moore, Andrew W. *Norfolk & The Grand Tour.* Norfolk Museums Service, 1985.

Morison, Stanley. *The History of the Times: 'The Thunderer' in the Making, 1785-1841.* London: The Times, 1935.

Murray, John. *Lord Byron's Correspondence: Vol I.* Cambridge: Cambridge University Press, 2011.

Nielson, Wendy C. *Women Warriors in Romantic Drama.* Newark: University of Delaware Press, 2013.

Nightingale, Joseph. *Beauties of England and Wales, Vol X, Part III.* London: J Harris, 1815.

Nightingale, Joseph. *Memoirs of the Last Days of Her Late Most Gracious Majesty Caroline, Queen of Great Britain, and Consort of King George the Fourth.* London: J Robins and Company, 1822.

Nightingale, Joseph. *Memoirs of the Public and Private Life of Her Most Gracious Majesty Caroline, Queen of Great Britain.* London: J Robins & Co, 1820.

Nors, P. *The Court of Christian VII of Denmark.* London: Hurst & Blackett, 1928.

O'Keefe, John, Kelly, Michael and Taylor, John. *Personal Reminiscences. New York:* Scribner, Armstrong, *and Company, 1875.*

Oldham, James. *English Common Law in the Age of Mansfield.* Chapel Hill: The University of North Carolina Press, 2004.

Oulton, C W. *Authentic and Impartial Memoirs of Her Late Majesty: Charlotte Queen of Great Britain and Ireland.* London: Kinnersley, 1819.

Pearce, Charles E. *The Amazing Duchess: Vol I.* London: Stanley Paul & Co, 1911.

Pearce, Charles E. *The Beloved Princess, Princess Charlotte of Wales*. London: Stanley Paul & Co, 1911.

Perceval, Spencer. *The Book, Complete*. London: Sherwood, Neely, & Jones, 1813.

Pergami, Bartolomeo. *Tales of the Baroni, or, Scenes in Italy*. London: J Bailey, 1820.

Plowden, Alison. *Caroline and Charlotte*. Stroud: The History Press, 2011.

Poser, Norman S. *Lord Mansfield: Justice in the Age of Reason*. Montreal: McGill, Queen's University Press, 2013.

Rappaport, Helen. *Queen Victoria: A Biographical Companion*. Oxford: ABC-Clio, 2003.

Reddaway, WF. *Struensee and the Fall of Bernstorff. The English Historical Review.* Vol. 27, No. 106 (Apr., 1912), pp. 274-286

Reeve, Henry (ed.). *A Journal of the Reigns of King George IV and King William IV, Vol II*. London: Longmans, Green, and Co, 1874.

Reynolds, George WM. *The Mysteries of London, Vol I*. London: George Vickers, 1846.

Richardson, Joanne. *The Disastrous Marriage*. London: Jonathan Cape, 1960.

Robins, Jane. *The Trial of Queen Caroline: The Scandalous Affair that Nearly Ended a Monarchy*. New York: Simon and Schuster, 2006.

Robinson, Mary. *A Letter to the Women of England and The Natural Daughter*. Calgary: Broadview Press, 2003.

Robinson, Mary. *Memoirs of the Late Mrs Robinson*. London: Hunt and Clarke, 1827.

Rosenthal, L Glück. *A Biographical Memoir of the Duke of Sussex*. Brighton: P Gardner, 1846.

Rounding, Virginia. *Catherine the Great*. London: Random House, 2007.

Rushton, Alan R. *Royal Maladies*. Victoria: Trafford Press, 2008.

Russell, Gillian. *Women, Sociability and Theatre in Georgian London*. Cambridge: Cambridge University Press, 2007.

Sanders, Margaret. *Intimate Letters of England's Kings*. Stroud: Amberley, 2014.

Sanders, Margaret. *Intimate Letters of England's Queens*. Stroud: Amberley, 2014.

Sheldon, Ann. *Authentic and Interesting Memoirs of Miss Ann Sheldon (now Mrs. Archer)*. London: Privately published, 1788.

Silson, Carol Shiner and Haefner, Joel (eds.). *Re-Visioning Romanticism*. Philadelphia: University of Pennsylvania Press, 1994.

Sinclair-Stevenson, Christopher. *Blood Royal: The Illustrious House of Hanover*. London: Faber & Faber, 2012.

Smith, EA. *George IV*. New Haven: Yale University Press, 1999.

Smith, William James (ed.). *The Grenville Papers, Volume 4*. London: John Murray, 1853.

Smyth, Gillespie. *Memoirs and Correspondence (Official and Familiar), of Sir Robert Murray Keith, Vol. I*. London: Henry Colburn, 1849.

Stanhope Taylor, William, and Pringle, John Henry (ed.). *Correspondence of William Pitt, Earl of Chatham, Vol IV*. London: John Murray: 1840.

Stelzig, Eugene. *Romantic Autobiography in England*. London: Routledge, 2009.

Stephenson, Raymond. *The Yard of Wit*. Philadelphia: University of Pennsylvania Press, 2004.

Stoker, Bram. *Famous Impostors*. New York: Sturgis and Walton, 1910.

Stott, Anne. *Hannah More: The First Victorian*. Oxford: Oxford University Press, 2003.

Stuart, Dorothy Margaret. *The Daughters of George III*. Stroud: Fonthill Media, 2017.

Taylor, Elizabeth. *Authentic Memoirs of Mrs Clarke*. London: Thomas Tegg, 1809.

Thackeray, William Makepeace. *The Works of William Makepeace Thackeray: Vol XIX*. London: Smith, Elder, & Co, 1869.

Thal, Herbert van. *Ernest Augustus: Duke of Cumberland & King of Hanover : a Brief Survey of the Man and His Times*. London: Arthur Barker, 1936.

Thoms, William J. *Hannah Lightfoot: Queen Charlotte & the Chevalier D'Eon. Dr. Wilmot's Polish Princess*. London: W.G. Smith, 1867.

Thorne, RG. *The House of Commons 1790-1820*. London: Secker & Warburg, 1986.

Tillyard, Stella. *A Royal Affair: George III and his Troublesome Siblings*. London: Vintage, 2007.

Tomalin, Claire. *Mrs Jordan's Profession*. London: Penguin Books, 2003.

Urban, Sylvanus. *The Gentleman's Magazine and Historical Chronicle for the Year MDCCXCIV: Part the First*. London: John Nichols, 1794.

Wade, John. *British History, Chronologically Arranged, Vol II*. London: Effingham Wilson, 1839.

Wake, Kidd. *The Case of Kidd Wake. Being a Narrative of His Sufferings During Five Years Confinement!!!*. London: 1801.

Wakley, Thomas (ed.). *The Lancet. MDCCCXXVIII-IX, Vol II*. London: Thomas Wakley, 1829.

Wallace, William. *Memoirs of the Life and Reign of George IV., Vol I*. London: Longman, Rees, Orme, Brown, and Green. 1831.

Wallace, William. *Memoirs of the Life and Reign of George IV, Vol III*. London: Longman, Rees, Orme, Brown, Green, & Longman. 1832.

Walpole, Horace. *The Last Journals of Horace Walpole During the Reign of George III from 1771-1783*. London: John Lane, 1910.

Walpole, Horace. *Letters of Horace Walpole, Earl of Orford, to Sir Horace Mann*. London: Richard Bentley, 1833.

Walpole, Horace. *The Letters of Horace Walpole: Vol I*. London: Lea and Blanchard, 1842.

Walpole, Horace (1846). *The Letters of Horace Walpole, Earl of Orford: Vol III*. London: Richard Bentley, p.369.

Walpole, Horace. *Memoirs of the Reign of King George the Second, Vol II*. London: Henry Colburn, 1846.

Walpole, Horace. *Memoirs of the Reign of King George the Third: Vol I*. Philadelphia: Lea & Blanchard, 1845.

Walpole, Horace and Doran, John (ed.). *Journal of the Reign of King George the Third, Vol I*. London: Richard Bentley, 1859.

Walpole, Horace and Le Marchant, Denis (ed.). *Journal of the Reign of King George the Third, Vol IV*. London: Richard Bentley, 1845.

Ward, Adolphus William. *The Electress Sophia and Hanoverian Succession*. London: Longmans, Green and Co, 1909.

Wardle, Gwyllym Lloyd. *The Investigation of the Charges Brought Against His Royal Highness the Duke of York, Vol I*. London: J Stratford, 1809.

Wardroper, John. *Kings, Lords and Wicked Libellers*. London: John Murray, 1973.

Wardroper, John. *Wicked Ernest: The Truth About the Man Who Was Almost Britain's King*. London: Shelfmark Books, 2002.

Watkins, John. *A Biographical Memoir of His Late Royal Highness Frederick, Duke of York and Albany*. London: Henry Fisher, 1827.

Watkins, John. *Memoirs of Her Most Excellent Majesty Sophia-Charlotte, Queen of Great Britain*. London: Henry Colburn, 1819.

Wharncliffe, Lord. *The Letters and Works of Lady Mary Wortley Montagu: Vol I*. London: Richard Bentley, 1837.

Wharncliffe, Lord (ed.). *The Letters and Works of Lady Mary Wortley Montagu, Vol. II*. London: Henry G Bohn, 1861.

Wharton, Thomas I (ed.). *The Law Library, Vol. XXXIII*. Philadelphia: John S Littell, 1841.

Wilberforce, Robert Isaac and Wilberforce, Samuel (eds.). *The Life of William Wilberforce: Vol III*. London: John Murray, 1839.

Wilkins, WH. *The Love of an Uncrowned Queen*. London: Hutchinson & Co, 1900.

Wilkins, William Henry. *A Queen of Tears, Vol I*. London: Longmans, Green & Co, 1904.

Wilkins, William Henry. *A Queen of Tears, Vol II*. London: Longmans, Green & Co, 1904.

Wilkinson, Tate. *The Wandering Patentee*. York: Wilson, Spencer and Mawman, 1795

Wilkes, John. *An Essay on Woman*. London: Gretton, 1763.

Wilks, John. *Memoirs of Her Majesty Queen Caroline Amelia Eliz, Vol. I*. London: Sherwood, Neely and Jones, 1822.

Williams, Thomas. *Memoirs of Her Late Majesty Queen Charlotte*. London: W Simpkin and R Marshall, 1819.

Willis, Geoffrey Malden. *Ernest Augustus, Duke of Cumberland and King of Hanover*. London: Arthur Barker, 1954.

Wills, William. *An Essay on the Rationale of Circumstantial Evidence*. London: Longman, Orme, Brown, Green, and Longmans, 1838.

Wilson, Kathleen. *A New Imperial History*. Cambridge: Cambridge University Press, 2008.

Woodall, William Otter. *A Collection of Reports of Celebrated Trials, Civil and Criminal, Vol. I*. London: Shaw and Sons, 1873.

Woodward, Horace Bolingbroke. *Memorials of John Gunn*. London: WA Nudd, 1891.

Worsley, Lucy. *Courtiers: The Secret History of the Georgian Court*. London: Faber and Faber, 2011.

Wraxall, Lascelles, Sir. *The Life and Times of Her Majesty Caroline Matilda, Vol. I*. London: WH Allen & Co, 1864.

Wraxall, Lascelles, Sir. *The Life and Times of Her Majesty Caroline Matilda, Vol. II*. London: WH Allen & Co, 1864.

Wraxall, Nathaniel William. *Historical Memoirs of His Own Time: Vol II*. London: Richard Bentley, 1836.

Wraxall, Nathaniel William. *Memoirs of the Courts of Berlin, Dresden, Warsaw, and Vienna, Vol. I*. London: T Cadell Jun. and W. Davies, 1800.

Wright, Thomas. *England Under the House of Hanover, Vol II*. London: Richard Bentley, 1848.

Newspapers Cited

All newspaper clippings are reproduced © The British Library Board; in addition to those cited, innumerable newspapers were consulted.

Bath Chronicle (Bath, England), Thursday, 5 March 1789; Issue 1475.

Bingley's Journal Or the Universal Gazette (1770) (London, England), Saturday, 4 August 1770; Issue 9.

Bingley's Journal (London, England), 2-9 November 1771; Issue 75.

Bingley's Journal (London, England), February 22, 1772 - February 29, 1772; Issue 91.

The Bury and Norwich Post: Or, Suffolk, Norfolk, Essex, Cambridge, and Ely Advertiser (Bury Saint Edmunds, England), Wednesday, 18 December, 1811; Issue 1538.

Evening Mail (London, England), 23 -26 April 1793; Issue 651.

General Advertiser (1744) (London, England), Tuesday, 23 July, 1751; Issue 5228.

Hereford Journal (Hereford, England), Wednesday, 29 October, 1806; issue 1897.

Hereford Journal (Hereford, England), Wednesday, 3 July, 1833; Issue 3286.

The Lancaster Gazette and General Advertiser, for Lancashire, Westmorland, &c. (Lancaster, England), Saturday, 4 February, 1809; Issue 399.

The Leeds Intelligencer (Leeds, England), Tuesday, 2 July, 1771; Issue 935.

The Leeds Intelligencer (Leeds, England), Tuesday, 20 August, 1771; Issue 940.

The Leeds Mercury (Leeds, England), Saturday, 16 December, 1809; Issue 2317.

Leeds Mercury (Leeds, England), Saturday, 28 November, 1829, Issue 3177.

Lloyd's Evening Post (London, England), 13-15 July, 1763; Issue 937.

London Chronicle (London, England), 23 -25 October,1760; Issue 598.

London Evening Post (London, England), 17-19 July, 1764; Issue 5728.

London Evening Post (London, England), 25-27 September 25, 1766; Issue 6071.

London Evening Post (London, England), 30 September – 2 October, 1766; Issue 6073.

London Evening Post (London, England), 1-4 November, 1766; Issue 6086.

London Evening Post (London, England), 28-30 August, 1770; Issue 6677.

London Evening Post (London, England), 5-7 November, 1771; Issue 6839.

BIBLIOGRAPHY

London Evening Post (London, England), 30 May-2 June; Issue 6928.

London Gazette (London, England), 8-12 January,1765; Issue 10486.

London Gazette (London, England), 16-20 May, 1775; Issue 11562.

Manchester Courier and Lancashire General Advertiser (Manchester, England), Monday, 4 June, 1866; Issue 2982.

Manchester Courier and Lancashire General Advertiser (Manchester, England), Friday, 8 June, 1866; Issue 2986.

Middlesex Journal or Chronicle of Liberty (London, England), 5-7 May, 1772 - May; Issue 484.

Middlesex Journal or Universal Evening Post (London, England), 31 – 3 November, 1772; Issue 561.

Morning Chronicle (London, England), Thursday, 25 April, 1793; Issue 7454.

The Morning Chronicle (London, England), Thursday, 2 February, 1809; Issue 12396.

The Morning Chronicle (London, England), Saturday, 28 December, 1811; Issue 13304.

Morning Herald (London, England), Tuesday, 13 May 1800; Issue 6131.

Morning Herald and Daily Advertiser (London, England), Friday, 5 January, 1781; Issue 57.

The Morning Post (London, England), Wednesday, 6 June, 1810; Issue 12279.

Morning Post and Daily Advertiser (London, England), Saturday, 12 February 1780; Issue 2288.

Morning Post and Daily Advertiser (London, England), Wednesday, 9 August 1780; Issue 2431.

Morning Post and Daily Advertiser (London, England), Friday, 3 August 1781; Issue 2710.

Morning Post and Daily Advertiser (London, England), Wednesday, 2 November 1791; Issue 5780.

The Morning Post and Gazeteer (London, England), Monday, 1 February 1802; Issue 10397.

New Morning Post or General Advertiser (London, England), Saturday, 14 December, 1776; Issue 35.

Newcastle Guardian, and Tyne Mercury (Newcastle-upon-Tyne, England), Saturday, 23 June 1866; Issue 1059.

The Norfolk Chronicle: or, the Norwich Gazette (Norwich, England), Saturday, 8 April 1809; pg. 4; Issue 2037.

Northampton Mercury (Northampton, England), Saturday, 18 March1809; Issue 2.

Public Advertiser (London, England), Friday, 8 November 1771; Issue 11553.

Public Advertiser (London, England), Monday, 17 February 1772; Issue 11639.

Public Advertiser (London, England), Friday, 18 September, 1772; Issue 11705.

Reading Mercury, Oxford Gazette and Berkshire County Paper, etc (Reading, England), Monday, 1 July, 1833; Issue 5835.

Royal Cornwall Gazette (Truro, England), Saturday, 21 November, 1829, Issue 1378.

The Standard (London, England), Monday, 8 February, 1830; Issue 853.

Star (London, England), Wednesday, 4 January, 1792; Issue 1152.

Star (London, England), Tuesday, 23 April 1793; Issue 1555.

Star (London, England), Monday, 13 May 1793; Issue 1575.

St. James's Chronicle or the British Evening Post (London, England), 15-18 July 1780; Issue 3018.

St. James's Chronicle or the British Evening Post (London, England), 21-23 March 1793; Issue 4999.

The Tamworth Herald, etc (Tamworth, England), Saturday, 25 November, 1876; Issue 431.

The Times (London, England), Friday, 18 November, 1791; Issue 2184.

The Times (London, England), Wednesday, 22 January 1794; Issue 2892.

The Times (London, England), Saturday, 14 March 1829; Issue 13826.

The Times (London, England), Monday, 16 March 1829; Issue 13863.

The Times (London, England), Tuesday, 9 February 1830; Issue 14145.

The Times (London, England), 29 May 1848, Issue 19875.

Trewman's Exeter Flying Post or Plymouth and Cornish Advertiser (Exeter, England), Thursday, 23 March 1809; Issue 2342.

Whitehall Evening Post (1770) (London, England), 13-15 July 13, 1780; Issue 5346.

Whitehall Evening Post (1770) (London, England), 12-14 October 1780; Issue 5383.

World (1787) (London, England), Friday, 5 October 1792; Issue 1800.

World (1787) (London, England), Monday, 7 April 1794; Issue 2270.

Websites Consulted

19th Century UK Periodicals (http://gale.cengage.co.uk/product-highlights/history/19th- (century-uk-periodicals-parts-1-and-2.aspx)

BIBLIOGRAPHY

British and Irish Women's Letters and Diaries (www.bwl2.alexanderstreet. com)

British History Online (http://www.british-history.ac.uk)

British Newspapers 1600-1950 (http://gdc.gale.com/products/19th-century-british-library-newspapers-part-i-and-part-ii/)

Hansard (http://hansard.millbanksystems.com/index.html)

Historical Texts (http://historicaltexts.jisc.ac.uk)

House of Commons Parliamentary Papers (http://parlipapers.chadwyck. co.uk/marketing/index.jsp)

JSTOR (www.jstor.org)

The National Archives (http://www.nationalarchives.gov.uk)

Oxford Dictionary of National Biography (http://www.oxforddnb.com)

The Proceedings of the Old Bailey (http://www.oldbaileyonline.org)

The Times Digital Archive (http://gale.cengage.co.uk/times-digital-archive/ times-digital-archive-17852006.aspx)

Notes

Chapter 1

1. *Newcastle Guardian, and Tyne Mercury* (Newcastle-upon-Tyne, England), Saturday, 23 June, 1866; Issue 1059.
2. George I married his cousin, Sophia Dorothea of Celle, in 1682 and from the start, the couple hated each other. Although they had two children together George and Sophia Dorothea's marriage was a disaster, marked by George's violent outbursts and public love affairs.

   Neglected and isolated, Sophia Dorothea took a lover in the strapping form of a dashing Swedish adventurer named Count Philip Christoph von Königsmarck. The handsome Königsmarck had no shortage of admirers and chief among them was the scheming Countess Clara von Platen, the mistress of George's father, Ernest Augustus. She also just happened to be an old flame of Königsmarck's.

   When Clara learned that the couple was conspiring to run away together, she convinced Ernest Augustus to agree to Königsmarck's arrest. As soon as he gave the OK, Clara had Königsmarck murdered. George's marriage to Sophia Dorothea was annulled on the grounds of adultery and she was locked away in Ahlden House. Here she remained until her death three decades later, forbidden to see her children. Her son, later George II, never forgave his father for the fate that had befallen her. He in turn would eventually become estranged from his own son, Frederick, the father of George III. A destructive cycle indeed!
3. Walpole is a legend of the era. A waspish diarist with connections seemingly everywhere, he is remembered today for his home of Strawberry Hill and his marvellous gothic novel, *The Castle of Otranto*.
4. Walpole, Horace (1846). *Memoirs of the Reign of King George the Second, Vol II*. London: Henry Colburn, pp.204-205.
5. Ibid, pp.204-205.

6. John Wilkes was a radical Member of Parliament, journalist and constant thorn in the side of the establishment. He is particularly famed for his association with *The North Briton*, a radical paper that pulled no punches.

7. George I and II were understandably at odds after George I locked his wife away for her liaison with the count. Sophia Dorothea predeceased her former husband and when George I died, one of his son's first acts was to take his mother's portraits out of mothballs. Sadly, after George II read Sophia Dorothea's private papers during a trip to Hanover, he put those pictures back into storage and never spoke of her again.

8. George II left Hanover for Britain when Frederick was just 7-years-old. Left behind in Europe to serve as the figurehead of the House of Hanover, Frederick grew closer to his grandfather, George I, and ever more distant from his father. When the pair met again nearly fifteen years later, they had grown irretrievably apart. Domestic dramas and political disputes contrived to keep them estranged for the rest of Frederick's days.

9. RA GEO/MAIN/54227-54232 Instructions from Frederick, Prince of Wales, to his son George, written at Leicester House, 13 January 1749. Royal Archives, Windsor.

10. St John is now known as Shadwell, and sits within the London Borough of Tower Hamlets.

11. *Star* (London, England), Monday, 13 May, 1793; Issue 1 575.

12. Boulton, William (1909). *In the Days of the Georges*. London: George Bell & Sons, p.90.

13. Elizabeth Chudleigh, Duchess of Kingston, was pretty scandalous herself. She was found guilty of bigamy in 1776 and fled for new adventures on the continent.

14. Howitt, William (ed.) (1861). *Cassell's Illustrated History of England, Vol I*. London: Cassell, Peter and Galpin, p.6

15. A morganatic marriage, sometimes referred to as a *left-handed marriage,* is a marriage between two parties of unequal social rank. The wife and children of such a marriage have no right to any titles or privileges as a result of the union.

16. Wraxall, Nathaniel William (1836). *Historical Memoirs of His Own Time: Vol II*. London: Richard Bentley, p.42.

17. Hester Thrale enjoys deserved fame as a diarist, patron of the arts and chronicler of her times. She was a close friend of Samuel Johnson and moved within the highest literary circles.

18. *The Tamworth Herald, etc* (Tamworth, England), Saturday, 25 November 25 1876; Issue 431.

19. *Manchester Courier and Lancashire General Advertiser* (Manchester, England), Monday, 4 June 1866; Issue 2982.

20. John Dunning, 1st Baron Ashburton, would enjoy a glittering political career. The reputation of the famed Prime Minister William Pitt, of course, precedes him.

21. Anonymous (1846). *The Eclectic Review: Vol XIX.* London: Thomas Ward & Co, pp.186-187.

22. Cockburn loved presiding over the most scandalous trials, so he must have *relished* this one.

23. *Manchester Courier and Lancashire General Advertiser* (Manchester, England), Friday, 8 June 1866; Issue 2986.

Chapter 2

1. *General Advertiser (1744)* (London, England), Tuesday, 23 July, 1751; Issue 5228.

2. *London Chronicle* (London, England), 23 October 1760 – 25 October 1760; Issue 598.

3. King Frederick V had married Louise of Great Britain, daughter of George II and sister to Caroline Matilda's father, Frederick, Prince of Wales.

4. *Lloyd's Evening Post* (London, England), 13 July 1763 – 15 July 1763; Issue 937.

5. Almost as soon as Frederick William and Elisabeth Christine were married in 1765, Frederick William was living it up with his mistresses. So shameless was he that Elisabeth Christine took a court musician as her lover. He was swiftly executed and rumours spread that Elisabeth Christine had been pregnant by him and procured a herbal abortion. Her husband was so incensed that he had his wife placed under house arrest and the marriage was annulled. As the years passed and the conditions of her captivity were relaxed, Elisabeth Christine became a popular and celebrated society hostess, beloved of both the people and her wide intellectual circle. Frederick William married Frederika Louisa of Hesse-Darmstadt and later, without any effort to end *that* marriage, he bigamously took a third wife, Julie von Voss, from among his wife's ladies-in-waiting. When Julie died he

made another bigamous marriage to another lady-in-waiting, Sophie von Dönhoff. If you're wondering what his *official* wife made of all this you might not be surprised to learn that there was little love lost between the eventual king and queen of Prussia, who regarded their marriage, which bore seven children, as little more than a business arrangement.

6. Titley began his diplomatic career in 1729 when he was appointed as Chargé d'Affaires in Copenhagen. Less than two years later, he had been promoted to the position of Envoy-Extraordinary and Minister Plenipotentiary. With the very real threat of a Danish-French alliance looming, the British needed a safe and trustworthy pair of hands in Denmark and Titley provided them. He became so fond of the country that he turned down a prestigious fellowship at Cambridge to remain in Copenhagen. He died in his adopted land in 1768, nearly four decades after he first took up residence there.

7. Louisa died in 1768 at the age of 19.

8. Wilkins, WH (1900). *The Love of an Uncrowned Queen*. London: Hutchinson & Co, p.47.

9. *London Gazette* (London, England), 8 January 1765 – 12 January 1765; Issue 10486.

10. Wilkins, WH (1900). *The Love of an Uncrowned Queen*. London: Hutchinson & Co, p.81.

11. Gunning took over the role of Envoy-Extraordinary and Minister Plenipotentiary when Titley died.

12. Wilkins, WH (1900). *The Love of an Uncrowned Queen*. London: Hutchinson & Co, p.81.

13. *London Evening Post* (London, England), 30 September 1766 – 2 October 1766; Issue 6073.

14. *London Evening Post* (London, England), 25 September 1766 – 27 September 1766; Issue 6071.

15. Elizabeth Carter made her name as a writer and translator and moved in the highest intellectual circles. Described by Francis Lord Napier as 'a fine old Slut', by the age of 21, Carter was already working on the classical translations that would make her name. She published her celebrated translation of *All the Works of Epictetus, Which are Now Extant*, in 1978. This philosophical work sealed Carter's reputation and provided her with security for life.

16. *London Evening Post* (London, England), 1 November 1766 – 4 November 4 1766; Issue 6086.

17. Wraxall, Lascelles, Sir (1864). *The Life and Times of Her Majesty Caroline Matilda, Vol. I.* London: WH Allen & Co, p.97.

18. Louise was fired by the king in 1768, as he believed she had conspired to create domestic discord. She and her charge were reunited following the queen's disgrace and exile.

19. It was to be one of Reverdil's final acts before Christian's decadent best friend and chamberlain, Count Conrad Holck, convinced the king to have his former tutor exiled. His efforts to oust Reverdil were supported by Christian's mistress, Støvlet-Cathrine.

20. Støvlet-Cathrine earned her nickname, which translates as *Catherine of the Gaiters*, or *Boots-Catherine*, because her mother was a bootmaker. Unsubstantiated rumours persisted that her father was none other than Prince Georg Ludwig of Brunswick-Bevern.

21. Rounding, Virginia (2007). *Catherine the Great.* London: Random House, p.198.

22. Walpole, Horace (1844). *Letters of Horace Walpole, Earl of Orford, to Sir Horace Mann.* London: Lea & Blanchard, p.215.

23. Wilkins, WH (1904). *A Queen of Tears, Vol I.* London: Longmans, Green & Co, pp.191-192.

24. Durham, Samuel Astley (1840). *History of Denmark, Sweden, and Norway, Volume III.* London: Longman, Orme, Brown, Green & Longmans and John Taylor, pp.179-180.

25. Wilkins, WH (1904). *A Queen of Tears, Vol I.* London: Longmans, Green & Co, p.263.

26. *The Leeds Intelligencer* (Leeds, England), Tuesday, 2 July 1771; Issue 935.

27. Brown, John (1818). *The Northern Courts, Vol I.* London: Archibald Constable and Co, p.113.

28. Brown, John (1818). *Memoirs of the Courts of Sweden and Denmark, Vol I.* New York: The Grolier Society, pp.128-129.

29. Tillyard, Stella (2007). *A Royal Affair: George III and His Troublesome Siblings.* London: Random House, p.192.

30. *The Leeds Intelligencer* (Leeds, England), Tuesday, 20 August 1771; Issue 940.

31. The rumours did Louise Auguste no harm whatsoever and she became a great favourite at the Danish court, where she became known as *the Venus of Denmark*. She later married Frederick Christian II, Duke of Schleswig-Holstein-Sonderburg-Augustenburg, and presided over a happy household, eventually giving birth to three children. Louise Auguste died in 1843, at 71.

32. Wilkins, WH (1904). *A Queen of Tears, Vol I*. London: Longmans, Green & Co, p.332.
33. They were the queen dowager herself, Prince Frederick, politician Ove Høegh-Guldberg, General Hans Henrik Eickstedt, Colonel Georg Ludwig Köller, whose regiment was in charge of palace security that night, and Jessen, Struensee's former valet, who could be relied upon to know his movements. Completing the group were two of Struensee's once-trusted associates, Rantzau and Magnus Beringskjold.
34. Tillyard, Stella (2007). *A Royal Affair: George III and His Troublesome Siblings*. London: Random House, p.219.
35. Wilkins, WH (1904). *A Queen of Tears, Vol II*. London: Longmans, Green & Co, p.161.
36. *Middlesex Journal or Universal Evening Post* (London, England), 31 October 1772 - 3 November 3, 1772; Issue 561.
37. *London Gazette* (London, England), 16 May 1775 – 20 May 20 1775; Issue 11562.
38. *Oracle Bell's New World* (London, England), Wednesday, 10 June 10 1789; Issue 9.

Chapter 3

1. Sheldon, Ann (1788). *Authentic and Interesting Memoirs of Miss Ann Sheldon (now Mrs. Archer)*. London: Privately published, p.128.
2. *London Evening Post* (London, England), 17 July 1764 – 19 July 1764; Issue 5728.
3. Urban, Sylvanus (1669). *The Gentleman's Magazine: Volume 39*. London: D Henry, p.612.
4. Sheldon, Ann (1788). *Authentic and Interesting Memoirs of Miss Ann Sheldon (now Mrs. Archer)*. London: Privately published, pp.70-71.
5. The couple's first child, Robert Grosvenor, was born on 22 March 1767. He followed the family tradition of entering Parliament as a Tory yet switched allegiances and became a Whig following the death of Pitt the Younger. Robert enjoyed some notoriety for hurling a bible at the head of King George IV in frustration at the monarch's behaviour towards his estranged wife, Caroline of Brunswick.
6. Urban, Sylvanus (1669). *The Gentleman's Magazine: Volume 39*. London: D Henry, p.607.

7. Anonymous (1771). *Copies of the Depositions of the Witnesses Examined in the Cause of Divorce Now Depending in the Consistory Court of the Lord Bishop of London, at Doctor's-Commons.* London: J Russell, p.251.

8. Sheldon, Ann (1788). *Authentic and Interesting Memoirs of Miss Ann Sheldon (now Mrs. Archer).* London: Privately published, pp.202-203.

9. Anonymous (1771). *Copies of the Depositions of the Witnesses Examined in the Cause of Divorce Now Depending in the Consistory Court of the Lord Bishop of London, at Doctor's-Commons.* London: J Russell, pp.251-252.

10. *Cornuto* is an Italian term that translates as *cuckold*.

11. Grosvenor never got his dukedom, though he became 1st Earl Grosvenor in 1784.

12. Hamilton, A (1770). *The Town and Country Magazine, Or, Universal Repository of Knowledge, Instruction, and Entertainment, Vol II for the Year 1770.* London: A Hamilton Jnr, pp.401-402.

13. *Bingley's Journal Or the Universal Gazette* (1770) (London, England), Saturday, August 4, 1770; Issue 9.

14. *London Evening Post* (London, England), 28 August 1770 – 30 August 1770; Issue 6677.

15. William Murray, 1st Earl of Mansfield, remains a colossus of legal history. He served as Lord Chief Justice for a monumental thirty-two years, championing many reforms that changed the face of British law and society forever.

16. D'Onhoff's identity seemed to confound the public, who had never heard of her. Happily the *Gazetteer and New Daily Advertiser* (London, Britain), Wednesday, 15 August 1770; Issue 12 935, had the answer.

    'As many of our readers may be at a loss to know who the famous Countess of Dunhoff [sic], who makes so great a talk in the late trial between Lord Grosvenor and the Duke of Cumberland is, we beg leave to inform them, that she is the daughter of the late, and sister of the present Earl of Tankerville. The above celebrated Lady married Count Dunhoff, a German nobleman.'

17. Anonymous (1771). *Copies of the Depositions of the Witnesses Examined in the Cause of Divorce Now Depending in the Consistory Court of the Lord Bishop of London, at Doctor's-Commons.* London: J Russell, p.306.

18. Anonymous (1770). *The Genuine Copies of Letters which Passed Between the Duke of Cumberland and Lady Grosvenor.* London: J Wheble, p.66.

19. Anonymous (1770). *A Full and Complete History of His R—l H—ss the D— of C—d, and Lady G—r, the Fair Adulteress, Vol I.* London: J Porter and T Walker, p.100.

20. *Junius* was the pseudonym employed by the author of a number of letters published between 1769 and 1772. Though the most commonly held belief is that the man behind the name was Sir Philip Francis, the 1st Marquess of Lansdowne, this has never been definitively proven.

21. Junius (1774). *The Letters of Junius: Vol I.* London: Privately published, p.236.

22. Brougham, Henry (1839). *Historical Sketches of Statesmen who Flourished in the Time of George III.* Paris: Baudry's European Library, p.60.

23. A sum worth more than £1.6million today.

24. *Bingley's Journal Or the Universal Gazette* (1770) (London, England), Saturday, 14 July 1770; Issue 6.

25. Donne, W Bodham (1867) (ed.). *The Correspondence of King George the Third with Lord North, From 1768 to 1783, Vol. I.* London: John Murray, p.34.

26. Ibid, p.35.

27. In 1819 Porter became 6th Baron de Hochepied after inheriting a Hungarian title. After this, he became known as George de Hochepied.

Chapter 4

1. Walpole, Horace and Doran, John (ed.) (1859). *Journal of the Reign of King George the Third, Vol I.* London: Richard Bentley, p.74.

2. Smith, William James (ed.) (1853). *The Grenville Papers, Volume 4.* London: John Murray, p.276.

3. *Bingley's Journal* (London, England), 2 November 1771 – 9 November 1771; Issue 75.

4. London Evening Post (London, England), 5 November 1771 – 7 November 1771; Issue 6839.

5. His easily-agitated state would not have been helped by mischievous speculation in the *Public Advertiser* (London, England), Friday 8 November, 1771; Issue 11553. The august publication impishly suggested that, 'It is now, happily for this Country, within the Limits of Possibility, that a *Luttrell* may be King of Great Britain.' Whilst not *impossible*, it was certainly highly unlikely.

6. Donne, W Bodham (1867) (ed.). *The Correspondence of King George the Third with Lord North from 1768 to 1783, Vol I*. London: John Murray, p.91.

7. Perhaps better known as Pitt the Elder, Chatham served as prime minster twice. His first term was from 1756-1761, his second 1766-1768. Alongside his son, William Pitt the Younger, he is amongst the pantheon of the long eighteenth century's greatest statesmen.

8. *Bingley's Journal* (London, England), 22 February 1772 – 29 February 29 1772; Issue 91.

9. *The Royal Marriages Act 1772* was eventually repealed by the *Succession to the Crown Act 2013*. Under this act, now only the first six candidates in the line of succession must seek permission to marry from the monarch, with others free to marry as they wish. Unlike the Royal Marriages Act, should any of those marry without receiving permission, they risk losing their place in the line of succession.

10. Augusta of Saxe-Gotha, the Dowager Princess of Wales, died on 8 February 1772 of throat cancer.

11. Donne, W Bodham (1867) (ed.). *The Correspondence of King George the Third with Lord North from 1768 to 1783, Vol I*. London: John Murray, p.89.

12. Wharncliffe, Lord (1861) (ed.). *The Letters and Works of Lady Mary Wortley Montagu, Vol. II*. London: Henry G Bohn, p.360.

13. All four children, Laura, Maria, Edward and Charlotte, survived to adulthood. Laura married Frederick Keppel, Bishop of Exeter, Maria married Prince William Henry, Duke of Gloucester and Edinburgh, and Charlotte married Lionel Tollemarche, Earl of Dysart. Edward remained unmarried until his death in 1771.

14. Walpole, Horace (1846). *The Letters of Horace Walpole, Earl of Orford: Vol III*. London: Richard Bentley, p.369.

15. Wharncliffe, Lord (1861) (ed.). *The Letters and Works of Lady Mary Wortley Montagu, Vol. II*. London: Henry G Bohn, p.360.

16. Those three girls, Charlotte, Elizabeth, and Anna, were later to be immortalised by Joshua Reynolds in his painting, *The Ladies Waldegrave*.

17. *Middlesex Journal or Chronicle of Liberty* (London, England), 5 May 1772 - May 7, 1772; Issue 484.

18. *London Evening Post* (London, England), 30 May 1772 – 2 June 1772; Issue 6928.

19. *Public Advertiser* (London, England), Friday, 18 September 1772; Issue 11705.
20. *Public Advertiser* (London, England), Monday, 17 February 17 1772; Issue 11639.
21. Donne, W Bodham (1867) (ed.). *The Correspondence of King George the Third with Lord North from 1768 to 1783, Vol I*. London: John Murray, p.222.

Chapter 5

1. The exact date of Mary's birth is disputed. In her memoirs, she attests to being born in 1758, whilst her baptismal record, in which her name is recorded as Polle, notes that she was born in 1756. More recently Mary's biographer, Paula Byrne, posits a birthdate of 1757.
2. One of those children, Elizabeth, died before Mary's birth.
3. Hannah was inspired by her father, Jacob More, who believed unequivocally that education was not only the right of boys and men, but of girls and women too. She established schools for the poor and became one of the most important women of her time. Hannah is depicted in *Characters of the Muses in the Temple of Apollo*, painted by Richard Samuel in 1778 (Hannah More is standing, second from right).
4. Powell was so loved that when he fell ill in 1769, the streets around his house in Bristol's King Street were covered in straw to mute the sounds of carriages and King Street itself was chained off, to ensure that no vehicles would disturb his rest. He died on 3 July and theatres went dark in his honour. His funeral was so heavily attended that it wasn't possible to admit all the mourners to the service.
5. Robinson, Mary Elizabeth (1827). *Memoirs of the Late Mrs Robinson*. London: Hunt and Clarke, p.17.
6. Ibid.
7. Some sources mention nine children, others five. Sadly, it isn't possible to definitely ascertain exactly how many children Grace and Francis had, nor how many survived.
8. One of those who was besotted by her legs was none other than the adolescent Robert Stewart, later the ill-fated Viscount Castlereagh.

Castlereagh, of course, would one day inspire Shelley's legendary poem, *The Mask of Anarchy*. He took his own life in 1822 by which time, one imagines, Dora Jordan's legs were long forgotten or perhaps, to the contrary, they were fondly remembered in moments of lucidity.

9. A few years later Mary encountered Lorrington again as a filthy, half-naked, drunken beggar. Ashamed of what had become of her, Lorrington refused all Mary's desperate offers of help and tragically, she later died in the workhouse.

10. Robinson, Mary Elizabeth (1827). *Memoirs of the Late Mrs Robinson*. London: Hunt and Clarke, p.28.

11. Boaden, James (1831). *The Life of Mrs Jordan, Vol. I*. London: Edward Bull, p.11.

12. Ibid.

13. Adolphus, John (1839). *Memoirs of John Bannister, Comedian, Vol. I*. London: Richard Bentley, p.127.

14. Anonymous (1784). *The Memoirs of Perdita*. London: G Lister, p.17.

15. Actor-manager Wilkinson was a leading light in northern England's theatrical firmament.

16. When the theatre famously burned to the ground in 1809, Sheridan sipped port as he watched it burn. He knew the fire would ruin him and commented with admirable sang-froid, 'a man may surely be allowed to take a glass of wine by his own fireside.'

17. *New Morning Post or General Advertiser* (London, England), Saturday, 14 December 1776; Issue 35.

18. *Morning Post and Daily Advertiser* (London, England), Wednesday, 9 August 1780; Issue 2431.

19. Malden assembled one of the finest collections of British art of his time, commissioning work from such legendary names as Joseph Mallord William Turner and David Wilkie.

20. *Whitehall Evening Post* (1770) (London, England), 13 July 1780 – 15 July 1780; Issue 5346.

21. Robinson, Mary Elizabeth (1827). *Memoirs of the Late Mrs Robinson*. London: Hunt and Clarke, pp.108-109.

22. A terrible one, as Caroline of Brunswick would no doubt be able to attest.

23. Robinson, Mary Elizabeth (1827). *Memoirs of the Late Mrs Robinson*. London: Hunt and Clarke, p.109.

24. *Morning Post and Daily Advertiser* (London, England), Saturday, February 12, 1780; Issue 2288.

25. Anonymous (1784). *The Memoirs of Perdita*. London: G Lister, p.98.

26. *St. James's Chronicle or the British Evening Post* (London, England), 15 July 1780 – 18 July 1780; Issue 3018.

27. *Whitehall Evening Post* (1770) (London, England), October 12, 1780 - October 14, 1780; Issue 5383.

28. *Morning Herald and Daily Advertiser* (London, England), Friday, January 5 1781; Issue 57.

29. Davenport, Hester (2011). *The Prince's Mistress: Perdita*. Stroud: The History Press.

30. *Morning Post and Daily Advertiser* (London, England), Friday, August 3 1781; Issue 2710.

31. Fortescue, Sir John (ed.) (1927). *The Correspondence of King George the Third from 1760 to December 1783, Vol II*. London: Macmillan and Company, p.269.

32. Wilkinson, Tate (1795). *The Wandering Patentee*. York: Wilson, Spencer and Mawman, p.136.

33. Anonymous (1795). *The Great Illegitimates!! Public and Private Life of that Celebrated Actress Mrs Jordan*. London: J Duncombe, p.32.

34. That child, William Henry Courtney, died when his ship went down with all hands in 1807. His mother's identity remains a mystery, but Dora treated him as though he were her own child. Dora and Clarence's sons all followed their father into a naval career.

35. *Morning Post and Daily Advertiser* (London, England), Wednesday, November 2, 1791; Issue 5780.

36. *The Times* (London, England), Friday, Nov 18, 1791; Issue 2184.

37. *Star* (London, England), Wednesday 4 January, 1792; Issue 1 152.

38. Allen, Walter Gore (1960). *King William IV*. London: The Cresset Press, p.52.

39. *St. James's Chronicle or the British Evening Post* (London, England), 21 March 1793 – 23 March 1793; Issue 4999.

40. Known as the *Wiltshire Heiress*, Catherine was the richest commoner in the country as sole heiress to a fortune worth millions. She married William Wesley-Pole, the Duke of Wellington's nephew, in 1812 and he promptly set about infecting Catherine with venereal disease almost as quickly as he started spending her money.

    Although he enjoyed royal favour at the court of George IV, William abandoned Catherine and fled to the continent to escape his creditors. Catherine died in 1825 but despite his best efforts, William was unable to get his hands on her fortune, which was inherited by the couple's eldest son.

41. Boaden, James (1831). *The Life of Mrs Jordan, Vol. II*. London: Edward Bull, pp.273-275.

42. Dora died in 1816, two years before the Duke of Clarence wed Adelaide of Saxe-Meiningen. They became king and queen in 1830. Together the couple had two daughters, both of whom died in early infancy.

Chapter 6

1. *World* (1787) (London, England), Friday, 5 October, 1792; Issue 1800.

2. George I had been placed on the throne as a result of the 1701 Act of Settlement. The Act decreed that, if no heir was born to William III, or his sister-in-law, the future Queen Anne, then the succession would leap-frog over the dozens of Roman Catholic Stuart heirs who stood in line and pass straight to the first Protestant on the list. At the time of Queen Anne's death that Protestant was George, Elector of Hanover, and from 1714, King of Great Britain. Also included in the Act was the not-at-all-small matter that the throne could not be inherited by a Roman Catholic and should any heir or monarch marry a Catholic, they would forsake their right to reign as sovereign.

3. Anonymous (1845). *The Annual Register, or a View of the History and Politics of the Year 1844*. London: F&J Rivington, p.343.

4. Thomas Erskine, 1st Baron Erskine, served as Lord Chancellor. As a lawyer he defended James Hadfield after Hadfield took a shot at King George III. Erskine successfully argued that Hadfield was not guilty for his actions by reason of insanity, a legal watershed.

5. Rosenthal, L Glück (1846). *A Biographical Memoir of the Duke of Sussex*. Brighton: P Gardner, pp.5-6.

6. *Morning Chronicle* (London, England), Thursday, 25 April 1793; Issue 7454.

7. *Star* (London, England), Tuesday, 23 April 1793; Issue 1 555.

8. Hutton, James (ed.) (1885). *Selections from the Letters and Correspondence of Sir James Bland Burges, with Notices of his Life*. London: William Clowes and Sons Limited, p.285.

9. Anonymous (1845). *The Annual Register, or a View of the History and Politics of the Year 1844*. London: F&J Rivington, p.344.

10. *Evening Mail* (London, England), 23 April 1793 – 26 April 1793; Issue 651.

NOTES

11. That child, Augustus, was born just a month later in January 1794. The couple's second child, Augusta Emma, followed in 1801. In 1809 the children took the surname of d'Este, a royal house to which both parents were able to trace their descent.

12. Sir Augustus d'Este, the couple's son, later attempted to prove the marriage legal and gain his rights and privileges as the son of a member of the royal family, including the inheritance of the title, Duke of Sussex, following his father's death. He case was rejected by the House of Lords. Sir Augustus can also claim the dubious honour of being the first recorded person to display the symptoms of Multiple Sclerosis, a condition which was not recognised during his lifetime.

13. *World* (1787) (London, England), Monday, 7 April 1794; Issue 2270.

14. RA GEO/ADD/43/3a Queen Charlotte's Diary for 'Month of January & part of February 1794'. Royal Archives, Windsor.

15. *The Times* (London, England), Wednesday, 22 Jan, 1794; Issue 2892.

16. Aspinall, Arthur (ed.) (1963). *The Later Correspondence of George III.* Cambridge: Cambridge University Press, p.176.

17. *Morning Herald* (London, England), Tuesday, 13 May 1800; Issue 6131.

18. Aspinall, Arthur (ed.) (1963). *The Later Correspondence of George III.* Cambridge: Cambridge University Press, p.245.

19. An influential politician and key figure of the Scottish Enlightenment, Dundas was also the last person to be impeached in the United Kingdom. Although he was eventually acquitted of the charge of misappropriation of public money in 1806, his career was over. When he was offered on Earldom in 1809, Dundas declined it. He died two years later.

20. The Lord Chancellor between 1793 and 1801.

21. Aspinall, Arthur (ed.) (1963). *The Later Correspondence of George III.* Cambridge: Cambridge University Press, p.259.

22. RA GEO/MAIN/36514-36515 Letter from Queen Charlotte to George, Prince of Wales, 30 August 1799. Royal Archives, Windsor.

23. *The Morning Post and Gazetteer* (London, England), Monday, 1 February 1802; Issue 10397.

24. *Hereford Journal* (Hereford, England), Wednesday, 29 October 1806; issue 1897.

25. His subsidiary title was Earl of Inverness, so this was a tacit recognition of the marriage.

26. Childe-Pemberton, William (1910). *The Romance of Princess Amelia.* London: G Bell & Sons, p.26.

27. Ibid, p.4.

28. *Bath Chronicle* (Bath, England), Thursday, March 5, 1789; Issue 1475.

29. George III even extended mercy to three assailants who tried to take his life, recognising that they were mentally ill during their assassination attempts.

30. Howard, John Jackson and Crisp, Frederick Arthur (eds.) (1897). *Visitation of England and Wales, Volume 5.* Privately published, p.87.

Chapter 7

1. On 18 May 1797 Charlotte, Princess Royal, married the Hereditary Prince Frederick I of Württemberg. He was a widower and father of three who was not only the son of a Catholic but had also been accused of infidelity and physical and mental cruelty by his late wife, Duchess Augusta of Brunswick-Wolfenbüttel. The Princess Royal fought a long and tireless battle to win the blessing of her parents and eventually it was forthcoming. Against all expectations Frederick proved to be a loving husband and the princess was popular with both the Württemberg courtiers and her new stepchildren. Eventually the couple became king and queen of Württemberg, living very happily together until Frederick's death in 1816.

2. Burney, Frances (1854). *Diary and Letters of Madame D'Arblay, Vol III.* London: Henry Colburn, p.294.

3. Burney, Frances (1843). *Diary and Letters of Madame D'Arblay, Vol V.* London: Henry Colburn, p.26.

4. When the Princess of Wales was forbidden permission to see her daughter other than on strictly scheduled visits, Frances Garth assisted in sneaking her into the nursery without the knowledge of the prince.

5. GEO/MAIN/36458-36459 Letter from Queen Charlotte to George, Prince of Wales, 23 January 1796. Royal Archives, Windsor.

6. By the time of his death in 1829, Garth had attained the office of General. He was such a trusted and valued member of the royal household that he eventually served as guardian to Princess Charlotte of Wales, the ill-fated only child of the Prince Regent.

7. Garth wasn't the only equerry to number royal princesses amongst his admirers. Brent Spencer and Charles Fitzroy were linked with Princess Augusta and Princess Amelia respectively.

8. Charles Greville's diaries are a treasure trove of the era and their publication was eagerly awaited by the public.

9. Iremonger, Lucille (1958). *Love and the Princesses. New York: Thomas Y Crowell Company*, pp.204-205.

10. Fraser, Flora (2012). *Princesses: The Six Daughters of George III*. Edinburgh: A&C Black, chapter 10.

11. Ibid.

12. As mother to fifteen children, thirteen of whom survived to adulthood, Charlotte knew a thing or two about childbirth.

13. Stuart, Dorothy Margaret (2017). *The Daughters of George III*. Stroud: Fonthill Media, chapter 5.

14. Iremonger, Lucille (1958). *Love and the Princesses. New York: Thomas Y Crowell Company*, p.190.

15. A career soldier, Taylor enjoyed a successful career in the royal household. He was private secretary first to the Duke of York, followed by the king and finally the queen, whom he served until her death in 1818.

16. Ham, Elizabeth (1945). *Elizabeth Ham, by Herself*. London: Faber & Faber, p.48.

17. Wardroper, John (2002). *Wicked Ernest*. London: Shelfmark Books, p.34.

18. Fraser, Flora (2012). *Princesses: The Six Daughters of George III*. Edinburgh: A&C Black, chapter 10.

19. The Dashwoods of West Wycombe were famed for their love of pleasure thanks to the exploits of Sir Francis Dashwood, who made such spirited use of the Hellfire caves on his property.

20. Lord Jacob Astley's personal life was so sordid that his request for a divorce was denied, for he could not lay claim to being blameless when it came to Georgiana's abandonment of him and their children. He had lost his wife *and* his reputation.

21. The two men eventually fought a duel in 1828. Though Sir Jacob fired, Tommy refused to return his shot and whilst the seconds were busy discussing their next move, the police intervened.

22. *The Times* (London, England), Saturday, 14 Mar 1829; Issue 13826.

23. *The Times* (London, England), Monday, 16 Mar 1829; Issue 13863.

24. Ibid.

25. *Royal Cornwall Gazette* (Truro, England), Saturday, 21 November 1829, Issue 1378.

26. *Leeds Mercury* (Leeds, England), Saturday, 28 November 1829, Issue 3177.

27. *The Times* (London, England), 29 May, 1848, Issue 19875.

Chapter 8

1. *The Leeds Mercury* (Leeds, England), Saturday, 16 December 1809; Issue 2317.

2. Du Maurier fictionalised her ancestor's story in her 1954 novel, *Mary Anne*.

3. Or perhaps Oxford, her nineteenth century biographers simply could not agree.

4. Again, the various references to Mary Anne cannot agree on the number of children she had, and she is variously claimed to have been mother to two, three or four offspring by Clarke. Two seems most likely, but like many things in Mary Anne's life, there remains an element of mystery.

5. This marriage inspired James Gillray to take up his pen and draw one of his most famous works, *Fashionable Contrasts;—or—The Duchess's little Shoe yielding to the Magnitude of the Duke's Foot*. This celebrated cartoon depicts the tiny feet of the Duchess of York in jewelled slippers, caught in an obviously compromising position between the large and ungainly feet of her husband, the duke, clad in sensible buckled shoes.

   The Duchess of York was famed for her tiny feet, which supposedly measured less than six inches in length. Copies of her shoes were sold as souvenirs and fashionable ladies squeezed their own feet into slippers that were too small just to get her look. Enough, said Gillray's print, forget the feet and let the couple get on with the business of producing heirs!

   Fashionable Contrasts was published by Hannah Humphrey on 24 January 1792. It remains one of Gillray's most iconic images.

6. Glover, Richard (1963). *Peninsular Preparation: The Reform of the British Army 1795–1809*. Cambridge: Cambridge University Press, p.12.

7. Chandler, David G and Beckett, Ian (eds.) (1994). *The Oxford History of the British Army*. Oxford: Oxford University Press, p.148.

8. Gronow was a dandy, a debtor and a bon vivante!

9. The Duke of York was *far* from a perfect beauty himself, with a bulbous nose and drink-reddened cheeks to his name. Of course, you won't find any trace of these distinguishing features in his official portraits!

10. Clarke, W (1809). *The Authentic and Impartial Life of Mrs. Mary Anne Clarke*. London: T Kelly, p.9.

11. He also provided her with an opulent residence in Weybridge, Surrey, close to his own residence of Oatlands.

12. Indeed, one biographer noted that 'it was acknowledged by the Duke, that she had more influence than the Queen.'
    Clarke, W (1809). *The Authentic and Impartial Life of Mrs. Mary Anne Clarke*. London: T Kelly, p.5.

13. Sadly, these letters never reached the market!

14. Hogan, Denis (1808). *An Appeal to the Public, and a Farewell Address to the Army*. London: G Gorman, p.56.

15. Gronow, Rees Howell (1862). *Reminiscences of Captain Gronow*. London: Smith, Elder and Co., p.42.

16. *The Lancaster Gazette and General Advertiser, for Lancashire, Westmorland, &c.* (Lancaster, England), Saturday, 4 February, 1809; Issue 399.

17. In fact, it took a little longer than that. He became Prince Regent in 1811.

18. *The Morning Chronicle* (London, England), Thursday, 2 February, 1809; Issue 12396.

19. Ibid.

20. Wilberforce, Robert Isaac and Wilberforce, Samuel (eds.) (1839). *The Life of William Wilberforce: Vol III*. London: John Murray, p.402.

21. *Northampton Mercury* (Northampton, England), Saturday, 18 March 1809; Issue 2.

22. *Northampton Mercury* (Northampton, England), Saturday, 4 February 1809; Issue 48.

23. *Trewman's Exeter Flying Post or Plymouth and Cornish Advertiser* (Exeter, England), Thursday, 23 March 1809; Issue 2342.

24. Clarke, Mary Anne (1810). *The Rival Princes*. New York: David Longworth, p.150.

25. Radical writer Pierre France McCallum wrote *The Rival Princes*, which told the tale of the conflict between the Duke of York and the Duke of Kent. When it was published, it carried Mary Anne's name.

26. Clarke, Mary Anne (1810). *The Rival Princes*. New York: David Longworth, pp.40-41.

27. Ibid, p.27.
28. Thorne, RG (1986). *The House of Commons 1790-1820*. London: Secker & Warburg, p.489.
29. Wardle eventually sank so deeply into debt that he had no choice but to flee the country to escape his creditors. He died in Italy in 1833.
30. This was a far cry from the days of 1809 when meetings had been held to honour Wardle at which motions were carried railing against York. One of them stated boldly, 'That any man, who should advise his Majesty to reinstate the Duke of York in his situation as Commander in Chief, was an enemy to his country.'

    The Norfolk Chronicle: or, the Norwich Gazette (Norwich, England), Saturday, 8 April 1809; Issue 2037.

Chapter 9

1. Anonymous (1833). *The Trial of Josiah Phillips for a Libel on The Duke of Cumberland*. London: J Hatchard and Son, p.4
2. Sellis was actually born in Corsica.
3. Cobbett, William (1810). *Cobbett's Political Register, Vol XVII, From January to June 1810*. London: Richard Bagshaw, pp.1007-1008.
4. In addition to the terrible head wounds, Cumberland sustained injuries from the sabre on his right hand, left arm and right thigh. His hand was so badly wounded that he almost lost a finger, though it was ultimately saved and the duke made a full recovery.
5. Bearing the no-nonsense title of *The Act for Murder and Malicious Bloodshed*, it was ruled that 'all inquisitions upon the view of persons slain, or hereafter to be slain, within any of the King's said Palaces or houses, or other house or houses aforesaid, shall be by authority of this Act, had and taken hereafter for ever by the Coroner for the time being of the household of our Sovereign Lord the King or his heirs, without any adjoining or assisting of another Coroner of any Shire within this Realm'.
6. Eleven of the jurists hailed from Charing Cross, with just one from St Martin's Lane thrown in to provide a little variety. They read like a perfect cross-section of Georgian society, each no doubt a fine and upstanding member of the community with an honest, respectable profession to complete the picture. Their jobs were listed as ironmonger, bootmaker, silversmith, carver and gilder, hatter, victualler, bookseller,

tallow chandler, bricklayer, grocer, coffeehouse keeper, baker and man's mercer (a supplier to tailors).

7. Anonymous (1810). *A Minute Detail of the Attempt to Assassinate High Royal Highness the Duke of Cumberland*. London: JJ Stockdale, p.55.

8. A stone was thrown at George III during a protest on 29 October 1795. A culprit named Kidd Wake was arrested and sentenced to be pilloried before enduring five years of hard labour at Gloucester Penitentiary. Pitt used the incident as justification for the introduction of the *Treasonable Practices Act* and the *Seditious Meetings Act*, which were notorious in Georgian society as the *Gagging Acts*.

9. Anonymous (1810). *A Minute Detail of the Attempt to Assassinate High Royal Highness the Duke of Cumberland*. London: JJ Stockdale, p.77.

10. Anonymous (1810). *La Belle Assemblée: or, Bell's Court and Fashionable Magazine, Volume 1*. London: John Bell, p.301.

11. *The Morning Post* (London, England), Wednesday, 6 June, 1810; Issue 12279.

12. Ibid.

13. Anonymous (1810). *A Minute Detail of the Attempt to Assassinate High Royal Highness the Duke of Cumberland*. London: JJ Stockdale, pp.103-104.

14. Ibid, p.103.

15. The verdict of *fell de se* literally means *felon of himself*, meaning that the victim died by their own hand.

16. *The Bury and Norwich Post: Or, Suffolk, Norfolk, Essex, Cambridge, and Ely Advertiser* (Bury Saint Edmunds, England), Wednesday, 18 December, 1811; Issue 1538.

17. *The Morning Chronicle* (London, England), Saturday, 28 December, 1811; Issue 13304.

18. *Philo Junius* should not be confused with the famed anonymous commentator, *Junius*, who made an appearance during the sorry saga of *another* Duke of Cumberland and Lady Grosvenor. Instead, Philo Junius wrote letters in support of the original Junius when his letters came under fire. Some suspect that Junius and Philo Junius were actually the same author.

19. Anonymous (1810). *A Minute Detail of the Attempt to Assassinate High Royal Highness the Duke of Cumberland*. London: JJ Stockdale, pp.91-92.

20. Garrow became a legend of the law and is noted for having introduced the phrase, 'innocent until proven guilty'.

21. James Scarlett, 1st Baron Abinger, was later appointed Attorney-General.

22. *The Standard* (London, England), Monday, February 08, 1830; Issue 853.

23. *The Times* (London, England), Tuesday, 9 February 1830; Issue 14145.

24. Anonymous (1833). *The Trial of Josiah Phillips for a Libel on the Duke of Cumberland*. London: J Hatchard and Son, p.2.

25. Ibid, p.6.

26. Ibid, p.8.

27. In 1834, Denman was elevated to the peerage as Baron Denman.

28. *Reading Mercury, Oxford Gazette and Berkshire County Paper, etc* (Reading, England), Monday, 1 July 1833; Issue 5835.

29. *Hereford Journal* (Hereford, England), Wednesday, 3 July, 1833; Issue 3286.

30. Merryweather, George (1838). *Kings, the Devil's Viceroys and Representatives on Earth*. New York: George Merryweather, p.98.

Index

DISCOVER MORE ABOUT PEN & SWORD BOOKS

Pen & Sword Books have over 4000 books currently available, our imprints include: Aviation, Naval, Military, Archaeology, Transport, Frontline, Seaforth and the Battleground series, and we cover all periods of history on land, sea and air.

Can we stay in touch? From time to time we'd like to send you our latest catalogues, promotions and special offers by post. If you would prefer not to receive these, please tick this box. ❑

We also think you'd enjoy some of the latest products and offers by post from our trusted partners: companies operating in the clothing, collectables, food & wine, gardening, gadgets & entertainment, health & beauty, household goods, and home interiors categories. If you would like to receive these by post, please tick this box. ❑

We respect your privacy. We use personal information you provide us with to send you information about our products, maintain records and for marketing purposes. For more information explaining how we use your information please see our privacy policy at www.pen-and-sword.co.uk/privacy. You can opt out of our mailing list at any time via our website or by calling 01226 734222.

Mr/Mrs/Ms ....

Address...

....

Postcode...................... Email address...........................

Website: www.pen-and-sword.co.uk Email: enquiries@pen-and-sword.co.uk
Telephone: 01226 734555   Fax: 01226 734438

Stay in touch: facebook.com/penandswordbooks or follow us on Twitter @penswordbooks